KRISTOFFER
HUGHES

THOTH PUBLICATIONS
Loughborough, Great Britain

A CIP catalogue record for this book is available
from the British Library.

Cover design by Avanson Design

ISBN 978-1-870450-67-6

Printed and bound in Great Britain

Published by Thoth Publications
64, Leopold Street, Loughborough, LE11 5DN

Web address: www.thoth.co.uk
email: enquiries@thoth.co.uk

Contents

Introduction

It is New Year's day, the first of January 2006, and I find myself sitting here at my dining room table in my home that I share with my partner and cat. The dining table and I are old friends; she has shared with me the constant pounding of fingertips on my keyboard. My books stare down at me, I can smell them, and memories of pages, stories and tales flood from them to infiltrate my mind. I still have the twinkling lights of Yuletide warming the room with their cheery glow but when I gaze up at the window I see nothing but darkness and my own fuzzy reflection staring back at me. I can see nothing of the beautiful island upon which I live; I cannot see the bare branches of the trees being battered by the winds that sweep across the Island from the Irish Sea. My partner Ian is in the living room watching repeats of "Charmed" on the TV! It is night time, and I sit here in silence, the darkness has long since draped itself upon the landscape and I can sense the discomfort of folk in the nearby villages nursing their overstretched stomachs and hangovers from the New Year celebrations. Upon my altar, just there to my right, an image of my Goddess, created from air drying clay stares at me inquisitively. *"What you up to?"* She whispers in my head, *"I'm writing a book,"* I reply. *"Your father is proud of you,"* She answers. Our one eyed cat Flora, gazes lazily from myself and then to the Goddess on the altar; and with a yawn resumes her endless cleaning regime. A single tear appears at the corner of my eyes and falls onto my laptop.

It has been a strange Yuletide, my Father lost his life three weeks ago at the age of 54 to cancer, and I found myself suddenly fatherless. And here in this room I reach out to him in the halls of the dead, within the ranks of my ancestors, and sense him there, he is proud. My father will never get to see my book in print, but he hears each word I write as it transfers from my mind to computer. I want to mention these thoughts that pass through my head with you, I want to write a book that is personal, intimate, where a portion of my personality can be perceived through these words of dry ink. My father taught me much about life and now he teaches me from beyond the realms of life, as an ancestor. The darkness at my window only reminds me of the potentiality that lies within us all, and the potentiality within Druidry.

I am no one particularly special; I have no direct lineage to the ancient Druids, no secret, ancient manuscript that only I will ever see. I am simply a Welsh man who is in love, in love with this land, sea and sky. Druidry to me is something that develops from that connection, from that embrace, a deeper kind of listening to the voices of this land. Yet initially this Druidry is akin to the darkness that lies at my window, a blank canvass of nothingness. It is us who breathes life into this tradition that we identify as Druidry, it is us who reach into the darkness and bring forth a tangible and living spiritual tradition that enriches the lives and experience of those who choose to explore it. The purpose of this book is simply to share my experiences, and I hope that this inspires you.

However if you are looking for a book on Druidry that provides historical and scholarly correspondences and essays, then this book is not for you. There are countless books available regarding the world of the ancient Druids and the Celtic people, this is not one of them; this is Druidry of the heart, and of the land. Druidry as it is applied and practised in my life, this is my Druidry, and all I can hope for is that my path through the forest will inspire your journey. This is my journey. There are plenty of 'how to' books available within the ever popular mind, body and spirit section of any bookstore, again technically this is not a how to book, there are suggestions, and sometimes exercises. Ultimately this book will not make you a Druid or teach you true Druidry, for I don't believe there is a definitive version of Druidry. Druidry is an evolving spirituality that is deeply personal and reaches and whispers to that secret place that hides within our very souls, the place where we hear clearly and listen intently to the song of creation, the lyrics and music of this wondrous universe we call home. Druidry, touches each of us in utterly different ways, it is moving, sad, filled with joy, pain and despair, with wonder of the sunset and the vast blue ocean. It speaks of the hidden people of the hills and the dark and wild places, of the treasures hidden in the forest, but above all it is transformation that lies at the very heart of Druidry.

Transformation must be the ultimate goal of anybody on a spiritual path, but this is never to suggest that the transformative process will easy. In fact it is quite the opposite. Sometimes I think that the so called "Muggles" of the world have it easy, the ability to move freely through life without thought of cause, effect, personal responsibility, and positive morality, never having to search within themselves, to discover the crap that lie within us all and having to deal with it, use it and allow that connection to ourselves and the world around us, to transform our very being. Bringing us closer to the sacred relationship we not only have with ourselves but with our land, our tribe, our people, our ancestors, and our heritage.

As I write, the words dance and flow on the screen of my laptop, I wonder who will read these words, what will they think of my version of Druidry? Who will they be, why are they reading this in the first place. Am I so far up my own arse that I feel confident enough and bold enough to write a book; have the authority to write a book? But I feel I need to, I feel the need to share my path through the dappled groves and share with you my world within Druidry. At the same time I have never written a book before, and the thought of doing so is initially daunting, but a friend of mine who is a writer shared with me some words of wisdom. The fact that she's a writer itself is daunting, but she is wise and inspired, and she told me to write as if I am writing to a friend, on a one to one basis, it being personal and relevant. Not attempting to write to an entire audience of faceless individuals. So this is what I have done, this book is written with one person in mind, you. And for the duration of this book you are my friend, and I am yours, and together we will travel through the pages of this book and through the adventure that is Druidry.

So this book is about my journey, but the more people I meet, and the more we talk and share, the more and more similar the experiences are, even though some of us have never interacted with other people of the Pagan way. Our spiritual experiences and that sense of connection is ultimately the same, we share so many parallels. So to those already on the path and those just starting out, there will be much in these pages that taste familiar.

My culture and heritage have been important to me, my identification as a Celt, a Welshman, and the richness of tradition, philosophy and literature of this nation have sent me spiralling into other worlds of vision and dreams, to strange and wondrous shores, to islands in the deepest darkest oceans, islands of magic and song, where the minstrel never tires and the bard sings for all eternity. As a child I would long for Cerridwen to tell me her secrets, I knew Bran and ran and made war games with Pwyll, chattered and flew with the birds of Rhiannon. This was my world, a world of wondrous beings, of sheer potentiality, a world of possibilities beyond human comprehension, and that awe and wonder and childlike surrender one feels when faced or confronted by the Gates of Annwn, the way to the deep, to that cauldron of inspiration and rebirth. And all this hid within the confines of my culture, I say hid, for that is what it is, hidden, not really spoken of or taught in our schools, but nevertheless there. We have forgotten so much of the truths that lie within the wonders of our heritage and culture, the old songs of mud and of rock, the red and the green, the blood and the sap. But do we truly forget? I doubt it. For I believe we carry within us the ability to shift from this realm of commercialism, imperialism and materialistic gain, to that space and silence within the forest, where we can no longer differentiate or define where we end and the grass upon which we sit begins. We still carry that knowing, the knowing of sheer connection that our ancestors possessed, but allowing the knowledge and wisdom of the twenty first century to filter through. We are not the old people, we live here and now, what was appropriate for one society and one time is not appropriate for another, but we are inherently, genetically the same. Call it what you will, species consciousness, a psychic link, regardless of what we call it, it is still a connection, and that connection is to this land, the land of Druidry.

Within the pages of this book there is one word that you will notice glaring out at you from the pages, *connection*. I do not apologise for the prolific use of this word which epitomises the importance of this concept within Druidry. Connection, connection, connection. You may well tire of seeing this word leap out at you paragraph after paragraph, yet in my view it is the lack of connection which fragments our society and facilitated man's fall into unconsciousness and apathy. We have forgotten the importance of the interconnectedness of life, and as a consequence have become lost in the illusion that density fabricates, creating a deep sleep that fell upon the people of the earth, each individual believing themselves to be separate from the sentiency of the earth and her creatures, a state which I refer to as the forgetfulness of life. Druidry evokes within us a memory, forgetfulness is a temporary state, it merely requires something to stir that memory within us and allow it to filter through, imbuing in us a sense of "Oh yeah!!! I remember!" And when that remembering is embraced and utilised within our lives, we begin to change, the world can no longer be seen through rose tinted glasses, but is illuminated by the blinding light of truth. We do not truly forget anything, the knowledge of connection and the truth of mystery lie inherently within us, all that is required is a little push in the right direction, in Druidry inspiration is the key to remembering. As we grow, our society subtly enforces the belief that we are separate, that there is nothing beyond that which we can gain materialistically, that we must strive to progress, to amass wealth and properties and be better than those around us. And we cease to remember that we are an aspect of nature and the mystery of life as we traverse the treacherous landscape of security and wealth, greed and pride.

I believe that society in general would rather keep us in a non lucid state, succumbing to the pressures and tribulations of modern life, falling into the trappings of non conscious living. As a by-product of this forgetfulness our planet suffers as disconnection becomes the normal state, resulting in ecological damage, war, terrorism and apathy. When we remember the mysteries of life we reconnect to the fundamental principle that we are all the same, priorities abruptly alter, and the world becomes a better place. Druidry facilitates this remembering, awakening the memory and knowledge of the universe within us.

So let me take you on a journey through the forest of the year, to and from each season and cycle of the Sun and Moon, the trees and the hedgerows. Druidry is the voice of this land, this nation, it is our heritage and culture, and is as precious as the sunrise, we nearly lost it once under the sword of Rome; let's make sure that never happens again. Listen, if you will, to the voice of one who walks the forest path, and thoroughly enjoys every bloody living minute of it!!

Kris Hughes,
January the First, 2007.
The Isle of Anglesey.

PART 1

shadows of the past

I am a harmonious one;
I am a clear singer,
I am steel, I am Druid.
I am an artificer,
I am a scientific one,
I am a serpent;
I am love,
I will indulge in feasting.

(The book of Taliesin)

odern Druidry does not attempt to recreate the past; rather it embraces it, seeking inspiration and truth from the darkness of the past. Druidry is the expression of that connection between the tribe and its land, that deeper understanding of who and what we are. Its song has filled the air of our beloved isles for thousands of years, and its lyrics can still be heard today; in the quiet places, the hidden places. Our forests and mountains sing the songs of our ancestors, and we hear them, but how many of us listen?

The bards and minstrels of our people carried this song within them, and I cannot over emphasise the importance of this song, the music of the universe and of nature. The entire universe sings in praise of itself, its music fills the distant galaxies, and resonates through our world, a song of oneness, of connection. We have temporarily forgotten the lyrics to this song, a song so powerful that it has the ability to shock us out of unconsciousness and disconnection, facilitating a deep awareness of our place in this universe and of the wonder of creation. No one can teach us the lyrics to this song; we must discover it for ourselves by re-connecting to our source, to the unifying voice of the universe. Druidry facilitates this awareness; it is an experiential spirituality that explores the many facets of human nature as an aspect and integral part of nature. We are not separated from it; it is only our modern society that instils in us a deep sense of individuality and ultimately loneliness. Druidry brings us back to that place of connection, of oneness, through the discovery of that primordial song of the universe and its beautiful lyrics. It sings to the rhythm of our souls, and of the soul of this world, the unified soul of the universe. Have we truly forgotten the lyrics?

We never really forget anything, all the memories of our ancestors continue to speak to us, through the land, the soft green earth of our beloved planet, the rivers and streams, deep silent lakes, tremble with ancestral memory and inspiration, we need only discover the stillness within us, that ability to release the mind from the confines of the 21st century and allow it to soar with the skylark. Our ancestors knew the song, were familiar with it, and had a deeper understanding of its meaning, a gift that has become lost in the mundane trivialities of modern life. This nation contains hundreds upon thousands of ancient tales, the stories of the bards of old, those who would travel, inspiring their people, keeping the old ways alive. Our ancestors left a legacy of fantastical tales which speak of beasts and fairies, of kings and poets, gods and goddesses, all relaying secrets and mystery and the history of our people. All of them contain within them the very essence of that song, as sung by the trees of our land, a song of simplicity and awakening.

History is generally written by the conquerors, they retell tales of victory and triumph, but we have another history, mythology. Mythology is our true history it is the history of the heart. Told by the bards of old, they kept the connection between the tribe and land alive and thriving. They tell of a time when two races interacted harmoniously, the gentle folk of the hills, and humans. Those of the hidden places would sing their songs in tune with ours, but man grew proud and greed clouded his eyes, man lost the respect for our mother the earth, and as a consequence the hidden ones vanished from our sight, man blinded himself from them. For two millennia we have roamed alone, unable to see those of the hidden places, but still they are there. They continue to watch, silently from the dappled shadows of the trees, and some of us hear them, for they are the spirits of place. It takes only one brave soul to tread the moonlit path and hear their voices, one brave soul to share that experience to retell the stories of our people.

Druidry embraces this connection, and strives to re-establish this relationship between us and the forces of nature. And we remember there, is a familiarity within Druidry that encourages a deep sigh of relief, of coming home. Most comment on how familiar it all seems, how natural it feels to follow the way of the Druid, simply because we have never forgotten that connection. We recall it through ritual, mumming and dancing, through ancient traditions that still prevail to this day, and something about it makes us feel good, we feel connected, not only to ourselves but to the memories of our ancestors, those of blood and of heritage.

The Druids of old were the priestly caste of the tribes of Britain, identified generally as those of the Iron Age people, the Celts. Here I will speculate a little. I see the Druids as a caste of priests that have always existed here in the British Isles from the Neolithic era through to today. The title "Druid" was given to them during the flowering of Rome, but did they exist before that, or were they simply a people of the Celtic tribe?

It is apparent through the sacred landscape of Britain that we have always had priests that walked between the worlds; to me they were the Druids. The Druids of the Iron Age were simply an extension of an older priesthood, guardians of ancient knowledge and wisdom, magic and wonder. Those who built the mighty temples of Avebury, Stonehenge, The ring of Brodgar, Bryn Celli Ddu, were one and the same, it is modern man who has emblazoned upon them an identity of culture and of a place in time. I speculate that the Druids were always there, silent watchers of time, observers and keepers of wisdom.

Druidry speaks of the trees and of knowledge of the trees, derived from the word "Drui" meaning Oak and "Id" meaning "To know". In Wales they are the Derwyddon, again derived from "Derwydd", meaning Oak, and also the "Gwyddon" or "Gwyddoniaid". I find this ancient Welsh word a preferable title to those priests of the Celtic people, 'Druid' has limitations, whereas 'Gwyddon' can be seen throughout the Welsh language and has attached to it a certain enchantment and mystery that seems to depict a relation between the people and the land. The word 'druid' has been dissected on numerous occasions in countless books. Let me explain the meaning and attributions of the word Gwyddon that many may not be as familiar with.

To begin to understand this word and its implications we must revert to another connected word, 'Gwybod', meaning 'to know'. Within its composition we see the prefix 'Gwy' which is merely a contracted form of 'Gwydd', even Taliesin spoke of this word when he said "Pwy a amgyvred gwydd," "who can understand Gwydd?" He implies that the word itself is worthy of comprehension, but what does it mean? There are three common interpretations of the word; firstly it refers to trees, shrubs, timber, greenwood and weeds. Secondly it refers to presence, the sight and knowledge, and finally to a wise man or woman, a sage, a prophet or soothsayer. The word 'Gwyddfa', again a derivative of 'Gwydd' refers to a place of presence, of spirit and mystery, a sacred place where bards would meet, these were normally prominent features in the landscape, mountains or hills, tumuli or mounds. The most significant which still carries its ancient name to this day is "Yr Wyddfa Fawr", Mount Snowdon, a mutated form of 'Gwyddfa Fawr', meaning the great place of presence or power where bards would meet. There are dozens of Welsh words which are composed of the root word 'Gwydd', one of the most interesting being its interpretation as 'Sage', these were known as the Gwyddon or Gwyddoniaid in the plural, and various place names throughout Wales reflect a connection between the land and these mysterious people of wonder and magic, Bryn Gwyddon, The hill of the sages, Nant y Gwyddon, the valley of sages and Craig y Gwyddon, the rock of sages. These words imply a connection to nature and to natural philosophy, yet it has another hidden aspect to it, that of understanding or an inherent wisdom, in my view I would translate the word as "He who knows the wisdom, science and presence of trees". Interestingly the modern Welsh word for 'Science' is Gwyddoniaeth, which translates as the "language of the trees, sage etc", again derived from the two root words of Gwydd and Iaeth (language).

Certain mythological figures found within the ancient texts of Wales also reflect the attributions linked to the word "Gwyddon", examples are "Gwydion", Gwyddno Garanhir, implying a connection between the character and the world of mystery and magic.

Another mythical, perhaps archetypal figure is also mentioned in Welsh folklore and tradition, 'Gwyddon Ganhebon.' It seems that Gwyddon Ganhebon was a protector and guardian of the wisdom and knowledge of the old Cymric people, and it is said that the pillars of Gwyddon Ganhebon are buried in a secret cave on the sacred island of Mona in north Wales, and upon them are written all the arts and sciences of the world. Local legend tells a tale of the Druids, during the time of the Roman invasion breaking their primary regulation and carving their wisdom and knowledge upon these pillars and subsequently hiding them in the depths of the earth, so their secrets would survive for future generations.

Another interesting derivative of the root word Gwydd is 'Celwydd', in modern Welsh this translates as; to lie. But in the old Welsh it was not quite as simple. It is derived from two words the first being 'Celu,' to conceal, and the second Gwydd. In its entirety it would have been interpreted as "To conceal the knowledge of the trees, sage etc." The Gwyddon were connected with a system of esoteric secrecy and it seems apparent from this word that those who understood the mysteries and lived by them, were the 'Celwydd', those who concealed the wisdom and knowledge of the Gwyddon from the general populace, it implies a sacred duty to protect the truth and only present it to the initiated, preventing its dilution. The Welsh poet Llywarch Hen speaks of the duty of Celwydd when he said: "Gwaith Celwydd yw celu rhin." "The work of Celwydd is to conceal rhin." It is speculated that rhin denominated the ultimate mysteries of the Gwyddon caste, those mysteries that were forbidden to be put in writing; I can only assume that the secrets of rhin would have been expressed poetically through verse and prose. Unfortunately the esoteric significance and meaning of the word Celwydd has crudely evolved into simply meaning 'To lie'. How sad that so much wisdom and knowledge has been nearly lost through our disconnection to the land and the language of our tribe, a language which expressed the wonder and awe the people felt towards nature and the natural world. However modern Druidry retains some of the old wisdoms of the Gwyddon, and the tradition awakens within us the knowledge of the trees and the mystery our forefathers saw reflected within them. Throughout this book I use the words Druid and Gwyddon interchangeably.

Druidry is that still, silent place within us, a place where we loose our minds. It encourages the shifting from the restrictions of the conceptual mind, and facilitates a journey through our non-conceptual minds to that point where we become one with the world, one with the universe. Through the observation and experience of nature we un-learn the restrictive and passionless attitudes of modern humanity and gently, slowly at first, begin to sway and dance to the rhythm of nature and the nature of the soul. In Druidry, nature is our teacher, the trees of our woodlands and forests speak to us, in subtle hushed whispers, and when we listen to that wisdom, we awake to the magic and mystery of life in all its paradoxical glory. Take the nature of a tree, it cares not for explanation, reason, logic, power or control, it is simply "tree", and it sings the song of tree. Quietly it watches, it absorbs and simply acts in accordance to its nature. It simply is. A mighty oak will allow a bird to perch for a while, and then to fly away, without ever attempting to call it back. If our hearts can become like a tree then we are closer to the truth, but truth is a treasure of the deep, dark recesses of the human soul, and the journey there takes courage, stamina, strength and integrity. We have been programmed by years of social breeding, its takes a lot to break through that learning and listen to the consuming truth of the soul, where we learn to know it, to love it and to maintain it.

Druidry brings us to the portals of truth, of understanding and of awareness, but the journey is both wondrous and harrowing. The wisdom of the trees takes us to parts of ourselves that we have ignored; it opens our eyes to the responsibility of life, and of its celebration. Confronted with our demons and slaying them one by one, we begin to hear the gentle plucking of harp string that sings to us from the origination of our souls.

Exercise

Contemplation

How do we contemplate, how do we still the mind to such an extent that it no longer had control of us? Druidry is a contemplative path. I ask you to consider life as a druid, what does it mean to you? What impact will it have on your life, your reality?

Before you start this exercise begin your preparations the evening before. It is always a good idea to keep a journal of your path through the forest, find yourself a little blank notebook, and in it record your journey through the world of Druidry. Start your journey by creating a sacred space within your home; build an altar to the spirits of your home and in honour of those you share that space with. This can be as elaborate or as simple as you wish a place of focus, of meditation and contemplation. A little table with some stones from the garden or beach, an old feather and candle is sufficient; your altar will grow with you.

Pamper yourself a little; take a long soak in a hot bath infused with delicate herbs and oils. If you do not have any oils, use your favourite bubble bath, or gather some local herbs, either from your garden or your local retailer. Lemon balm and mints, lavender and rose are wonderful for calming the mind and instilling a sense of tranquillity. Place the herbs in an old sock, tie it in a knot and cast it into your bathwater. Whilst soaking in the warmth and delicate aroma, contemplate the path of the Druid, travel in your mind to a place in the distant past and allow your imagination to draw images of the priesthood, their rites and celebrations. Do not restrict your imaginings, allow them to flow freely through you, see the colours, and sense the shadows and voices of the past. Your imagination is a powerful tool for the invocation of truth, play with it, enjoy this time, alone with your thoughts.

Before retiring, light a candle on your altar, burn some sweet smelling incense, sit before it and watch the flickering dance of the candle flame, feel its warmth and light as it illuminates the room. Allow yourself to become aware of the room, the house, other people within it, still your body and mind, and let the images of your previous imaginings to infiltrate your consciousness. Settle into the warm feeling that this time is your time, a time to be with yourself. Eventually retire to dream of ages past, of trees whispering their secrets.

Before dawn take yourself off to somewhere quiet, preferably with nature, a quiet grove in your favourite forest, your garden, somewhere where you can observe the slow passing of nature. Ensure you are warm and comfortable and find a spot that feels right. Lean against the security of a tree if you like.

Now shift your consciousness, the technique is quite simple, instead of antagonistically fighting against the interfering thoughts that inevitably pollute the mind. Observe them, watch them dance as they enter and leave, don't attempt to focus on their content or meaning, simply watch them. The intention here is to free yourself from the confines of the ordinary mind. Do not focus inwardly, instead become ultra aware of everything. Begin to listen to the natural sounds around you, the creaking and groaning of wood and bark, the shuffle of small animals in the undergrowth, the breeze, wind and rain if present. Gently reach down with your hands and allow your fingertips to caress the ground around you, feel the textures allowing that sensory input to seep gracefully into your brain. Again ignore what your thoughts are telling you, simply watch them.

Now choose a tree, it could be the one that you are leaning on or sitting closer to, sense its presence, its subtle breathing, the slow steady drawing of water through its body, sense the presence of its roots as they search the deep dark earth for nutrients. Allow these impressions to absorb passively into your subconscious, do not force this conjoining with the essence of the tree, and be passive and receptive to sensing it only. Explore every aspect of the tree, allowing your essence to join with it, becoming a part of it. What does it feel like to be this tree, what has it witnessed during its life, what animals live within it and nest upon its secure branches? Watch the thoughts; do not attempt to force them in any way. Your connection to the tree will facilitate a deeper, subtler form of communication that we are unused to in modern life, flow with it, and swim with the sap of the tree.

What of the nature of Druidry can this tree teach you? Why the trees? What significance do they have to us and the spirituality that we call Druidry? Contemplate these questions, passively, receptively. Be the tree, whilst simultaneously being you; sense that connection of spirit to spirit. Now begin to listen to your thoughts, you will now have achieved an altered state of consciousness, a place of clarity and connection, your body having melted into the surrounding area, becoming a part of it. What does it mean to be a Druid in the twenty first century? How will this change your life and affect those close to you? What does this connection to nature actually mean? Ponder, think, ask and contemplate. Be with nature and understand that human nature is simply an aspect of Nature.

Having expanded your consciousness, become one with nature and her creatures, return slowly to the sense of density and singularity, slowly detach yourself from the connection you have established with honour, send out blessings and gratitude as you mind returns to the density of your human body. Take a walk, contemplate the experience, dance and sing if you wish to the rhythms of that place. Finally gather yourself together and return home for a well earned cup of tea!

Druidry is the art of stopping, listening and being. And its most transforming quality is that of inspiration, which brings us to the very heart and mystery of Druidry, the concept of the three rays of Awen.

PART 2

chapter 1

awen: the heart of druidry

The Awen I sing, from the deep I bring it,
A river while it flows,
I know its extent,
I know when it disappears,
I know when it fills,
I know when it overflows,
I know when it shrinks,
I know what base
There is beneath the sea.

The Hostile confederacy, The Book of Taliesin

t the heart of Druidry lies a unique concept of spirit and connection, epitomised in one single word; Awen, pronounced "A-Wen". Awen is a Welsh word that is sometimes translated as flowing spirit; however this interpretation hardly does the word justice. Welsh is an unique language where some words of its vocabulary have attached to them an emotional connotation. The mere utterance of some particular words instils in the speaker a sense of feeling, of connection and emotion, the very word quickens the heart and causes the lungs to gasp momentarily. A primary example of this is the Welsh word "Hiraeth", this word immediately stirs a sense of longing, a deep homesickness that only the Welsh can feel for Wales. It is a sense of home, of belonging that sings to the soul, causing it to cry in desperation, pain and love for the mountains and the streams, the dappled forests and coastlines of Wales, the land of inspiration.

Of course the entire fertile landscape of Britain was once home to the people that we now refer to as the Cymry, when this Beloved Island of ours was knows as "Clas Myrddin", Merlin's enclosure, also known as Ynys Prydain, The Isles of Britain. In those long lost times of ancient sunlight we all spoke the same language, shared the same visions and dreams, our language was Brythonic, the precursor of three later languages of the P Celtic tribes. Today the Brythonic languages exist as Welsh, Cornish and Brittanic.

Awen is not only a philosophy, a spiritual concept, but also a term which links us to the inspiration of our ancestors and the wisdom they held. For many it seems rather an insignificant word, small, unassuming, falling gently from the lips of the speaker like a deep heartfelt sigh. The word itself can be seen in the various texts of ancient Wales, significantly those written by the hand of the remarkable Taliesin, as seen in the opening quote of this chapter. I do not intend to give a history lesson as to the origins of Awen, but rather attempt to explain its significance at the heart of Druidry. The understanding of Awen comes from its experience, from its flowing as it sings and dances within us, it is of this awakening to Awen that this chapter will focus. To those who understand the meaning and expression of Awen, the mere mention of the word summons a storm within, transports him or her to the shadows and darkness of sheer potentiality. The mere utterance of this sacred word causes the stomach to churn and the heart to race, it instils within the listener a sense of home, of homesickness and longing. The word speaks to an ancient, primordial part of our spirit that understands, that constantly hears and is illuminated by the three rays of Awen, and swims in the deep, utter nothingness beyond its rays.

Awen is the essence of modern Druidry; it is the spirit behind the tradition, the spirit of unification which binds us to the entire universe, that which is seen and unseen. But what in fact is it and can it truly be adequately articulated into words? No explanation could ever truly do it justice, I have seen so many descriptions of Awen, but none of them ever really come close to describing what one feels when that connection to Awen consumes you.

Traditionally Awen is a word which describes a symbol, this symbol being three lines, one vertical which corresponds to the sun at winter and summer solstice and one line either side of the first at an angle, each corresponding to the suns position at Spring and Autumn equinox and is drawn thus: / | \ . In Neo-Paganism three dots may also be seen above each ray, these dots represent the three blessed drops of Awen that erupted from Cerridwen's cauldron to inspire the future Taliesin, Gwion Bach. It is entirely personal preference whether or not you use the dots, some people have an affinity for them others do not. The rays themselves emanate from above and they represent the voice of the universe, but they are not to be confused with the concept of the Christian or other God. Awen is beyond the concept of God, if Awen could speak to us in English it would say: "Before God was I am!" Another way of thinking of Awen is to imagine all the Gods and Goddesses of the world playing football, Awen is the deep, green pitch upon which they play and the bright blue of the sky above them, it is the gentle cotton like clouds which grace the vast blueness above them. Awen is the light of the sun that shines upon them, the warm rays of sunshine that the Gods feel upon their skin is its voice. Awen is the very spark of life, which connects all of creation. It is the dance of the sun's rays upon our atmosphere, the light of a distant nebula, the embrace of a galaxy, the death of a star. It is the sense of wonder which we feel when the buds of spring explode into an array of green life.

Awen is the spirit of unification, it inhabits every part of the universe, known and unknown, that which can be perceived and that which is invisible, it is the energy and force behind all things, yet this energy is constant, unchanging, it simply is. Awen is neither negative nor positive, good or bad, it has no motive other than to be and sing its unique song of connection, and it is the voice of the universe speaking to itself, celebrating itself in all its wondrous expressions, we being an integral part of that expressive force. In humans its expression can only realistically be creative in nature, these being the sacred arts of creativity as expressed through Bardism; the arts of poetry, prose and storytelling, writing, the art of voice and song, painting and crafting, dancing and music.

The principle of these three almost insignificant looking rays is often intellectualised to such an extent they become too complex for the majority to grasp. We become transfixed and almost obsessed to seek out its meaning as a word, discovering its source, pondering over ancient texts for years in the hope that all will suddenly become illuminated, and a deeper understanding will descend upon us. In actuality those who intellectualise it to such an extent rarely experience the wonder of the rays, and remain in the dappled shadows of cerebral comprehension without the experiential vision that melts the heart and burns the soul. Our overcomplicated society has become so engrossed by complexities that we assume all things of any value, including matters spiritual, to be complex and difficult to comprehend, taking years to master. This is not so of Awen.

When we create, be it through music or poetry, something comes from nothing, one second it never existed, suddenly there it is; a painting in living colours on the soft surface of fine canvas, or in the enchanting words of the Bard. The un-manifest abruptly manifests itself on the physical plane, having traversed the void, the primordial darkness, that place where anything is possible. All potentiality exists there, and we reach into that void, and from it pull forth a tiny strand of the essence of Awen, and we express it through our creativity. We become inspired, and that inspiration touches others, a certain painting, the words of a song, a piece of music can move the heart and cause a deep feeling of wonder, of love, joy or pain. For through these methods of creativity and their sharing we share our connection with the source of all things, reaching back through nature, through the Gods and sinking deep into the cauldron of Awen. It is here within the cauldron of Awen that we discover true inspiration, and our creativity expresses that connection.

When we sit and listen to the Bard who feels the Awen, his words stir something within us, and that stirring awakens a connection, it is that connection that we strive to develop and experience within Druidry, that sense of singularity, of oneness. It is neither complicated nor difficult it is simply a matter of waking up to the lucidity of life and the encompassing, flowing spirit of the universe, Awen.

The sheer beauty of Awen lies within its simplicity, it is not a faceless deity out there watching, it has no need for prayer and it cannot be worshipped, for how can you worship what you already are. We are all an expression of Awen, as is everything else on this planet, living, animated or non-animated. The force of Awen runs through everything that exists. It is the living soul of the universe, and we are an inseparable component of the universe learning about itself. The simplicity of Awen lies in its omnipresence, its presence is everywhere, as your breath leaves your lungs, to travel through moist bronchi and mingle with the air outside your body, the Awen is there around and within each molecule of air. It sings within the leaves of the trees, within and around each greening bud, as each and every single leaf on every tree in the entire world sings, each piece of music different, sung in accordance to the singer's experience, yet the lyrics always remain the same. We all sing the same song, only to a different tune. Each tune an unique expression of our individual lives, the way we look, walk, talk, our personalities, likes and dislikes, the simple fact I like chocolate and someone else doesn't. I hum to my tune, but the words I sing, deep within my spirit are the words of Awen, it is the song that has been sung since the very before time, in that place of nothingness.

But man has separated himself from the song, from the lyrics that bind us to creation and the universe. Through greed and pride, we distanced ourselves from nature, from the entity we depend upon entirely, an entity that does nothing but sing the song of Awen. And slowly our ears and hearts closed to the delicious song that nature emanated, a tree simply became tree, a blade of grass simply grass, meaningless, we lost our connection to the very thing that give us the pleasures of life. But how did this disconnection come about?

When our spirit is born into this world, having come from singularity, it continues to experience that sense of oneness as a new born child, it is the universe. But suddenly trapped within the density of matter and physiology and the developing mind attuning to its environment, it senses something different. It develops a sense alien to the spirit; a sense of self and of other; and that rift between connection increases, duality ensues. As we journey through infancy and childhood, this rift grows wider, we sense a separation from the world around us, and our individuality increases as we develop an identity through the experience of being. No longer can we seemingly control the universe which we inhabit, we become separate from it, and as we ascend through childhood that sense of self and other increases further; we are alone, we become "Me". The sense of "Me" escalates during adolescence when we develop an awareness of our uniqueness and individuality, a knowing that no one else in the world is like us. We soon venture onto a path of self exploration, searching the world for who we are, for the illusion of self. As a consequence we broaden the gap between connection; distancing ourselves further from the truth of singularity, ignorant to the fact that the answer, the return to oneness, already exists within us. Separation, duality is metaphorically man's fall from grace, our society inadvertently encourages this illusion of duality and promotes disconnection, facilitating mankind's fall into unconsciousness, increasing the distance between ourselves. Consequently, violence, disrespect, indifference and injustice evolve naturally. Awen allows us to see beyond the illusion of self and other, to the truth within the rays.

The Truth Against The World

Iolo Morgannwg, the infamous author of a collection of works, which was published after his death and titled, "Barddas, a collection of original documents, illustrative of the theology, wisdom, and usages of the bardo-druidic system of the isle of Britain", edited by J. Williams ap Ithel, devoted an entire section of his manuscript titled "Awgrym" (Symbol) to the concept of Awen. When describing the three rays he said:

> "...*That is to say, they are the three columns, and the three columns of truth, because there can be no knowledge of truth, but from the light thrown upon it; and the three columns of sciences, because there can be no sciences, but from the light and the truth.*"
> (*Bibliography reference*).

Iolo also attributed the phrase *"Y gwir yn erbyn y byd"* (The truth against the world) to the three rays, in fact this phrase can still be seen today on the banner of the "Gorsedd of Bards of the Isles of Britain" at the National Eisteddfod of Wales. Iolo Morgannwg was the instigator of the Gorsedd of Bards which have ever since been associated with the annual celebratory festival of Welsh culture, the Eisteddfod. This festival celebrates the rich culture of the Welsh people through poetry and music, arts and crafts, and continues to carry a rich tradition of Druidry within its structure, however the Druidry of the Eisteddfod is not Pagan, and is practised within a

Christian construct. The concept of Awen however still lies deep at its core. Interestingly this simple phrase, "The truth against the world" together with the primary triad of the three rays, "To know truth, to love truth, to maintain truth", imply that within the rays lie the entire truths of the Universe and all it contains, truth which can only be understood by developing a relationship with Awen. All knowledge is derived from the three rays, when we are not in tune with Awen, there only exists a cerebral knowledge that cannot touch and move the spirit.

The knowledge of truth can only be perceived and understood once the light of Awen illuminates it. The truth however is constantly there, and only the ignorance of our conceptual minds can hinder its radiance and understanding. But beyond the rays in the void, the darkness before the bursting of light lies the essence of that truth and the potentiality of its knowledge. Truth is after all a treasure of darkness. All things in this world are illuminated by the light of truth, it is simply man's arrogance and ignorance that fails to comprehend that truth and act upon it. In Druidry we seek not only the knowledge of the rays, but utilise that knowledge to reach the darkness beyond them. After all once something has become illuminated, it can no longer change, it simply is what it is, but in the void, in the cauldron of the Gods, that vast and eternal primordial abyss, it is there that our connection originates, where all things are one, before their illumination by the three rays.

Darkness is a vital aspect of exploration within Druidry, as is light, but obviously not within the modern concept of darkness being somehow 'bad'. We are taught to fear the dark; to an extent our ancestors feared it, when predatory, opportunistic animals would hunt under the camouflaging cloak of darkness, threatening tribal communities. Today it is Hollywood's influence that causes us to see demons and malignant spirits that hide in the shadows, ready to pounce upon us, and the subsequent insecurity most feel within the dark hinders their exploration of it. The sheer potentiality of the darkness before the light relays to us the mysteries of the universe and brings us closer to a deeper understanding of our origination, of that part of us which is a part of the whole. Meditating on the darkness, the void allows us to swim in that primordial soup of nothingness, allowing us unique opportunities of glimpsing the known universe from that point of initiation, looking from the inside out. Our sense of singularity increases and our connection attains a lucidity that was otherwise absent.

Many in the neo-pagan movements seek out only the light, a process which requires very little commitment and very little exploration of the truth behind the scenes, and it is the quality and connection to that truth which brings about transformation. Through trance and meditation we can traverse the three rays of light, basking in their luminosity and knowledge, swimming within the tides of life and arrive unhindered with clear intent and integrity at the cauldron from which they spring forth. There we descend into the abyss, into the womb of the One Whole, where our concepts of the spirit are shattered into a billion pieces, and the questions "Who am I? What am I?" fall into irrelevancy as the darkness of Awen consumes us, transforming and releasing us into a state of bliss and rapture. But actively exploring the dark requires stamina and a depth of spirit unknown to most non lucid path walkers, the consequences of having been No-One and All-Things tears apart our ideals and aspirations, forcing us to see our place in the world from a different angle, from someone who has been on the inside looking out. Courage is also needed to travel to the primordial darkness, for in there we find "our demons", the demons we have created through childhood and adolescence, through our interactions with humanity and the dark side of our own nature. For in that darkness we become, initially, the only point of reference available and it is our own demons we project onto those blank walls of nothingness. It is here that we confront our years of programming, allowing them all to fall away like the leaves of an autumn oak, enabling us to explore the dark as a place of sheer potentiality. The darkness which inhabits most of our universe is a place of nourishment and understanding, comfort and connection, mystery and knowledge. It is here that we discover the ultimate truth, the truth of soul, hidden as a treasure in the utter darkness of nothing.

Our ancestors understood the vitality of the darkness and the balancing rays of light, and provided for us a vital and important tool in its exploration, the concept of Awen. Part of the mystery of Awen is its appearance, three rays of light; they act as an illusion to the mystery that lies behind it, the darkness. To know it we must flow with it, up and down the rays of light to and beyond their source. Enveloped in both light and darkness, moving in balance with the energies of the universe, drawn neither to one more than the other, our lives consequently develop a balanced pattern, where the radiance of Awen shines like a beacon from our brows.

The concept of Awen may be something new and fresh to you, something inherently British, an indigenous philosophy that offers richness of culture and tradition. Gone are the days when we need to look to other lands for inspiration and connection. There is so much of value here on our great island. Ironically people remain ignorant in regards to the value of spiritual tradition we have hidden within our own culture and land. A tradition that is not so easily found, to explore it one must seek it out and this requires hard work, dedication and commitment. Qualities that few have in an age of quick fix spiritual tourism, surely it is so much easier to read the teachings of another society, another tradition? Perhaps so, but the easy route is hardly fulfilling. When we venture out into unknown terrain, poring over the tales of old, seeking wisdom and inspiration, when we listen to the whispers of the rivers and the forests and loose our minds and identities, that is when the spirit sings with clarity. The exploration of Awen is a bed of roses, fragrant, soft and filled with beauty, with the brightest colours tempting the senses, but its thorns are also sharp and merciless as they stab into your back. The way of Awen is not easy, but its rewards far outweigh the hard effort involved in its understanding. Perhaps this is what gives the pursuit of Awen such connection of spirit, the simple fact that it must be worked at, hard, each individual must be responsible for his or her own connection to it. There is no guidebook, no guru who can take you there, it is a perilous yet wondrous journey to the very edge of the spirit and beyond into the vast darkness of nothingness.

You may already be familiar with Awen and have already incorporated it into your spiritual life, if so then these words may feel familiar to you. We have no proof as to the initial origination of the three rays in their symbolic form. The word itself however, can be traced back centuries, and we will never know if it was old Iolo who invented the symbol. What we do know is that it has power. Awen has been empowered by centuries of use throughout Britain and now the world, as more and more people tap into its mysteries. I would imagine the Bards of old would smile incredulously to realise that today people as far flung as the United States of America and Australia embrace the concept of Awen, keeping the tradition alive and well across the globe

In the following chapters you will notice me referring to "Spirit" occasionally and "Soul" at other times, allow me to explain why I seem to change from one term to another. According to personal experience within the tradition I define the make up of life as follows. Firstly we have a body and that body contains within it a mind, the mind is then bifurcated into two separate entities, the conceptual mind, which is firm, experienced, it knows what is what and likes for everything to remain that way! Secondly we have the non-conceptual mind, the aspect of our mind that is open and receptive, in tune with spirit and the unseen worlds around and within us, some may prefer to refer to these mind states as the finite or infinite mind. Above these we have the spirit, the driving force behind our human incarnation, the energy within us that responds and develops through the uniqueness of experience. The spirit is that aspect of us that survives the demise of the mortal form and journeys onto the subtler realms of energy, retaining the richness of experience it encountered during incarnation. Does the spirit retain human form; does the realm of spirit resemble the human, material world that we are familiar with? In my opinion, it is simply a matter of personal perspective, our own world is a reality created by our own experience of it, each individual perceives the world in a unique manner. I believe the world of spirit is no different, a realm of infinite realities, each one an aspect of the billions of spirits that have encountered experience. Each aspect uniquely contributes to the essential experience of the universe as it learns about itself. Beyond the spirit yet inexorably linked to it and the mind, swims the soul, that aspect of us that is the universe in its entirety. It is here that we first see the bright illumination of Awen as the rays emanate from the primordial void beyond human comprehension.

In the next chapter we will explore techniques of deep connection with Awen, but as an introduction I offer some techniques of familiarisation and contemplation.

Exercise

To begin with, spend time in gentle meditation whilst drawing the symbol over and over on a piece of paper, try not to think too much about the activity, simply allow your mind to become lost in the process of "Doodling". Keep drawing until your mind is still and all that exists within your consciousness is the symbol itself. Have you placed the dots above the rays, or excluded them? Spend a little time each day in this gentle contemplative state, doodling to your heart's content, you will find that you enter a daydream state, where your mind wonders freely, liberated from your skull, allowed to roam freely to wherever it chooses. Although you will not be actively thinking about the symbol, subtle messages will enter your subconscious during this time as you connect to the essence of the symbol these will become clearer to you later when you return to a lucid state.

Next, plan to take yourself to a place where if possible sky, sea and land meet, if you are too far from the sea, or cannot get there for one reason or another, then use a local river or lake. Go under the cover of darkness so that the borders of each realm melt and blend into each other so that you are unsure of where one ends and the other begins. If you are able cloak yourself in shadows by using a cape, robe or shawl then do so. Absorb the ambience of the environment surrounding you, allowing subtle impressions from each realm to infiltrate your consciousness, imprinting gentle, invisible messages into your mind. Slowly approach the realm of water, sensing its presence as you move towards it, feel its ebb and flow, the pull of the moon upon its mass tugging at your own heart. Feel the flowing spirit of Awen spilling from its waves, cascading onto the shore joining the Awen that sings in the land, feel the stars above you like fairy lights in the sky blinking down upon you. You are an integral aspect of this beauty and wonder, it is yours, sense it, feel it, with every footfall you take towards the water, feel it tugging and calling the water that exists within you. Offer your reverence to the spirits of water, reach down and touch them, allowing the water to gently wash over your skin. What does that feel like? Break it down to its vital components and truly feel and experience the water upon your flesh, hear the great song that sings within it. With one finger wetted by the sea, trace the three rays upon your forehead, with deep intention, each stroke determined and felt, feel the coolness of the water on your head, and the burning, searing Awen which sings from the ocean emblazoned on your body, burning its song deep into your being. Allow your brow to shine with the light and power of Awen. Enjoy the moment; be there with the land, sea and sky, the Awen shining from you.

These seemingly simple rituals offer a depth of transformation to the practitioner, they are neither difficult to remember nor logistically complicated, yet they can move the spirit to new heights of understanding and perception. Obviously the depth of the experience is utterly dependant upon your connection and ability to remove yourself from the humdrum of life. Remember, there are no tricks, no ancient formulas that must be adhered to, to experience Awen, all we require is the ability to stream our consciousness with pinpoint accuracy and intent, knowing where we are going, and what we aim to achieve when we get there. The way of Awen is experiential, therefore we need not rely on the words of others for validation, we experience, therefore we know.

Since a child I have been in love with Awen, it has been my friend and companion, my lover and nurturer, my nothing and everything. Whenever I utter the word "Awen" my heart breaks into a thousand pieces, although I am aware that it is I who gives the word such power, such influence over my human mind, it has become a reality that I treasure and love with such passion, that hopefully is transparent in these words of dry ink. Awen is an aspect of my culture that remained hidden from me until one day it invoked me. In my early teens, lost in the turbulence of puberty, emotionally troubled and confused I experienced what Emma Restall-Orr in her book *Living Druidry* refers to as the Shamanic wound, that deep cut to the soul that opens the floodgates to spirit and allows it to sing so loudly that your mind shatters into insanity. Awen brings us back from the cliff of insanity, preventing us from plummeting over the edge to be lost in madness. All this time it has been there, lost in the wisdom of our culture, so few listen to its music that tugs at the harp strings of our hearts, yet still it sings; in tune to the rhythms of the earth and nature. Awen is magic beyond articulation, and although I have written several thousand words in this and the subsequent chapters, they do not and cannot convey the rapture of its experience. I have cried tears of Awen, tasted the harsh salt that falls from my eyes, not tears of sadness but tears of being in the midst of such rapture, tears of connection. In sharing these words I hope we can cry together.

ChAPTER 2

AWEN AND The ShaMANIC WAY

"I have been a myriad of shapes,
Before I assumed this present form,
I have been a narrow edged sword,
I have been a breath of air,
I have been the furthest star,
I have been a word within letters,
I have been a book in the making,
I have been the light of lanterns.
I have been a course, I have been eagle,
I have been a coracle upon the seas,
I have been compliant in the banquet,
I have been a raindrop in a shower,
I have been a sword, held in hand,
I have been a shield in battle,
I have been a string on a harp.
(Cad Goddeu, The book of Taliesin VIII)

ithin the profound, yet paradoxically simplistic philosophy of Awen; hides the mystery of transformation and shape shifting, a common trait in ancient Celtic culture, as presented in the words of Taliesin above. Taliesin speaks of having been in many forms before attaining consistency. Many who read the words of the chief Bard assume that he refers to several incarnations where he encounters the life experience of each individual phase of existence stated. But this common assumption fails to take

into consideration the nature of Awen, the nature of which Taliesin was more than familiar with. Taliesin's experience of not only connection to Awen, but being it, allowed him to experience anything in the physical and non-physical world as simply an extension of himself. When duality is removed and singularity takes hold of the liberated mind, we arrive at an abrupt realisation that we are everything! We can be the toad that croaks for his mate on the edge of a damp pond, we can be the aroma that the rose emits around its delicate petals. We are everything, and through the liberation of the conceptual mind, this simple conclusion becomes reality and no longer armchair philosophy. Awen brings us to this state, through harmonious connection with the flowing, divine energy of our universe and beyond.

A spell must have been cast upon our people, an enchantment of illusion born from the apparent disconnection of modern society, owing to greed and pride, material gain and wealth. For in ages past our people, like Taliesin, moved freely from this world to the other, crossing that thin, silk veil that separates us from the world of spirit, the world of the *Tywlyth Teg*. And those of the hollow hills travelled here, to our world, inspiring, interacting and sometimes marrying human folk. This interaction can be seen in the ancient tales of our nation, wondrous tales of the fairy folk, of Gods and Goddesses walking among mortals. They speak of humans transforming into animals, birds and fish. This casting away of the restrictive human mind, allows profound experience of enchantment, magic and primordial connection to ensue. Our ability to see clearly increases.

This ability to see beyond the veil and travel there and to alter our shape and form seems to have become a lost art to us in the modern world, or has it? Is it simply that we haven't as yet reconnected to that aspect of ourselves that has the knowledge and skill to magically transform? And are we looking at these tales from the wrong angle, what in fact are they telling us? Did these people actually change their physical forms, or was it something beyond that? Can we do it today?

Shamans, those who wonder between the worlds, those who converse with the spirit world and offer healing, prophesy and guidance to their communities, have been an aspect of human society from the beginning of time. And Britain was no exception. Shamanism and the techniques for loosing the mind continue to be a vital component of Druidry today; in Wales the Shaman is known as the "Awenydd" (A-Wen-ee-th). Through techniques that free the mind from the confines of the body, allowing it to soar with the hawk, swim with the salmon and run with the wild horses we continue to serve our communities through the ancient art of Shamanism. Using the principle of Awen can act as a focus for the freeing of the mind, thus allowing us to tread those unseen places and share the corporeal and spiritual bodies of other entities that can guide and assist us in our earthly quest.

Liberating the mind from the confines of our cerebrums is the key to successful spirit communication and shape shifting. We have become so dense in our corporeal bodies, that we assume it to be the only reality that exists, everything else, the invisible, and the supernatural must be illusions, fantasy. Our consciousness for the 99 per cent of the time we are aware of it, is stuck, firmly rooted somewhere within our heads, trapped by bone, being sensible, cautious, reasonable and guarded. Its main focus is our protection, sustaining the status quo; it dislikes our attempts to leave it behind, and will attempt to prevent interference by any means possible. But for a priest of Druidry to learn the sacred arts of Shamanism we must break loose from the confines of the mind, and run free with the wind, to sip from that consuming cauldron of inspiration and connection. Allow me if you will to tell you a story that reflects this connection to the wondrous rays of Awen.

*Before the reign of Arthur, and deep within the mountains of
the great white kingdom of Gwynedd lived a noble and gentle
man by the name of Tegid Foel. His humble homestead stood
beside the still, dark waters of Llyn Tegid in the village of Bala.
His wife Cerridwen was greatly skilled in the arts of magic, and
would often be found gracefully meandering by the lake's shore,
whispering to its sacred waters, and listening, listening to its subtle
mystery and secrets, casting her spells into its consuming depths.
The trees spoke to her, and she knew their secrets and the wonders
of the herbs that festooned the hedgerows and forest floor.*

*But there was a deep sadness in Cerridwen's heart, for her
only son Morvran, meaning 'SeaCrow' was the ugliest man
to have walked upon Gwynedd's fair and fertile land, so ugly
was he in fact that his parents changed his name to Afagddu
meaning 'Utter Darkness'. How was Afagddu to be accepted
amongst the noble gentlemen of Gwynedd, would he find a wife
who could see beyond his ugliness and love the creature that lay
within? Cerridwen resorted to the magical arts. One morning
she awoke early to consult the 'Book of Fferyllt', those who bore
the wisdom of the entire magic of Britain. And there within
those blessed pages she discovered a spell, a magical brew of
inspiration, of Awen.*

*For a year and a day, the ingredients would have to be
simmered in a giant cauldron and the remaining liquid at the end
of the given time would bestow upon the receiver the knowledge
of all things. Cerridwen reasoned that this would compensate for
Afagddu's ugliness, finally his unrivalled intelligence would earn
him the respect of the men of Gwynedd.*

*Cerridwen scoured the land for the secret ingredients of the
magical brew. All across the land she travelled in her quest,
chanting and singing to the plants as she gathered them. She set
a massive cauldron upon the fire and found a young boy from the
village called Gwion Bach to tend it, and Morda, an old blind
man from the village was summoned to stoke the fires. For a
year and a day that cauldron bubbled and steamed, as the herbs*

within worked their magic, for a year and a day Cerridwen continued her task of gathering, adding to the cauldron's great belly.

On the final day, Cerridwen fell into an exhausted slumber, when suddenly the cauldron shuddered and cracked, and as it split the three drops of that magical brew soared into the air and landed promptly on Gwion Bach's thumb. Gwion, startled at being burnt quickly thrust his thumb into his mouth to quench the sting. In an instant all knowledge was his, as the Awen coursed through his veins, causing his brain and mind to explode with the rapture and bliss of all that the universe beholds. The remaining brew turned to poison, and contaminated the rivers nearby, polluting the land and killing the horses that drank from them.

Cerridwen awoke, but Gwion anticipated her reaction, her son had been cheated of the only gift she could bestow upon him and the fury rose within her, a tumultuous storm of great strength and rage. Gwion took to the hills like the wind and knowing that Cerridwen pursued him he transformed into the shape of a hare, his long hind legs thrusting him forward deep into the valleys of Snowdonia. Cerridwen relentlessly transformed into a greyhound and pursued the hare with great speed. The hare grew weary of the chase and bounded towards a lake in the distance, with a great leap it soared into the sky and dived into the murky depths, in an instant the hare transformed into a salmon, scales and fins took the place of fur and legs. Through the dark depths it swam, faster than the current around its body, navigating tendrils of underwater plants and vegetation. But Cerridwen came, in the shape of an otter, she gave chase. The salmon knowing it could not out swim the otter bolted for the surface, and as it burst through into the sunlight, it rose into the air, scales became feathers, gaping mouth became beak, and a delightful song burst from its body, as a wren Gwion took to the clouds. But Cerridwen followed, this time in the guise of a great and fierce hawk, and the two birds chased and dived and hurtled through the sky, the tiny wren soon grew tired of the chase, and below in a farmer's field he saw a pile of winnowed corn, and towards it he flew, transforming as he landed into a single grain. But Cerridwen was a wise and knowing witch, in turn she transformed into a great black hen and began pecking at the corn, until finally she pecked at Gwion himself and ate him.

But Cerridwen fell heavily with child, and knowing that this child was not of her husband's, she realised that a deeper, older magic had occurred, Gwion Bach lay within her womb. For nine months she carried the child vowing to kill it at birth. But when the birthing came, there beside the shores of Llyn Tegid, she beheld a wondrous child of such beauty, her heart melted and she could find no evil within her that could kill this child. And so a coracle she made, and wrapped in soft leather she placed the child within, and set him afloat upon the lake, placing him at the mercy of the elements. For a year and a day the coracle sailed through the kingdom of Gwynedd, until eventually it was caught in the weir of Gwyddno Garanhir in the estuary of Aberystwyth.

It was Noson Calan Gaeaf, Samhain, All Hallows Eve and tradition had it that upon this night a catch of salmon worth a hundredweight in gold could be found in the weir, but when Gwyddno Garanhir's son Elphin descended upon the waters he found nothing, nothing but a dirty coracle caught in the traps. Dejected and miserable he opened it and unwrapped a bundle which hid within it, a baby boy lay within, and from his brow a radiant light shone upon Elphin and sent his heart racing. "I shall call you Taliesin. He with the shining brow," said Elphin. And Taliesin spoke, even as a baby, words of wisdom emanated from his lips and the wonder of Awen was bestowed upon the world.

The above story of the life and history of Taliesin, retold in my own words, plays an important role in modern Druidry, it continues to be a source of inspiration and wisdom for those who walk the forest path, deep in the dappled shadows of the wise all knowing trees. It is an allegorical description of an individual inadvertently waking to the encompassing nature of

Awen, where clarity and strength of vision allow us to move instinctively through the world, transforming, shifting, and changing in accordance to each situation we face. It actively describes the shamanic initiation as Gwion transforms three times before he enters the primordial womb and transforms forever, becoming a changeling, a seer, he who has the sight and wisdom of all things, simply through the process of awakening to mystery. Gwion and Taliesin was always the one and the same creature, it was simply Gwion's awakening that facilitated the understanding of connection. After the initiatory process Taliesin was able to articulate through poetry and verse the strength of that connection.

Central to the story we have Cerridwen, the witch who became a Goddess, the all-knowing mother, nurturing yet cruel, simultaneously merciless and merciful. She forces Gwion to progress through various initiations until finally he descends into her womb, into the darkness where all becomes one. Cerridwen is an allegory for the creative force behind the universe, the primal mother. She is in essence the Awen that initiates the lucidity of Taliesin's connection to the universe. And the story teaches us that we are all capable of this connection, capable of knowing Awen, of becoming it. Cerridwen is also the patron Goddess of all magicians, witches and practitioners of the magical arts in Britain, magic plays an important yet sometimes controversial role in Druidry and Cerridwen is the guardian of that knowledge. Magic transforms the practitioner and Cerridwen stands at the gates to the cauldron that allows us access to the depths and darkness of magic. She does not only represent the magic of simple spell casting and folkloric magic which both have validity in their own rights, but she also represents the magic of true transformation, deep, primal magic from the very origination of our soul. Her magic requires work, dedication and a level of commitment that most are unwilling to give, in approaching her cauldron many run terrified by her awesome power and ability to facilitate and speak to us on an instinctive all-knowing level to transform the mind and break the mould of ignorance and unconscious living. Achieving a better, experiential knowing of Awen calls for stamina and intense connection, there is no belief involved here. It is a knowing. We experience therefore we know. To simply stand around the glowing embers of Cerridwen's cauldron, soaking in the ambience and warmth and prancing around like a bunch of new age fluffs is not enough to embrace Awen. The way of the Awenydd, the Shaman, requires vision and strength, we must be warrior and pacifier, hunter and hunted. If we remain in the light of all that's sugary and nice, where we eventually become so fluffy we will need back-combing, we will become trapped in the outer mysteries of Awen, never experiencing the wonder of being it. To experience it we need to get down and dirty, immersing ourselves in the transformative qualities of the wondrous rays, becoming them, being them!

Generally Pagans are comfortable with the invocation of energies and deities within their rituals, but how do we invoke Awen? Can we in fact simply call on this force and expect it to grace our ritual with its presence? Ultimately it is a matter of perspective and personal experience; I can only offer my method for the connection I achieve with Awen during my own rituals. Because Awen is a part of us and we a part of it, its simple invocation seems rather insignificant for something of such enormity. Rather than simply calling feebly on the flow of Awen to attend your rituals, becoming, and assuming the form of Awen gives an extra degree of connection to your rituals, resulting in creativity and transformation. When we comprehend that we are the flow of Awen, which runs within our veins, which is in the firing of the neurons in our brains and lies deep within that void between our very molecules, we attain an understanding that renders its simple invocation unnecessary. We only need to alter our consciousness to such a level that we feel the flow of it, become it. We do not call the Awen for the Awen is already calling to us, its song permeates every molecule and space within us, it cares not if we recognise or acknowledge it, it sings regardless. For humans to believe rather arrogantly that we can call on such a force and suddenly perceive it I find rather absurd, when the light of Awen is perpetually calling to us. By assuming its form we are acknowledging its existence and influence upon matter and the physical world. In its assumption we open our ears, minds and spirits to the ever present song that invokes us!

Our minds however, are our very worst enemies, to achieve the state of flowing inspiration, and to feel the warm light of the rays encompassing your body and soul, it is necessary to loose the conceptual mind. When this occurs, we enter the realm of the non-conceptual mind where our spirit sings blissfully of singularity and connection. Awen, although it exists as a concept its actual understanding through connection can only be successfully achieved via the non conceptual mind, where the bondages of society, upbringing and environment no longer hold sway, their ties become weak, and we enter the reality of our very essence. Within that purity and oneness we hear the lyrics of the blissfulness of Awen. Each night we move close to this state, this state of simply being a part of all things. When we wake up from restful sleep, what memory do we have of that experience? Can we remember being asleep? Other than the odd dream every now and again what do we remember of that deep slumber? Normally, unless plagued by nightmares or a restless night, we awake refreshed, revitalised and a residual emotion remains with it, a sense of bliss. Not happiness, or contentment, simply bliss, a feeling of near rapture, a sense of having been in a place of un-thinking, of not being 'Me'. And we go there every night, to that deep nothingness of all things, where the rays of Awen wait to explode in an array of enlightenment and illumination. It is to this place that we move to when assuming the form of Awen. Rapture is the best word I can think of to convey what we feel when we become Awen, our language is too inadequate to adequately articulate the depth of sensing and feeling that we encounter in the rays. Sensing and feeling? It's beyond that, those words do it no justice; words cannot convey the blissfulness of Awen connection.

We have no need of transport to get there, there is no suggestion of a journey, or a long trek into the other world to find Awen, it is here, a constant, within and without us, we only need to become aware of it, and that awareness awakens us to the understanding of 'Not I' and moves us to the place of 'Being'. And within the rays, feeling them course through our very souls, we become like Taliesin and can quote as he did those long centuries ago: "I have been". The wonder of singularity is the ability to be in all places simultaneously, the past the present and the future. Streaming our sub-consciousness during this time allows us the privilege of entering another form, another physical entity's experience, where we shift our shape and journey within the experience of something else's reality. We are ultimately already there!

Even the enchanting world of Quantum Physics mirrors to some extent the all encompassing nature of Awen within its theory of the Zero Point Field. Allow me to explain, imagine if you would you have in your hands the most powerful magnifying glass in the universe. With this glass you look at a friend's finger, and through it you can see deep within their flesh, through skin and bone and down, down deeper into the world of cells, even there you can see further, further than the mitochondria and the nuclei of cells to the very atoms that create them, and there between those tiniest of structures there is a space, an emptiness. This void that inhabits the space between everything that exists, a space that links up with distant stars and galaxies, with the butterfly happily foraging in your garden, they all have within them the same space, the Zero Point Field. It is within this space that Awen exists, from the darkness before time, before manifestation, there it lies, its light radiating forth to illuminate the atoms, molecules and cells that extend from within it. It is *all* things but yet *no* thing.

Quantum physics describes how the act of observing something changes the inherent behaviour of the observer's matter, therefore observing the flowing of Awen, not only has a profound effect on our minds but alters the behaviour of our physical make-up, resulting in balance. When you consider that illnesses and disease often result from states of mind, stress, anxiety and other often trivial worries that exist in our predominantly unconscious society it gives credence to the fact that observation affects matter. Observing the negativity and cruelty and depth of ignorance in our world alters the behaviour of our physiology, the "I am sick of…blah, blah, blah…" comment that we hear so often affirms this state of mind affecting matter, where we positively confirm something's effect on our bodies. When our minds perceive something as fundamental and unifying as Awen its effect on the material world is neutral. This allows us to see matter for what it truly is, just another reality, we have no need to control it; we simply need to be in balance with it, where energy and matter and their observation serve to coexist in harmony through connection.

Somewhere, deep within the vast, all knowing nature of our spirits we remember this connection, this singularity that Awen teaches. It is simply a matter of remembering, when we live with lucidity and are free from the bondage of society's brainwashing we awaken to a new connection, but this connection has a side effect. When one assumes singularity it has a knock on effect on our ordinary physical lives. This lucidity, living in a state of wakefulness facilitates a distancing from society as a whole, where the practitioner feels both a part of this world, yet subsequently apart from it, living on the edge if you like looking into a world inhabited by so many unconscious minds. The normal world inhabited by a constant state of unconsciousness becomes dense and ordinary, and we feel a sense of separation from it. Yet underlying this sense of separation lies the inherent quality of Awen, that of singularity, and through this we feel a paradoxical connection to those who have not attained a sense of lucidity in their lives, after all we are in one sense a part of them. It is only our lucidity that separates us, displaying that even through connection we may still encounter the illusion of duality. An old Welsh triad; the relaying of ancient wisdom in rhyming triplets, describes this paradox of Awen: *"To be aware of all things, to endure all things and to be removed from all things."* The Awenydd are of this world and simultaneously not of it, this can lead to confusion and conflict. Inspiration, the fundamental tenet of Awen, is the link that shatters that illusion of "Me" and "Other". And that inspiration causes us to express in a transformative and positive manner, creating ever increasing circles of Awen, like the ripples on the surface of a still and tranquil pond, each far reaching ripple touching, moving and affecting its surrounding environment and the creatures that inhabit its space.

EXERCISES

Exercise 1: Familiarisation

Connecting to the rays of Awen profoundly alters our perception and development within Druidry, initially begin with a simple meditation, familiarising yourself with the symbol of Awen, which acts like a key to the subconscious, non conceptual mind. On a plain piece of white card draw the symbol of the three rays thus / | \ in bold black ink, and enclose the symbol within a circle. You will be familiar with this practise from the exercise in the previous chapter, but this time we take it one step further. Use this symbol as a visual focus to open your awareness to the rays and their nature. Sit quietly before the symbol, which should be conveniently placed at eye level to avoid straining of the eyes. Extinguish all light in the room, except for one small candle which should be placed behind the symbol, just out of view, to prevent the eyes from tiring due to the brightness of the flame. The effect is rather atmospheric, the Awen symbol on its card will radiate from behind with a dull glow, allowing enough light to focus on the image, yet not too much to distract from the meditation. If you wish, burn some sweet smelling incense.

After allowing your vision to clear and relax to the surroundings, ensuring that enough light is present to allow you to adequately see the symbol, begin by simply staring at the symbol. Breath slowly and deeply, focusing on your breath, the rise and fall of your chest. Do not construct any thoughts regarding the symbol, simply look at it. If you focus your eyes somewhere at the midpoint of the central ray, your field of vision will allow you to clearly see the adjacent rays and the circle enclosing them. In your head or out loud begin to repeat the word "Awen", over and over in the form of a mantra. If any thoughts invade your consciousness simply observe them, pay them no heed, they are of no importance. Allow the symbol and word to infiltrate your very being, feel the rays coursing through your mind and body as the mantra resonates through your skull. Become aware of the origination of your thoughts, where do they come from? See the utter darkness that exists within your head, where your brain sits, a place that will never see the light of day, yet a place of infinite wisdom and illumination. Allow the darkness within your head and the lights of the three rays to meet, see the glowing light of the Awen blending with the darkness within your cranium, each aspect a vital component of inspiration, the light and the dark. Do not allow your eyes to move from the image of the Awen before you. Now, depending on the thickness of the lines that you have drawn, when you close your eyes you should still be able to see an imprint of them, burnt onto your retinas. If not try and draw the rays as outlines in thick black pen, this should increase the effectiveness of the illusion. With your eyes closed see the rays within the darkness of your mind, illuminating that space, feel yourself filling with inspiration and creativity as slowly the rays are absorbed by the darkness behind your eyelids and vanish into the abyss of your consciousness. When they have finally disappeared be aware that they are potentially still there, invisible, but present none the less.

The purpose of this simple meditation is to familiarise yourself with the three rays, the outcome of the meditation is that of relaxation and inspiration. I would suggest daily meditations of such nature, to free the mind from the everyday world and focus the attention on the divine rays of inspiration.

Now that we have familiarised ourselves with the Awen and formed a relationship with its physical appearance, let's break the mould and become it!

Exercise 2:
"The Awen I sing, from the deep I bring it."

Three vowels identify the resonating sounds of the three rays. Their vocalisation is believed to connect us to the eternal song and vocalisation of the universe, bringing us closer to the true nature of our spirit. The vowels are the song of Awen and they are the way in which the universe speaks inwardly to itself. Awen is the voice of the universe within all things, and this simple technique allows us to hear the song of Awen singing within us, by merely harmonising with it. Sound has a profound effect not only on our minds but also on our physiology, our very cells resonate and react to sound in different manners, each individual tone affecting different parts of our bodies, tapping into differing aspects of our minds. The vowel sounds of Awen are used to liberate the mind and in conjunction with their effect on the body they assist a powerful shift in our state of consciousness. Most people are familiar with the eastern techniques of utilising mantras to alter the state of mind, however many do not realize that we have a similar system of equal, if not greater value. Owing to the cultural significance of Awen, it not only facilitates a change in consciousness but affirms our relationship with the land. Why use a technique that has no cultural significance to our people?

The vowel sounds of Awen are as follows:
First ray / "O" pronounced 'Ohhhhh.'
Second ray | "I" pronounced 'Eeeeee.'
Third ray \ "W" pronounced 'Oooo.'

These vowel sounds are inspired by the works of Iolo Morgannwg in "Barddas" where a complete description of their mythology and usage can be found. Originally the vowels are depicted as "O", "I" and "U", but the last vowel changes to "W" later on in the book owing to the difficulty non Welsh speakers would have in pronouncing "U". However the change of lettering does not in any way alter the sound, it is believed that the letter "U" in middle Welsh was pronounced as "W". We may not be one hundred percent certain if Iolo invented these vowels and their attachment to Awen or if indeed they are older, in reality it does not matter, they are an effective manner of focusing the mind to a concept that is fundamentally true.

Now assume the Awen pose. In a quiet area where you are not likely to be disturbed, stand with your feet firmly together, arms stretched out on either side of your body at a 45 per cent angle to your body, palms forward. Your body now represents and mimics the pattern of the three rays /|\. Close your eyes and imagine a darkness somewhere above your head, a blackness darker and denser than night, do not force the image or succumb to an insecure judgement that the image must be vivid and cinematic. Simply imagine it, allow the image to float gracefully into your mind. Create it; see the density of the darkness. How big is it? What shape is it? Is it moving? Allow your imagination to be as wild or as subtle as you choose. Now within this darkness something stirs, a movement, subtle at first yet distinguishable. From this movement a shaft of light erupts, imagine the light bursting forth from the darkness you have created, forming the first ray, watch this ray as it emanates from the void and courses through your right arm to sink into the earth beneath you. See in your mind's eye this shaft of light radiating from the darkness through your arm and into the ground. As you imagine, allow the first vowel "O" to gently rise from your lungs, repeat this vowel at least three times or in multiples of three, until you feel comfortable with the vocalisation. Feel the resonance of it course through your body like a river. Which parts are they affecting? Is it the throat, the chest, the groin? Continue to visualise the light as your focus turns to the second ray.

Now imagine a second shaft of light bursting from the darkness, again to impale your body with its radiant quality, this time straight through the top of your head, through your torso, your legs and into the earth. Vocalise the second vowel "I". Again feel its resonance, observe its effect on your body and mind. Finally focus on the darkness above once more and watch as the third ray bursts forth to beam through your left arm and into the ground. Allow the final vowel to rise from your body, through your vocal cords and out into the world, "W".

Now you are Awen in its entirety, begin to vocalise the three vowels one after the other, decide for yourself in accordance to what feels right regarding speed and key. Let go of any inhibitions you may have. Allow the sounds of the vowels to blend and swim together, forming a cacophony of tone and music. Continue to imagine the beams of light connecting you to the darkness above and the earth below. After a few minutes of vocalisation your consciousness will begin to loose its cohesion. Your body will naturally respond to the effect of the technique, do not hinder it in any way, and simply allow the song to consume your being. Owing to the nature of the posture, with feet together your body will want to sway and possibly shake. Go with it, begin the dance as you respond to the natural music of the universe. Continue through this experience for as long as it takes to attain a state of singularity, a few minutes is not sufficient for profound connection, I find between twenty to thirty minutes sufficient. However you may find that an hour or more may pass in this state. You are Awen, feel your spirit expanding to encompass the entire universe which it inhabits. See, feel and be Awen.

When your body calls you back into corporeality, extinguish the rays, allow them to gently return to the void, to the cauldron from which they sprung. Transform the vocalisation into mere sighs, gentle, unobtrusive. Depending on how your body reacted during the exercise, you may feel stiff or exhilarated. Become aware of your body and allow your consciousness to fall softly back into the confines of your skull. Having been in the cauldron of inspiration, known the secrets of the universe, you must create, express, share. Do anything you can to express that connection, prophesise, divine the future, remember for the last minutes or hours you have been the past, present and future, use it to serve your community.

For what I refer to as "The quick Bardic fix", for a sudden surge of inspiration, use the initial stages of this technique to reaffirm the connection to Awen, you need only spend a moment or a few minutes maximum in the process. However this method of invoking inspiration is not a substitute for the previous exercise, and should be used in addition to it. The more frequently you practise this technique the more adept you will become at assuming the form of pure inspiration. Tapping into the creative energy and power behind the universe, return and create.

Another version of the above technique can be successfully utilised in a group setting, preferably the group should be a minimum of three or multiples of three. This version requires three people to lie together on the ground with their heads in contact with each other. You may lie in the pose of the three rays or in a star shape to facilitate maximum contact. Each person vocalises one vowel, initially in turn, then finally as a chorus. This technique allows each individual to feel the resonance of the vowels from all parties present, creating a unique vibration within the body. Use the above exercise as a foundation for the visualisation aspect of the exercise, altering it to suit your needs. The effect of this technique is twofold, as specified previously, each person feels and senses the resonance from the other people present, and also develops a sense of deep connection with each member of the party. Also, a sense of connection to the other people emerges relatively soon in the exercise, easing each individual into the connection they will ultimately sense as they enter the rays of Awen and become them. Sharing such experiences strengthens the relationship of a group or grove, developing trust and integrity between individuals who practise their spirituality together as a community.

Exercise 3: Shape and form

When we purposefully wonder, with integrity and with honour into the shape and form of another it is a profound and exhilarating experience. Shape shifting, the assuming of another form, transports us to realms and places, unfamiliar, alien, filled with wonder and magic, healing and wisdom. Like the Shamans of old, and Gwion Bach in the previous tale, we also have the capability of assuming the form of another, tapping into the life experience and wisdom of that being, and utilising that knowledge to serve our communities. Remember that this exercise is a spirit experience, our bodies remain unchanged and it is our consciousness projected into spirit that assumes another form. By using the previous exercise and assuming the form of Awen, we instantaneously become aware, on some level, that we are indeed all things that exist, it is this understanding that allows us to enter the experience of another. By streaming our consciousness with pinpoint accuracy and intent we enter the state of oneness, using it as a method of transporting the spirit into the form of another. Time has no relevance here, the creature you have chosen may well have died hundreds of years previously, its spirit may well still exist and remembers that experience, and it is this magic that we use during shape shifting. Its soul is your soul; you are simply tapping into the experience of its corporeal form, its existence in the physical world, its memory of 'being' immortalised in its spirit, contributing to the vitality of the universe.

Many practitioners of Druidry will have a totem animal, or the spirit of an animal that meets with them during meditation and trance. This relationship with the spirit of another creature cannot be forced; it must develop over time, gradually and subtly. In time the creature will come to you, when it is ready. To assume the shape of this or any other creature or spirit, I suggest you allow a considerable amount of time to familiarise yourself with it. If you choose an animal, for example a raven, observe it, study its nature and behaviour, and create a relationship with this creature. If the creature does not exist in this reality, draw it, paint it, and write to it. Remember there are spirits in the other world that have encountered experience or life in forms that we may never comprehend. They may seem beyond our ability to understand, giving them the feel of deities but that may not be necessarily the case. There is more to this universe than we will ever know in our limited human form. The aim here is to form and develop a sacred relationship with your chosen totem. It is rather impertinent to suddenly decide on a whim to become a wren when you know very little about them! Their soul may share the same singularity as yours, but its life experience differs, its interaction with its world and community vary greatly from our own, it is this wisdom and knowledge that assist us and our communities during shape shifting.

When you have developed a relationship with your chosen object, perform exercise 2, with the prior addition of a few minutes meditation, focused on your intent to share the experience of another. When you have assumed the form of Awen and are deep in trance, allow the image of your chosen creature or spirit to infiltrate your being, hear its call, see it in all its glory allow your spirit to integrate with it, becoming it, shift your entire focus away from your corporeal form and into its shape. At this point the visualisation of the three rays of light will diminish, as you assume form within the spirit experience of another. The trick here is to remember that you are both one, you were never separate, the illusion of duality shatters. Allow the universe and the world of spirit to invoke you, not the other way round. Deep in trance, deep within singularity, focused on intent, the body evaporates as spirit to spirit you become the form of another. Do not attempt to construct anything; simply allow the experience to consume you. The illusion of self no longer holds truth; you and the other become one. In time your awareness of its spirit will arise, it will become aware of your spirit and its attachment to a human form, the process is a two way thing, whilst you experience it, it experiences you! Spirits collide in harmony.

Live this experience; learn from the wisdom and knowledge of another. When the experience draws naturally to its conclusion, see again the illuminating rays of Awen, and conclude the session as described in exercise 2. Gives thanks and honour to the spirit and experience of the creature you have shared with, integrate this relationship into your everyday life. You have been touched by the experience of another, honour it.

Exercise 4: Songspells

A Songspell transports and liberates the mind, pinpointing our focus and intention for whatever ritual or magical practise we intend to perform. A Songspell is primarily a set of words that focus the mind on a particular goal, these can be taken from historical texts or invented on the spur of a moment, and it is not so much the content that matters but rather the intention behind the words. A Songspell behaves in a similar manner to an eastern mantra; they are repeated over and over, each repetition affirming the quality and intention of the words and their symbolic significance to the individual. They can be utilised for almost every act of ritual or magic that exist, whether we wish to simply reach a state of contemplation, or to attain clarity from the realm of spirit connection. Perhaps we wish to become entranced, to change our form and shape, or to travel beyond the mists of time to another place and another people. Sometimes we need to journey to the other worlds, maybe to the depths of Annwn to encounter the cauldron of inspiration, or to seek counsel of the ancestors and the Gods. A Songspell can take us to these places. Formed, created or taken from the ancient texts and repeated at a fairy mound or sacred site, with deep integrity and conviction they will facilitate our journey beyond the veil.

Many Druids practise magic and the raising of energy to change or manipulate a situation by forces beyond the understanding of the "Muggle" world; Songspells are effective tools for this type of transformation. We can see many examples of Songspells in the works of Taliesin as demonstrated in the opening verse of this chapter, his "I have been…" poems not only relay to the reader an esoteric mystery as to the nature of Taliesin, but also act to affirm his experiences, each retelling or rendition transports the mind to the truths of those statements and the experiences encountered there. In the modern world they act in the same way; however, you will notice that the Taliesin poems in the English language are not metered; they do not follow a set pattern of rhyme. In the ancient Celtic languages all poetry rhymed, for one simple reason; they spoke to a deep part of the mind that thrives on patterns. A rhyme is just that; a pattern that repeats, it becomes familiar, the mind remembers them with ease, and their repetition alters the consciousness. If a verse does not rhyme, it is not a Songspell and will not be effective. So when creating a Songspell try to ensure it rhymes, the effect is subtle yet immensely powerful. This presents a problem when we wish to use an existing Songspell from the old texts, maybe a poem from the Black of

Carmarthen or the words of Taliesin speak to us. If we use the existing English translation, we are dependant on the integrity and accuracy of the translator; some of them were not that good! We also sacrifice the metered, rhyming quality of the old language, a quality that offers such richness of spirit and connection, but to use the old language takes effort. Spirituality however is an effort, it is something that requires work and dedication, to continuously rely on the works and words of others is to sacrifice our own abilities and skills. Concerning Songspells, if you can use the original Welsh then do so, if you can't then try and learn, it is not as difficult as you imagine. The original Welsh versions of all the poems and songs from the old books are available from a myriad of sources, books, libraries and probably the most comprehensive resource is the internet. Compare the original Welsh to the many translations available, and learn to phonetically recite the verses. The unfamiliar sounds will instantly affect your consciousness, combining with an understanding of what you are actually saying; they are powerful, ancient tools for transformation and the attaining of an altered state. If you must perform your Songspell in any other language, try to ensure they rhyme. Some may argue that the language is irrelevant, to a degree this is true. Yet language has powerful attributions, it connects us to the very essence of a people and their culture, being the primary key of identifying a culture, language opens doorways that were previously bolted shut. It is not necessary to become fluent in middle Welsh or modern Welsh, but to be able to adequately pronounce and recite some of the old verses is an useful tool for anyone on the Druid path, it links you directly to ancient memory and culture.

Visualise yourself sitting at an ancient monument and using the same words as Taliesin and Cerridwen to alter your mind, in their tongue, speaking as they would have spoken all those centuries ago, the mists of time will dissolve around you, words have power, ancient words connect us to ancient memory. Our words, whether they be ancient or modern, when Awen filled open the gateways to spirit and connection, allowing us to move at will between this world and that of the soul and its experience.

Here are some examples of ancient and modern Songspells that you can use.

"Awen a ganaf, (Ah-wen a gan-av)
O ddwfn y gayaf." (Oh th-oovn u gay-av)
"The Awen I sing,
From the deep I bring it."

"Seith ugein ogrfen, (Saeeth ig-ain o-ger-ven)
"A sydd yn yr Awen." (Ah see-th un ur Ah-wen)
"Seven score Goddesses,
There are in the Awen."

"Awen fy, (Ah-wen vee)
Awen aeth, (Ah-wen ayth)
Awen row'n, (Ah-wen row-n)
Yn ol 'ir daith." (Un all eer die-th)
"The Awen was,
The Awen went,
The Awen we return
To the journey."

Whether you practise your Druidry alone or within the sacred relationship of a grove or group, assuming Awen and developing an intimate, singular relationship with it profoundly affects your development and connection to the spiritual heart of Druidry, creating a steadfast foundation upon which your entire spiritual life will stand. Bonding with and being Awen brings us to the inner mysteries of Druidry, to the temple of inspiration and singularity, allowing us to become one with all things, sharing, changing and shifting, becoming an integral part of nature. Blinded by the light of truth and the darkness of potentiality, our lives change as a consequence, our life experience enhanced by sacred relationships, and we move forward into the world as priests of Druidry, priests of Awen.

CHAPTER 3

BECOMING AWENYDD

See me as the sun on the mountaintop,
Feel me in the power of the seas,
Hear me in the laughter of the stream,
Power of nature, power of the trees.
It is you, who are broken,
You are part of me,
Some of you have awoken,
But others might never be free.
This is my song, this is my voice,
These are my words, this is my choice,
Hear me now; take heed of my words,
Love me now, and your spirit will fly.
(Extract from "The Song of Awen" by Damh the Bard)

ruidry transforms the practitioner and challenges the spirit. Responsibilities and obligations mutate and alter as we venture deeper into the rays of light and its initiatory darkness. This awakening and sense of lucidity causes the spirit to fly to heightened states of consciousness, searing the spirit and scorching the heart. Those who are touched by the rays are never quite the same again. This is the path of the awakened, those who have been forever touched and inspired by the consuming fire and potentiality of Awen. The transformative elements of Awen and our sacred relationship with it, with the very song of our essence, instigates a change within the practitioner, summons a tumultuous storm within the heart.

Life takes on a new energy, a lucidity previously unknown to the unconscious mind grasps the soul and catapults us into a new state of being, we become the Awenydd. The doors of the unseen world creak open to reveal a Priest within, a Priest of Druidry with the illumination of the three rays at its core, with radiant brows and fire in the head, we venture into the world of the Awenydd. Becoming the inspirer!

Before there were cities, before there was industry there were those priests of tradition and wisdom, knowledge and magic, those who would venture into the unseen worlds to assist, heal and counsel the community and its peers. They were the wise ones, those in tune with the inner mysteries of soul and being, the adventurous walkers between worlds, not seeking answers, but relaying mystery and counselling to the people. They were the priests of tribal gods and goddesses, mediators between community and the spirits of place, those of ancient memory whispering through bark and stone, river and hill. These priests paradoxically separate from their tribe, yet an influential and important aspect of the community, arranged and officiated at seasonal celebrations of honour and reverence, prophesied the success of battle and government. These were the 'Awenyddion', the Druids, the priests of Awen.

When consulted it is said they would shake and sway as if possessed by spirits, their eyes empty and their expression vacant. From them a torrent of riddle like answers would stream, not in any logical form, but in a manner which challenged the soul of the seeker and spoke to the heart, by-passing the mind, and inserting truth into the very being. They would achieve this state of trance by many methods, the repetitive beating of the drum, the crashing together of stones within the palms of the hand, or the steady mantra of chant or song. They were the enlightened ones, those who serve, those who inspire to bring others into the mystery of spirit and the great song, not through acts of conversion or proselytizing, but by inspiration.

This fundamental tenet of the Awen filled heart applies today, the Awenydd goes forth not to preach Druidry as a way to oneness, but to inspire the many faceted souls to not only hear the great song, but to listen. It is that listening, the sublime, intentional journey into lucidity, where the mind verges on the borders of insanity that sings the soul back home, back into singularity. This profound awakening alters perception, where each spirit on our earth is acknowledged as a vital aspect of the universal soul, of which we as priests serve to inspire. The Awenydd facilitates the breakdown of illusionary duality inspiring connection where disconnection prevailed. All things are perceived as aspects of the One, sacred in their own right; our world reflects the wonder and lyrical music of the universe, sacred, divine and inspiring.

The path of Awen awakens us to the realisation that other realities, other worlds of spirit and soul shine through our own realm of density and matter. It is this acknowledgement that melts the heart and brings us to the wondrous wisdom of the trees, the wisdom of Druidry. Druidry is the worldly expression of Awen, practised within a cultural framework that links us to ancestral memory, to the connection between tribe and land and it is those three rays of light that connect us to the essence of soul, to the song of our origination.

Let us explore the worlds of the Awenydd, bearing in mind that this is my own perspective, developed over years of practise, they work for me, and perhaps they will inspire your own journey. Paganism is unique in the manner that it allows personal exploration and the creation of personal tradition, where we invent through inspiration the rituals, rites and philosophies of our spirituality, sharing them with others to inspire. I have not entirely invented the following; it is inspired by the past with the addition of my personal experience.

The Worlds Of The Awenydd

Awen connects us to soul, to the very energy behind and throughout the universe and as stated previously, it lies at the very heart of Druidry. But the rays of light also illuminate our world and the beauty and wonder of nature, of the trees and hills, the vast and blue oceans, the temperamental skies. This is our world, the world in which we express our Druidry, our creativity and connection. In Druidry we see the world as three distinct realms, land, sea and sky. We interact and form relationships with each realm, each one effecting us on many different levels, each one vital for our survival on this planet. Our rituals and rites honour the great spirits of these realms as they present themselves within our locality, dictating the way in which we live our lives; we are at the mercy of these powerful forces, but we are also of them. In Druidry there is no antagonism between us and the land, sea and sky, our relationship is one of honour and respect, reverence and humility.

Becoming an Awenydd, a priest of Awen, requires us not only to have a divine and sacred relationship with the rays themselves but also with the world that they illuminate, our world. Our experience is locked here on this planet, trapped by density we encounter physical life and Awen permeates that life. We see the wonder of the rays throughout the natural world; our perspective alters dramatically as we see the sacredness in all things, as we see our spirit reflected in the beauty of our home, Earth. Nature inspires us, and as we move closer to her and understand that human nature is only an aspect of nature, we develop an intimate relationship with her. Attuning to the cycle of the year, the great wheel of birth, life and death reflected in land, sea and sky, our awareness of nature increases; our susceptibility to perceive her mood, her ebb and flow strengthens. We eventually begin to feel the great wheel, the cycle of land, sea and sky coursing within us. When we clearly hear the song of Awen singing through the land, sea and sky, we naturally form a sacred relationship with the earth, a relationship which affects our vision and ultimately our lives.

We shall explore the realms of land, sea and sky in conjunction with the additional three worlds of existence common to Druidic practise, these are the three worlds expressed by Iolo Morgannwg in his "Barddas." He described three worlds symbolised as three circles one within the other, they are called, Abred, the innermost circle; Gwynfyd, the central circle; and Ceugant, being the outermost. Many may argue of the dubious nature of this philosophy, or indeed any of Mr. Morgannwg's work, and that in fact they have no relation to the Druids of old. In my opinion they work, they have been a part of our culture since the 18th century, and there is little doubt that Iolo was a genius, one of the most remarkable bards since the age of Taliesin. Without him and his works Druidry would have a very different face, I personally admire and love his work, having applied some of his philosophies to my own personal spirituality I have found a depth of magic and intense transformative quality to them. He was a man in love with this land, in love with its people and in love with inspiration. Look closely and his Awen is apparent within his words. His concept of the three worlds tie in beautifully with the three rays of Awen and the common three realms of modern Druidry, land, sea and sky.

This philosophy speaks of spiritual progression, a concept not unique within the Celtic nations but mirrors the beliefs of other ancient civilisations. Meditating on this concept can bring about some remarkable realisations, and again it connects us to our land, to our people, it speaks of the sacred relationship between tribe and land.

The first world is that of Ceugant, the realm of the One. This is infinity, singularity, the world of wholeness, where the primal moving force behind the universe exists, it is the collective subconscious, the soul of the universe enriched by the experiences of the billions of spirits that have encountered the physical universe. Having existed in matter, these spirits separate yet linked to the one, experience existence in shape and form, an existence that enriches the soul experience of the universe. This world can be equated to sky, far reaching, all encompassing. In the Awen pose of exercise 2 in the previous chapter; it equated to the darkness you imagine beyond the rays. This is our origination, the point of initiation; it is the all present darkness beyond the rays of Awen, where the un-manifest exists, swimming in the void of nothingness. It is the place of not-being, in this state there is no identity; we are the One, the all. From this state of being the One chooses to fragment, it reaches out into the universe it has sung into existence and facets of it embark upon that initial movement, away from the One, into the world of spirit and consciousness. Yet umbilical tendrils of darkness connect each individual facet to the One, it is only our earthly programming that de-sensitise us to this inherent connection.

Akin to the sky, to air and breath, Ceugant is constant, ever present, invisible, but can be sensed and felt. Like the soft whispers of a summer breeze through our hair, we feel our connection to the wholeness of Ceugant. The sky exists within us as air, the molecules of oxygen traversing our lungs and arteries, it is not a separate entity, it envelops and permeates all life on this planet, like Ceugant, it is everywhere, all prevailing, omnipresent.

The dancing spirits of air, those spirits of hydrogen and oxygen, nitrogen and methane, forming great clouds of rain and of snow, dance and sing to the rapture of being, of existence and of connection, acting simply in accordance to their nature. Having never been disconnected from the world of the soul, they simply sing their song, with no need to reaffirm connection and re-establish relationship with the soul of the universe, unlike mankind. It is our sense of disconnection that instils in us a need to seek the truth and the nature of the soul, where we shift into the unity of Ceugant.

The second world is Gwynfyd, the realm of spirit or energy, eternally flowing, moving, it can be equated to the sea, its ebb and flow, rising and sinking, penetrating our world. In the Awen pose it is represented as your body from head to ankles. Gwynfyd represents the otherworld of Celtic legend and lore, it is where the hidden people reside, those of the invisible realms, the world of our gods, of our honourable dead. It is the residence of spirits, those who continue to serve the whole, the One, yet continue to grasp and experience the residual effects of having been mortal, of incarnation. This is the realm of spirit which has assumed form, be it through experience from material existence or in response to the exaltation by thought, where mankind has created its gods and other beings. This is also the summer land, the place of rest, contemplation and reflection. It is here that the spirit chooses its physical experience and embarks upon it, attaching itself to a chosen subject, birthing with it into the world of matter, of density and illusion.

It is within Gwynfyd that our spirit resides prior to reincarnation, if that is the spirit's will. The gods and goddesses also reside here, those who have been revered and honoured by humanity, and choose to continue their service, when we call upon our ancestors it is from this realm that they speak to us. The interaction between this world and ours is relatively easy owing to the nature of the veil that separates both worlds. This realm does not exist outside our universe, but permeates our world, it exists just below it, just out of sight, vibrating at a frequency much slower than our own world, preventing us from seeing beyond the veil with our human eyes. It is only an intense connection with our own spirits, who inhabit both worlds that can allow us to see beyond this veil. However, surrounding this world of spirits is the all prevailing darkness of Ceugant, constantly present, waiting, watching, its tendrils of darkness reach into this world, connecting the billions of spirits within it to itself. Ultimately that aspect of the One within us calls us home and we pass from Gwynfyd into the darkness beyond, and become once again the soul of the universe, enriching it with experience. After all we are the universe learning about itself.

Gwynfyd is the world in which we explore the relationships between spirits, where we can move into the experience of another form. It is where we encounter the spirits of nature, the spirit behind the trees, the winds and the seas. It is here that we seek the counsel of elders, our ancestors, those who continue to reside there, and who have not as yet returned to the darkness. Time does not exist in Gwynfyd, it is not confined within matter, it exists just on its borders, and therefore it cannot degrade. It is the corridor between the world of matter and the great soul of the universe. I refer to it as the 'Departure Lounge,' humour me for a minute as I explain!

Imagine a departure lounge at an airport, people milling around, laughter and chatter filling the air, people leaving for exotic locations, people returning to home and to familiarity. It has an air of apprehension, expectation, anticipation, excitement. Numerous gates opening and closing as folk take to their planes, the sudden cries as loved ones meet again, long lost friends finally coming together in tight joyful embraces. This is how Gwynfyd presents itself to me, immensely busy, spirits moving into incarnation, others resting a while, reflecting on previous experiences, others sighing as they return to the blissfulness of Ceugant, the spirits of incarnate humans moving between them, seeking wisdom and news of home. Here we still retain aspects of our humanity, residual remnants of our personalities persist, but as we are closer to the true nature of our spirits they are no longer limiting. It is here that we see the rays of Awen in all their glory, emanating from the darkness beyond, illuminating a world of spirits and the physical world just beyond the veil.

The innermost world, Abred is referred to as the realm of necessity, it is the physical world in which we exist and experience, and can be equated to the land. Within the Awen pose, this world is represented as the base of the rays, where your feet touch the ground. It is firm, stable, nourishing and physical; it is the glorious world which we look upon each day. Abred is the realm of experience, where we live our earthly lives, our spirits observing and absorbing the encounter, relishing every moment of it. But Abred is a necessary stage in the experience of the spirit, for it is here that we experience the illusion of duality, that sense of separation from the omnipresent soul of the universe of which we are an integral part.

It is within Abred that we experience those aspects of life that would otherwise not be encountered by the spirit. In Abred we encounter, love and joy, happiness and sadness, grief and the dark night of the soul, hopelessness and failure and the plethora of human emotions that go into the making of a human being. It is these emotions and the interaction with the natural world that enriches our spirit, our eventual returning to the source contributes to the experience of the One.

Within Abred, those who live lucidly feel the spirits of nature. As we develop our inner senses and increase our ability to perceive the hidden world of Gwynfyd; we begin to notice the spirits that have attached themselves to aspects of nature.

There was a time when mankind and the spirits of nature existed in harmony, in ages past, long before the circles of stones were constructed upon our soft green earth, a time when man was not blinkered by material wealth and gain, and moved amongst nature with reverence and honour.

Developing a sacred relationship with Awen and the subsequent awareness of the unseen worlds, transforms us into Priests of Awen, we become the Awenydd, those who are inspired. And our Druidry springs to life, in touch with the sacred heart of our spirituality; listening to the great song within nature we begin our journey, as our ancestors did before us, along the dappled path of mystery, and into the groves of our inspiration.

Supplementary to Iolo's concept of the three worlds lies another realm, Annwfn, also commonly referred to as Annwn, (A-noon), derived from the Welsh for "An" meaning "Un" and "Twfn" meaning "Deep", the Un-deep, the depth of nothing and all things. In the old tales this world is vividly described and resembles earth, many believe it to be a dimension of parallel worlds, containing the memories of the human dead and all other life forms that inhabited the earth. Others believe it to be the realm of the dead, or Gwynfyd. The arguments are conflicting and ultimately lead us away from the experience of Annwfn as the realm of the universal soul's amalgamated experience. In my own personal visions and journeys to Annwfn, it is the darkness and the light; it is a generic term for the combination and inter-relationship between all three worlds, it is where our stories are held, our mythologies enacted and lived, it is where the universe lavishes in the experience of itself. Basically Annwfn is whatever you want it to be, wherever you want it to be. Annwfn is one subject that Iolo and I disagree upon; he describes it as some kind of Christian Hell or limbo, whereas the old tales do not. The "Preiddeu Annwfn" (The spoils of Annwn) in the Book of Taliesin, describes a world of wonder and fantasy, highly recommended reading for vision quests and inner journeying. Annwfn also features in the first branch of the Mabinogi, ancient Welsh tales of magic and mystery, where Pwyll the Prince of Dyfed travels through a grove into the midst of Annwfn to exchange places with King Arawn for a year and a day. Again vital reading for any aspiring Druid.

I do not offer the concepts of these worlds as a defined structure or basis to which Druids must adhere. They are offered as a method of exploration and connection, they lead us to the multi faceted nature of reality and spirit, they are tools that enable our feeble human minds to articulate and thus understand the mystery of spirit, Awen and the nature of the universe reflected within us. They are a method by which I connect to my ancestors and the spirit of this land, this nation, and ultimately the one great soul of the universe. Explore them, experience them for yourselves, and define them accordingly, you may find that they bear a resemblance to my own experience.

The Priesthood

When we are touched by those fingertips of darkness and the delicious, wisdom filled rays of light, we must inspire. To withhold that inspiration would utterly consume us, and eventually break the heart. As Awen filled priests of nature, we are imbued with a duty, an obligation to share that inspiration, without prejudice, without proselytizing, aiming to share that overflowing cup of Awen and expressing that connection to our communities. As Druids we do not absolve ourselves of worldly responsibilities and obligations. The role of the Awen filled priest is one of integration, where the spiritual and physical compliment the other, knitting the two inexorably together. It is the dance of matter and energy in love with each other. When we combine the sacred with the seemingly mundane aspects of corporeality, the illusion of mediocrity shatters. And as a consequence each gentle step on our green earth, each hand lifted to help or offer a skill, each ear that leans intently to listen to the worries and anxiety of another transform into acts of sacredness. We walk with intent, each silent footfall honouring the beauty and awe filled wonder of our home world and those creatures that inhabit her. When we awaken to awareness and transcend the ordinary, a state of balance emerges from the gloom of unconscious living, this is the beauty of 'Becoming', of living with lucidity, this is how we inspire.

Balance

To live in balance is perhaps the most difficult of all our tasks, the ultimate test and proof of our connection to the universal source. This balance may sometimes feel elusive, a distant aspiration that we long for, and in truth is an arduous task, for as priests of Druidry we are not unaware of the difficulties of living a spiritual life. Living in tune, seeing, feeling and awake to the paradox of life, whilst simultaneously getting up each morning and embarking on the tedious journey to the office; can sometimes undermine and appear contradictory to our spiritual values and inspiration. How many Druids in the 21st century work in an inspiring environment? How many of us have surplus time on our hands to wander the forests and hills, living a life of deep connection twenty four hours a day, seven days a week. Life in the modern world is never that simple, we have other obligations and duties to attend, and they should not be ignored for some utopian concept of living as a priest. A priest is an individual who acknowledges the sacredness of each moment, regardless of its nature, integrating the spiritual with everyday life. Seeking balance where once there was chaos, seeking unification where once there was only separation. A Druid priest does not absolve himself of living in the world to sit on a mountaintop surrounded by the trappings of guruship, seeking only enlightenment. Druids move amongst the world, we are of it; this is an experience that enriches the spirit and contributes to that eternal learning of the universe. To remove ourselves from this world would be an abomination against the source. This removal, a characteristic relatively common in eastern religions, is akin to taking a cruise to the Caribbean, where the sun shines on azure blue seas, and green fertile islands poke provocatively from the gentle waves, then spending the entire holiday locked up in your cabin worrying about home! We see nothing of the experience we have chosen to embark upon, only images of home, consequently missing out on experiences that enrich the spirit. Druids seek balance, of living in the world and being inherently in tune with the flowing current of soul that cascade throughout this stuff we call matter. In this manner we have the best of both worlds. The danger here is that we do not separate ourselves from the world by believing that we are far removed from it. Yes we are different our senses heightened and alert as we walk between the worlds of matter and spirit. But we seek a healthy balance of integration where we serve both the experience of the soul and serve our world, living with honour and integrity.

Becoming priests of Druidry we simultaneously adopt the rank of priest to the people, and with it comes responsibility, not only for the preservation of the tradition and inspiring others to hear the great song, but a responsibility for our planet. The earth serves as our home, our teacher and our playground, upon her green flesh we move gently, each sacred footfall telling a story. We teach by the way which we live our lives, with honour and respect for the earth and her creatures. In tune with the subtle energies of the unseen world and the visible world we serve our communities in many varied ways. Many Druids work relentlessly with environmental matters, local and national politics and charitable organisation, serving both the physical aspects of our planet and the wellbeing of soul connection. There is much that we can do within our own localities that may well affect the entire planet in generations to come. Being actively involved in ecology, tree planting programmes, heritage and conservation not only empowers us as individuals, but benefits the world at large, the effects of which may not be instantly recognisable, but the ramifications of those actions will send ripples through time, influencing the future.

Serving our communities with physical and esoteric skills, brings a sense of balance to life, many reawaken the ancient skills of our ancestors to benefit the tribe. The sacred use of natural hedgerow materials and vegetation for healing and wellbeing, resurrecting the art of herbalism, it is not as difficult as you would imagine. Our perception of natural energies that inherently lie within nature will guide us to the usage and attributions of plants and their healing properties. Backed up with a reliable crash course in natural remedies and plant identification, which are readily available throughout the country, we can once again empower the tribe, working with nature rather than antagonising her. Becoming the wise men and women, in touch with nature, caring for her as she cares for us, and walking between the worlds to guide our people and offer counselling in times of tribulation and anxiety brings us in balance with the earth and her nature.

Within Druidry there are traditionally three avenues of expression, each one serving the community in a unique and inspired manner, the Bard, Ovate and Druid. Each caste imbued with Awen, each one an Awenydd in its own right, in touch with the sacred heart of Druidry. This is not to suggest that one must choose a rank he or she feels an affinity towards. We can have attributions of all three harmoniously swimming within us, each one applicable to a different time or situation. Some however may discover that their talents lie predominantly within one area, a singer songwriter may remain a Bard for the duration of life, singing the essence of the tradition to the people, whispering the secrets of Awen whilst strumming a guitar. Another may be instinctively drawn to the sacred gift of sight and vision, healing and counselling, and remain firmly within the green aura of the Ovate. We cannot enter the tradition with a predisposed concept of our role; it is something that evolves gracefully over time, ripening like the bramble in autumn to colour the soul and fill the heart with vision and purpose.

I identify the three castes of Druidry with three different yet complementary attributions each one applying itself to one of the three realms or worlds of Druidry.

The Bard. Seeing, The land. Abred.
The Ovate. Feeling. The sea. Gwynfyd.
The Druid. Being. The sky. Ceugant.

Let's briefly explore the role of each rank and their purpose within the priesthood.

The Bard, Seeing

The Bard is the observer of the tradition, he who sees beyond the normality of everyday life and using skills of memory and art, craft and music he relays the deeper mysteries of Awen to the people. Preserving the teachings of the old ways in a manner that can easily be relayed and digested by the human mind, the Bard transmits knowledge and mystery through the medium of poetry and art. Through subtle, connective observation the Bard sees the world through a myriad of colours and hears the sweet music of the landscape filtering through rock and mud to the ear of the listener. Owing to the nature of Awen and that we can only realistically relay it's meaning poetically the Bard is a vital component of Druidry a guardian of the tradition. Please note however that I am not simply referring to the Bards of old, but also to the Bards of the modern day, those who sing the music of the great song, and speak of mystery and truth through their works. The Bards never truly left the scene at all, they have always been here, whispering from the edges of society, inspiring those who hear their words and dance to their music and listen to the secrets of spirit and soul.

Filled with Awen we find the bard within and allow him to sing, listening to the pulse of harp strings that ring within our spirits, for these connect the Bard to the earth and to the primordial home of the soul. Sometimes we fail to hear the voice of our inner Bard; and the ripples of rhythm and movement that reach out to the world from our essence, but it is there, hiding within us. As we develop that inner understanding of soul connection, the Bard awakens and we cannot help but sing of mystery and become aware of the effect we have upon our world and environment, and upon others within this world. Our words have power and energy beyond belief; we should never underestimate the power of the Bard and of his words. It is said that the Bards of old could bring down Kings with their mocking and with their truths; our own words and the foolish use of those words can ultimately destroy us, use them carefully and wisely. This is the power of the Bard, of the storyteller, singer and minstrel, the power of the word, and their effects upon the physical world. In our song spells, we use words enveloped in raw and directed emotion, wrapped in an energy that forces our will and projects it towards a specific destination. Invoking we call to the Gods and the spirits with clear voice and intent, the intention that something will be transformed, altered, its reality changed or it perception enhanced. This is the voice of the Bard within us.

We do not all have the confidence to stand before an audience and sing, play the harp and tell tales, the expression can be subtle, gently moving those close to us, reaching out with soft fingertips of inspiration. We can all be bardic; do not listen to anyone who says your work is poor or inadequate. If your work was inspired and it touched something within you, the depth of spirit and integrity will be felt regardless of quality or style. We are all capable of inspiring and being inspired. Regardless of your ability to sing or write poetry, the Awen filled heart is still capable of inspiring and touching another.

As Bards of the Druid tradition we should be creating new stories and new allegories for life and its mysteries, singing of our deep relationship with the land and the spirits. The old tales of tribe and land however wonderful and inspiring, I believe are not being utilised to their full extent, they were meant to be retold, over and over, each retelling applicable to each tribe, each time and each society. As soon as the old tales were rendered in written form, they became stagnant, unchanging, forever fossilised in their form. Although they speak to us on a primordial level and inspire us to reach out through the mists of time to our ancestors, as Bards we should be applying them to our own culture and time, in a manner that continues to inspire from the shadows of the past. Allegorically they touch us and awaken a deep memory within us, causing us to journey into the recesses of spirit, and teaching us the fundamental truths of life and soul. The great gods and goddesses portrayed in the old tales continue to live as long as we give them the necessary energy to survive. It is the Bard that keeps them alive and well, and bridges the river between this world and the world of spirit.

Within the vast chronicles of the Celtic people a myriad of supernatural entities exist that mankind have known for millennia, but sometimes their nature and indeed their tales can be elusive. Take for instance the mother Goddess Modron, who had her son Mabon taken from her at birth and imprisoned for centuries. Who was she? What is her story in its entirety? Rather than fall into the complacent attitude that we just do not know, I suggest we tell it in our own words, initiating the process of story creation that can inspire others, stories that contain within them the essence of truth. This is the duty of the Bard, by connecting to these sources of inspiration, we no longer require a previously written tale that we simply retell, deep connection will enable us to hear the story first hand, it is already there, it simply requires listening to. When new legends combine with the ancient tales, we initiate a plethora of Bardism that speaks of truths ancient and modern.

The Bards of old were capable of memorising up to twenty thousand triads, and countless tales of varying content. We cannot be excused in the modern world. Developing our cognitive skills enable us to memorise and retell the allegories of our connection and people easily and inspiringly. The

Bard becomes the walking, talking keeper of wisdom and knowledge, opening the gates of awareness to those who hear his words, who are hypnotised by a painting, or moved to tears by song and music. By utilising skills of mind, memory and imagination the Bard is able to draw upon the unlimited potentiality of Awen and relay it to the world at large.

Our Bardic ancestors were masters at relaying wisdom in triplet form, known commonly as the 'Triads', there are literally thousands of these triads in existence, reaching back into the shadows of the past. Following are examples of triads which speak of Awen and its value taken from *Cyfrinach Beirdd Ynys Prydain. (Secrets of the Bards of the Isle of Britain)* taken from the original Welsh with English translations by myself. The Bards would have memorised them and used them for contemplation and education. Contemplate on the meaning and images that each of these triads transmits, and then devise your own that speak of your connection to Awen and its relevance to the modern world. These triads are among some of the many written to express not only the qualities of Awen, but its effect on the Awenydd.

> *"Tri pheth a wnant brydydd; Awen, Gywbodaeth a Chynhyrfiad."*
> "Three things an Awenydd requires; Awen, Knowledge and stirring Excitement."

> *"Tair cyneddf Awen; Hardd feddwl, priodol feddwl, ag amrywedd fedddwl."*
> "Three qualities of Awen, a beautiful mind, an appropriate mind and an open mind."

> *"Tair effaith Awen; Haelioni, Gwarineb, a Charedigrwydd."*
> "Three effects of Awen; Generosity, Civility and Kindness."

> *"Tri anhepcor Awen; Deall, Ystyriaeth, ag Amynedd."*
> "Three indispensabilitys of Awen; Understanding,

Consideration and Patience."

"Tri pheth a gynnydd Awen; ei hiawn arfer, ei mynych arfer, a llwyddiant o'I harfer."
"Three things that increase Awen; its rightful usage, frequent use and successful usage."

"Tri pheth a dderchaif Awen; dysg, ymgais, a pharch."
"Three things that initiate Awen; education, effort and respect."

"Tri nod Awen; anghyffredin ddeall, anghyffredin ymddwyn, ag anghyffredin ymgais."
"Three aims of Awen; uncommon understanding, uncommon behaviour and uncommon effort."

Contemplate the role of the Bard and the voice of Awen within you and create. Take pen and paper, instrument or paint and allow that connection to express itself freely through you, creating works of wonder and beauty that move the heart and sing of the magic of nature and unity. Enter the sanctity of nature, under a sharp moon and listen to the song in all its beauty. Allow that song to rise from your own lips and reflect the immense beauty of this rank within Druidry. Sing; sing until your heart will burst!

The Ovate, Feeling.

The Ovatic rank is perhaps the most mysterious and misunderstood aspect of Druidry, elusive and secretive, dark and mysterious. There is a dark deliciousness to the role of the Ovate, and it is their eyes that betray their rank. For there, in the very physical make up of their eyes, lies an intense darkness, a void of vision and knowing, of experience and mystery. Ovates are those who have the sight, the gift of vision, discernment, prophesy and communication, of feeling between the worlds. Both the Bard and the Druid have aspects of the Ovate within them for it is this rank that enables them to see or sense the spirit worlds and the subtle energies that lie hidden in our world, allowing them to channel that essence and bring it into manifestation. Yet some remain Ovates and only Ovates, choosing the world of shadow to move amongst, affecting this world from its fundamental base, by influencing and shifting the very energy that exists within physicality. It is perhaps the most difficult path in Druidry, for it opens the doorway of the soul, causing the practitioner to Ovate see one foot clearly in the world of spirit and the other firmly in the world of matter.

The Ovate is a frequent visitor to the halls of the dead, he who communes with the spirits that the sees with clarity of vision, sometimes to distraction. Akin to the traditional shaman of folklore and history, the Ovate traverses the otherworld in search of answers and advice that serve the community and the development of the Ovates' connection to spirit and Awen. It is the Ovate who at Calan Gaeaf (Halloween) sees the actual boundary between worlds, and is able to reach gently into it, travelling through spirit to divine the future and offer prophesies to the people. The Ovate is the quiet one of the tribe, the mysterious, feeling figure standing just on the edge of the circle, an expert actor who can elude the true nature of his spirit. People are often drawn to their energy, aware that something within them is different, almost peculiar, and aware of the air of mystery that surrounds them. When one spends so much time in that place where personality and earthly trappings hold no power, it alters them, and changes their very persona.

The role of the Ovate is elegant and beautiful, experts at the arts of glamoury they are often proficient actors able to conceal their function from general society. Glamoury, the magical art of creating illusion to suit a need or situation, to move unseen through humanity, visible only to their tribe and to nature, Ovates are powerful and inspiring people. They

are the manner in which the tribe communicates and learns
the ability to see beyond the boundary of manifestation and
into the world of spirit. They are the teachers of the sight
and the gentle arts of feeling, counselling and healing. The
Ovate exists within everyone that walks the Druid way, for it
naturally arises from a direct experience of Awen. But that
paradox of light and darkness can sometimes cause a person
to revert into the shadows forever, affecting change from the
perimeters of life, subtly and quietly. In olden days, the Ovate
would have been the wise man or woman who lived on the
edge of the tribe, alone and in solitude, where the villagers
would instinctively go to in times of need and comfort. Allow
me to offer a vision I experienced of an encounter with an
echo of a distant Ovate.

*Deep in the mountains of Snowdonia lies a small lake of rugged
beauty, a tiny island floats in its centre, a single hawthorn tree,
its branches made horizontal by wild winds and storms, clings
precariously to its western rocks. Late one night I wandered
silently, a gentle humming tune emanating from my closed lips, as
snowflakes of intense white descended from the moonlit sky, each
one gliding to earth in a chorus of music and light. On the opposite
shore of the lake and in the shadow of the mighty mountain that
hung like a matt painting from the snow filled sky, a small hut
glowed warmly through the darkness. The pale orange glow pulsing
through the night drew me towards it; I wrapped my cloak tighter
against my shivering body and slowly walked around the lake.
Somewhere in my rational mind I was aware that no such hut
existed in the present day on that side of the lake, only the ruins of
an old village. As I approached a figure draped in shadow its cloak
streaming behind it like wings in the wind quickly ran past me and
into the warmth of the little hut. I neared the threshold and offered
an emotional greeting of honour and reverence and slowly stepped
into the warm interior.*

*The small hut, with earthen floor and strewn with straw
combined with the various herbs that hung drying, emitted a*

pungent aroma that was welcoming. A cauldron steamed wildly, hanging by three chains from a crooked tripod that flanked the stones of a central hearth, the fire beneath it licking the fat bottom of the cauldron. Beside it sat an old woman, her body swaying and shaking, her eyes as black as coal, only the flickering of flames occasionally betraying the life that hid within them. Her visitor sat, perched on the edge of a stool, staring at her intently. The old woman, reached down and took a handful of herbs from a basket beside her and cast them into the cauldron, a dense steam, heavy and fragrant rose from its depths, her eyes widened, emptied of any emotion or intent as she glared into the dense pillars of blue vapour. And she spoke, in a language that was familiar to me, older than my own, perhaps as old as the circle of stones that graced the valley below. And in that mist, I could see the shimmering images of spirits that relayed the answers the visitor had sought. And she smiled, relieved, grateful as the Ovate sung a song of ancestry and wisdom. And I remembered having seen this same old woman in another vision on the sacred Isle of Mona (Anglesey), during an echo of an ancient Druid rite, and there she was too, her arms outstretched, reaching into the otherworld, the doors to the west opening at her command, seeking guidance for the community during the feast of the dead.

As the glowing fire of the Ovates home slowly vanished, leaving me sitting alone, in the empty ruinous village with snowflakes covering my cloak, her name floated through the cold, biting wind, Eryrwynt (Eaglewind). May she be remembered.

This vision burned into my spirit, whispering of ancient ways and the wisdom of those who sought the sanctuary of the hidden places, whilst simultaneously being integral parts of their communities. In my own peculiar way I have often thought that the traditional witches of Britain retained some of the knowledge of the Ovates of the ancient people, preserving the arts in their folk magic, spell crafting and conjuration. In this manner I have always perceived true witchcraft to be an extension of the old Druid ways, not as a structured tradition or in the manner of the mysteries of Wicca as developed by Gerald Gardner, but a folkloric method by which some of the knowledge could be preserved and handed down from one generation to another. Preserved for all time in the memory of our people, through our mythology and local histories, after all mythology is history of the heart, of the people. It was the skill of the Ovate that relayed the myths and magic of connection to the lips or hands of the Bard, either through inspiration or by means of the Bard connecting to the Ovatic gift within him.

The Ovate was also magician, sorcerer, conjuror, spellcaster, he who knows the mysteries of magic. The old King of Gwynedd, Math, was a figure I identify as an Ovate, a pre-eminent magician who knew the secrets of nature and how to utilise their power in the ordinary world. The ancient tales of Wales portray many such figures of magic and mystery, Ovates of the Druid tradition.

But how are the wisdom and skills of the Ovate appropriate to modern society? The Ovates of today's Druid tradition serve to re-establish a deep, ecstatic connection to the world of spirit, providing a vital link that society does not perceive as a necessity let alone a reality. It is the Ovates' duty through deep connection to inspire the tribe to awaken to the truths and mysteries that lie within our universe and speak of our origination and nature. Providing a balanced service of physical and spiritual wellbeing the Ovate heals and nurtures the spirit of the tribe and the ailments that inflict the body and mind. Their duties can range from the simplicity of applying a healing calendula salve to an infected wound, divining the future from the pattern of clouds, to the trance state of opening the doors of the other world during intense ritual and celebration. However as previously stated this path is neither easy nor comfortable and requires deep and intense commitment to the mysteries of spirit and unity, taking years if not decades to master any degree of proficiency within the craft. Yet the benefits far outweigh any negatives, becoming an Ovate is an immensely transformative and highly rewarding path that strengthens the spirit and increases vision. These visions can then be applied for the benefit of the tribe or our modern communities. With the increasing interest in natural remedies and healing the Ovatic skills are once again required in our world.

Traditionally identified with the colour green, their robes of rich forest hues reflect their qualities and skills, enveloped in the aura of nature, aware of her secrets and able with ease to listen to her and to the connective threads that reach back into the world of spirit, they wander freely through the world, inspiring those who meet them. They become the person at the end of the street that the community instinctively turns to when a child has chicken pox or a maiden's womb remains barren, or when a person requires advice regarding a career change. And when the tribe gathers for ritual, it is he or she whose eyes empty and the darkness of spirit bleeds from them as they observe the myriad of spirits that descend upon the circle.

Develop your skills of divination and prophesy, listen to the voice of your dreams and the whispers of the yew tree, for it is here that the song of the Ovate sings to you. Commune with the trees and plants of your vicinity and use their powers to effectively heal others around you. Open those invisible doors and step through to become a walker between the worlds.

The Druid, Being.

"A large number of men flock to them for training and hold them in high honour. The Druids are wont to be absent from war, nor do they pay taxes like the others. Attracted by these prizes many join the order of their own accord, or are sent by parents or relatives. It is said that they commit to memory immense amounts of poetry. And some of them continue their studies for twenty years."

Caesar, Gallic War VI.

The Druid is an amalgamation of both Bard and Ovate, with the added virtues of maturity, wisdom, skill, prowess, leadership and discipline. The Druid is he who has attained some of the wisdom of the trees, who has grown steadfast in his spirituality and moves with strength and conviction through the world, subtly affecting all those with whom he comes into contact. As a teacher and keeper of the tradition Druids are the flowering crowns of Druidry, they are simultaneously wisdom filled and humble. Clothed in the traditional white robes that reflect the flowing, ever moving dance of the clouds in our sky, they relay wisdom and understanding pertaining to the tradition. Having attained a state of being, their inspiration streams from them like flowing rivers through a mountain range, touching those who come close to them. Yet within the role of the Druid there lies an immense responsibility, teaching comes at a great price, not only does it make teachers vulnerable by giving so much of themselves away, but they take responsibility for the spiritual wellbeing of their students.

Of the nature of the ancient Druids we know very little, we rely entirely on the writings of the classical authors and the occasional vernacular text to offer us an insight into the ancient world of the Druids. It is believed that the Druids of old had several duties, each Druid being an expert in his or her own field of study, be that law, spiritual leader, teacher, philosopher, astronomer, astrologer or scientist. Caesar himself refers to the learned attributions of the Druids: *"They have also much knowledge of the stars and their motion, of the size of the world and of the earth, of natural philosophy, and of the powers and spheres of the immortal gods."* This suggests that the Druids not only studied the esoteric arts but were experts in the field of science and mathematics, combining knowledge of the esoteric with the natural.

To work with the subtle energies of nature one should also be familiar with the physical attributes of nature, learned in the arts of natural science, expanding the mind and the intellect. For instance many pagans work with the movement of the moon around our planet, but how many have any understanding of the science behind this function, why does the moon wax and wane, where is she when she is dark, how does she pull the waters of our planet? The Druid understands the powers of nature on two levels, physical and metaphysical. Balance is the key to effective spirituality, where one function does not hold importance over another, the Druid embraces this balance. Having an understanding of natural science one is more able to tap into the energies that lie behind the physical face. When we learn to identify the trees and watch their transformation throughout the year, familiarising ourselves with their mood and the way in which they interact with their environment we begin to see more. Beneath the surface of things, beneath their physical characteristics we begin to sense the life force that drives them. Knowing them on both levels heightens the relationship we have with them.

The Druids, masters of esotericism and science, walked in balance upon the earth serving the people and the gods. Most importantly they were the caste that ensured the fluid like cohesion of the tradition, keeping it alive and well, offering up sacrifices to the gods when necessary and appeasing the powers of nature, able to reassure and explain natural phenomena, firmly bonding the chaotic nature of a tribal community.

The Druids are the elders of the tradition, those who have spent years if not decades treading the forest path. Having spent time in silence and isolation, deep in conversation with the gods, they attain the state of mediators, able proficiently to journey to the realm of the gods and the spirits to seek advice and assistance to those on the earth. The Druids are experts at 'Being', their personalities reflect the endless and boundless nature of the sky above us. And like the clouds, they change and transform in accordance to their specific role; each Druid may well be very different from the next one. The true nature of existence and the mysteries of the universe and the shining rays of Awen are known to them, they are the epitome of the tradition. They share an invaluable relationship with local gods and the spirits of place, offering a starting point for those new to the tradition, teaching the skills required for communication with deity. It is not often that one stumbles across a Druid of experience and knowledge but when one does, it is quite apparent. Druids have a certain air around them, each movement of the body is precise, each word has great impact, and the eyes shine with the fires that burn in their heads. They have overcome the restrictions of the profane body, and know the secrets of the subliminal realms.

Modern Druidry presents a problem; we know from ancient literature that the Druids were an initiatory tradition, where does this leave us in the twentyfirst century? We have no apostolic succession or lineage that directly links us to the initiatory knowledge of the old priesthood, no ancient Druids to pass on the baton, to offer intense training to those who choose to follow the way of Awen. In truth, we have had to start over again, forming our own tradition, applicable to the society and time that we now live in. The Druids of today, those capable of preserving and teaching the tradition that has flourished over the last three centuries, are more or less self proclaimed, or belong to insular orders or to large national organisations. However this neither nullifies nor invalidates the tradition; we have to begin somewhere. We may well never attain the ranking or social kudos that the Druids of old held, and we may not particularly want to either! Many of the Druids today have been taught by their own experience and have climbed their own developmental ladder, attaining clarity and wisdom of spirit. We can learn much from these people and they can learn much from those just starting on the path. Our Druidry today is very different to the Druidry of the ancestral past, yet it has value and integrity, it is the unique process of creating something new, something that invokes the essence of the past without becoming lost in the mists of time.

PART 3
Ritual

chapter 1
the need for ritual

ithin different cultures, with different tongues and varied social structures there lies a universal language, the language of ritual, rich with intention, conscious and subconscious, traditional, ingrained into the heart of every society on Earth. Since the beginning of time man has performed ritual, even in modern society we inadvertently enact rituals on a daily basis. It is simply a structure that gives form to human activity, emphasising a function or situation as being somehow different from normal daily chores, giving it a depth that allows it to stand out amongst other mundane activities. The sitting down to a meal with the family is a ritual, the blowing of candles on a birthday cake, funerals, weddings, court appearances, competitions, school activities all have a ritualistic template that instils a sense of familiarity in the practitioner, informing the subconscious mind that something different, special or unusual is to take place. Even when human beings come together informally or formally, it is generally in the form of a circle, attention and focus is heightened as we prepare for some form of ritual. These are the rituals of every day life, routine, a structure that imbues a sense of comfort and familiarity. Then of course, we have religious or spiritual ritual, which differ only in the respect that the spirit of a situation or activity is acknowledged as an innate aspect of the rite, its purpose to connect to something that would normally be intangible.

Ritual is the outward expression of connection; it is the sacred art of listening, of stopping momentarily and acknowledging that deep heart felt, soul fulfilling connection to the spirit behind our Druidry. Ritual is the integration of matter (physical) and energy (spiritual) with a fusion of intention and vision that slowly crumbles the dense walls that seemingly separate the two worlds of density and spirit. Modern life does not educate its people to see, feel and listen to the subtle energies that inherently lie around us each and every day of our existence. Ritual re-establishes that link not simply to the world of spirit, which is not necessarily the purpose of deep ritual, but rather it promotes the amalgamation of both worlds, where the two aspects are seen as simply one side of the same coin. Ritual enables the 'sleeping' to subtly sense the movement behind all things, throughout all things, teasing the mind to possibilities and connection undreamt of, waking us to the unified nature of spirit and matter. The rituals of Druidry are creative in expression, not only the energy transference and expression within the ritual, but also its formation. The simple act of creating a sacred space, of delineating a specific area and acknowledging its inherent divinity and holiness is an act of inspired creativity. This notion of creating sacred space should not be assumed to mean that the act makes an area sacred. It does not, all of nature is sacred, and the delineation of sacred ritual space is simply an affirmation of its sanctity.

Druids work in nature, and our rituals are performed within the sacred kingdom of nature, there is no "carpet witchery" (as I call it!) in Druidry. Although our homes are ideal for daily practise of honouring the spirits of that place and of the hearth, deep ecstatic rituals where the body and spirit collide together occur in the natural world. This is the world of the Druid, the world of the elements, the ancestors, the spirits of nature that inhabit a place. They assist our rituals, allowing deep and utter connection through heritage, land and blood, to that place where our bodies and our spirits become one, and are acknowledged as such. Within a space designated as sacred and honoured as such, the sun shining upon us, or the moon's silvery light caressing our skin, or the torrent of raindrops that beat relentlessly we adjust our perspective, our consciousness shifts to that altered state where boundaries blur and energy and matter become one.

Acknowledgement, honour and celebration are also vital factors of Druid ritual, where we gather as a tribe or alone to celebrate the wonders of life, acknowledging our ability to see and listen. Ritual is a time where we honour the spirits of our ancestors and their connection to this earth as we feel their ancient pulses beating within our very arteries, singing the old songs of tribe and of land, matter and spirit. Ritual is not hocus-pocus, where a group of foolish looking people are gathered to make complete lemons of themselves; but of course that is what society sees! When folk gather in public rituals or Gorseddau the observers do not have the ability to feel the connection which the participants sense. Focused only on matter, they cannot see beyond the physical and feel the pulsing energy of the universe beating in harmony with us. As a consequence it seems to them ridiculous or entertaining and does nothing to inspire the connective nature of ritual. We inspire by the way we live and rituals allow us the time to pinpoint and integrate the world of spirit with the material world around us. It is that two way conversation between us and the spirit, not an act of pleading or pacifying some external unknown deity, rather we listen and act upon the immanent conversation with the living universe that speaks within us. The frequent practise of ritual take us ever closer to singularity and the understanding of mystery; rituals change us as we develop an acute awareness of the beating heart of our universe, increasing our proficiency to sense the spirits of nature and beyond culminating in completion, the commingling of matter and energy. It is this coalescence through the sacred art of ritual that enables us to be inspired and inspire others to awaken to the subtle voice of unity.

Within Druidry there are two specific forms of ritual practise. Personal ritual, where the practitioner reaches out to his own connection and moves through the worlds of spirit, acknowledging and singing to the music he has formed through personal development and sacred relationship. Then there is group ritual, the coming together of a community or tribe to celebrate and honour the various rites of passage that affect us and the ever moving cycle of the seasons. The two are quite different both in structure and intention. Our personal rituals strengthen our relationship with our gods, with Awen, and with the spirits of our locality with which we form relationships. Group ritual is the honouring of sacred relationship between the tribe, the land and its Gods.

Ritual does not necessarily require construction or structure; many Druids perform subtle rituals throughout their day. The simple acknowledgement of the rising sun, the lighting of the hearth fire on a cold winter's evening, and stopping for a moment, allowing the humdrum of everyday life to fall gently away, the awareness focused simply on the stimuli observed. We reach out, spirit to spirit, offering acknowledgement and praise, with honour and integrity, and as energies collide, each sensing a familiarity within the other and recognising kin. For a moment we are touched, embraced by the enveloping arms of the universe as we join, merging as one. As one grows sensitive to the vitality and hidden world of spirit and connection, where everything is seen as a habitation of the divine force behind our universe, sacredness becomes ever more apparent, and worthy of praise. A wren's song becomes a thing of untold beauty and serenity, the rowan at the end of the garden a plethora of music and story. It is to these attributions that we take time out to honour and acknowledge as contributing factors that enrich the song of our world, the song of Awen. The more familiar the sublime energies of the seen and unseen become, the more open we are to perceiving the wild inspiration of nature and that force which drives it.

Our daily lives become honourable as we see the enchantment and awe of Awen behind all things. A short walk on a cold and damp winter's evening transforms into a profound journey of connection, each footfall and crunch of frost ridden ground transmitting pulses of sacredness into the very heart of our spirit. These subtle yet profoundly moving rituals confirm the sacredness of all things and the inter connection of spirit. Our personal rituals enable us to wander into the arms of nature and the spirits that reside there, to the counsel of the gods and ancestors and ultimately to the singular aspect of all souls.

There is a time and a place for elaborate ritual also, but our personal daily rituals facilitate the melting away of human constructs that can sometimes inhibit our focus and intent. It is simply not enough to fixate on the ever turning cycles of life, honouring them only eight times a year when each and every moment of our lives are sacred in their own rights. If we do not integrate our experience of the sacred into daily life, we become no different from a Christian attending mass each Sunday. Through the medium of subtle ritual and the increasing nature of our sensitivity we perceive so much that is inherently holy. It is this awareness that takes us deeper into the gloomy forest and sun drenched groves of our spirituality and increases our vision. Acknowledging the divine essence of each and every experience allows us to see clearly, listen intently and open the heart to the elegant music of life. How many people in the twenty first century actually acknowledge this song? I often find myself on long train journeys through the British countryside, gazing out of the windows, watching the symphony of nature speeding past, each aspect of it reacting to its surroundings and the other creatures and greenery which share its space. I adore this sudden influx of so much activity and expression, happening right there, the tender campion its body blasted by the slipstream of the train. The oak ignoring the strange metal bullet speeding past it, its reflection slow, in years it will recall the peculiar object filled with spirits that sped past it. Each scene, vibrant and colourful emblazons itself on my mind, and then the bizarre awareness that there are others in the vicinity, people sharing this space unaware of the story swiftly passing by. Untouched by the awe inspiring streams of colour they are bound by the illusion that the carriage is the only reality in their lives at that time. How tragic that our society has fallen into a state of unconsciousness, each person trapped within a set reality that they feel powerless to change, fumbling through life, secure in their insecurity.

To adequately alter our lives; we need ritual with deep connection, where our rites become the outward expression of that relationship. As Druids in tune with Awen we must become like children, innocent and receptive able to see the heart breaking beauty of a new season, or the simple shadowed life of a woodlouse. When we gather fresh vegetables and herbs from the garden and slowly simmer them, transforming their essence into a hearty winter stew to sustain and nourish our tribe, this too can be an act of ritual. Honouring the sacred nature of earth's bounty, the bursting of deep purple as the elder sighs into berry, that vibrant green of a carrot leaf dancing in the wind and offering gratitude for their sustenance and beauty we move closer to their essence. Such clarity of vision enables us to sense the subtlety of the universe expressing itself in wondrous form. When we enhance our daily lives with these momentary, simple rites the ordinariness of their nature suddenly become extraordinary. The Awen filled heart of the Druid cannot help but see the wonder expressed in our world, which becomes a stage for the drama of existence and life in all its sheer beauty. Density becomes translucent and those pulses of energy can be clearly seen as currents beneath the illusion. It is this great song that we celebrate in our daily rituals, simple, unplanned yet focused.

Late one evening, unable to sleep, tossing restlessly in my warm bed, much to the annoyance of our cat and my partner attempting to sleep next to me, I rose to listen to the cold musical fingertips of the dense fog that slowly devoured the outside world. The cat, with a heavy yawn of resignation followed me into the dark unseen field that sloped towards the house, the trees surrounding it rejoicing in the sudden cloak of invisibility offered by the fog. A song floated from my mouth, the cold tendrils of fog greedily lapping the lyrics like nectar, the cat purring curiously beside me as we walked the steep hill to the borders of the wood. We could see nothing outside the circle of ten feet or so that reached out before each footstep, the dense wall of deep grey fog surrounding us, creating a nemeton of sacredness with every footfall. Each gentle step acknowledged the sleeping grass, the plantain and clover silently lying in slumber beneath the hard brown earth waiting for the calling of spring. My bare feet, cold and damp suddenly sunk into soft brown mud, like liquid chocolate oozing through my toes. We had inadvertently wondered into a large area of muddy ground, the look of distaste on the cat's face slowly vanished into a vision of curiosity as I removed my clothes and sat bare bottomed in the cold sludge. My hands found the embrace delightful as they took on a life of their own, swilling through the soft semi liquid texture of mud and sheep droppings!

The world around me vanished, the house merely yards away fell into insignificance, it was me, mud and cat, laughing and purring, the subtle, slow singing of mud rising slowly to join us. The tiniest bacteria and life forms, giggled at the daft human and its feline companion. But the connection was deliciously divine, two creatures of different species in tune with a million spirits that resided in mud, each of us dancing together, aware of the strands of soul that reached back into the darkness of wholeness. The shining rays of Awen illuminated our connection, our song in harmony, dancing and swirling amongst the dense fog. Suddenly the cat, startled, with hackles spread jumped to her feet, as a face of untold mystery appeared through the fog, its bright orange eyes glaring at the human and its companion. As more faces appeared I reached out through the nemeton touching these strange alien creatures as a bleating pierced the night air. They were sheep!

Surrounded by a heard of fluffy white sheep, the cat and I, mud and wool rejoiced in the party of souls, the silent earth pulsing its appreciation at such a spectacle. Laughing we returned to the illusion of normality, sighing as warm water cascaded from the shower head over cat and human, the nymphs tickling fur and skin, teasing, pleasing, before retiring invigorated into bed and to a deep, dream filled sleep.

Have you ever found yourself in your grove, the full moon shining above you and a cloak full of ideas burning next to your skin? You prepare yourself and your space, and suddenly all you can do is collapse to the floor and cry, cry until you feel your heart will tear beneath the strain, beneath the sheer beauty of it all. As that sense of connection completely shatters your soul into a billion pieces each one connecting with the world in a different way, no longer is the tree behind you a separate being, you are it, you feel its bark and the bark of the furthest tree on the furthest continent. You feel the light of a distant nebula caressing the very essence of your soul, as you dance with the tides and the rivers, with the stars and sky. The world becomes one with you and the universe is you! And with this vision comes clarity of connection and your soul flies to heights beyond comprehension, and suddenly snap! The dense weight of your body shocks you back to existence, the claustrophobic embrace of skin and flesh, the drum of your heart beating, your neck pulsing rapidly under the pressure of blood that's rushing to your brain, a brain that is screaming in horror at the release of the mind, and struggles to cling on to it as it returns to the body. You kneel there panting, tears streaming down your cheeks and dripping onto pine needles that stab your knees.

This is solitary ritual in all its spontaneous wonder, without structure, without planning, simple and inspired. This is the power of connection and ritual that enables us to celebrate connection, to honour it, evidently displaying that ritual regardless of structure can move the soul to heights beyond imagination. However structure is good, arriving in a space, affirming its sacredness and going forth into the unseen worlds with intention and honour also offer intensity and vision. No one form of ritual is better than the other; they each fulfil their purpose by intention and offer a unique format for vision and the liberation of the mind.

The intensity of vision-filled ritual, where we commune with the spirits of place, acknowledging our inert position within the universe, and seeking guidance and clarity from the ancestors, is most effectively achieved during solitary ritual. However this does not nullify the value of group ritual which can itself provide moments of ecstasy and intensity, they are simply different

Whether our solitary rituals are focused on personal spiritual development or the attuning and celebration of the cycles of life, they substantiate our sense of sacred relationship and the relevance of our spirituality. Ritual enhances our understanding of the tradition and its wisdom. They are the process by which we grow and mature and flourish into the priesthood. They are the vision-rich times we take out of human life to explore its sacredness and vitality; and to reach into the unseen, communing with our gods and the ancestors, the moving forces of nature and the one great soul of the universe. Our need for ritual has been apparent throughout human history, that deep need to connect to mystery, and we are no different today. Druidry and its rituals, help heal the rift between man and the nature of the soul, affirming our place within the universe, affirming the sacred, moving us closer to the very energy that lies within us, adjusting our perspective and affecting the world. Ritual brings back that sense of singularity that our modern society finds abhorrent. It prevents us from absolving ourselves of worldly responsibility; instead our passion and compassion escalate beyond the unconscious mind of those who are 'sleeping', creating a need to seek balance within our fractured society.

Ordinary every day rituals of humanity, whether they are the decorating of the Yuletide tree, or the casting of a coin into a wishing well, invoke a memory within us, a memory of the sacredness of life symbolised and captured within everyday objects. As children we remember and accept the wonder of magic and the unseen world, knowing that fairy folk reside in the garden, but the illusionary sensibility of adulthood and its influence soon penetrate the receptive mind and destroy the magic of the sacred. Druidry and its rituals seeks to resurrect that sense of wonder, by honouring interconnection and the sacredness in all things, our minds, reluctantly at first, bloom into acceptability, but without naivety. Due to the experiential nature of Druidry, matters of spirit are never taken on face value. We cannot claim to believe in anything, rather, we have a sense of knowing, for what we experience becomes our reality, we accept that which we experience as a fundamental truth of spiritual wisdom and knowledge. Knowledge arises from direct experience, belief relies on faith, and faith is generally blind. Our rituals eliminate the need for gurus and spiritual masters; we are capable of discovering truth for ourselves. If one embarks upon a well worn path through the forest, then we are not walking our path but rather relying on someone else and their perception of truth. In Druidry we create our own path, even though all these paths ultimately lead to the same grove of truth; we take inspiration from others, but do not rely upon their truths. Truth must be experienced alone, stumbling into tree roots and struggling through the brambles, our ankles stung by nettles. Reliant only upon the guiding, knowing nature of the spirit and the whispers of nature to reveal to us the essence of truth we delve deeper into the mysteries and our rituals mirror this journey. Alone we develop and learn in the shadows of the mighty oaks, discovering that the sense of loneliness is simply an illusion, when we are surrounded by a universe of which we are an integral part, in truth there can be no loneliness, it is only the social nature of our species that senses this isolation. When we gather as a community to celebrate and share, we gather as a whole, each human individual aware of that subtle glow in another's eyes, a glow that betrays their experience of wholeness and unity, a glow that is instantly recognisable to one who has been there, in the deep abyss of unity. As a community we share and inspire.

Tribal Rituals

A full moon shines brightly on the dense, black surface of the lake, its reflection shimmering like liquid silver in the night. The old barn owl turns her head to watch curiously as the humans gather beneath her, their drums beating a steady pulse that echoes through the shadowed landscape, words stream from the lips of one who stands amongst them, and the owl shivers as she senses a familiarity within the speaker, his words tickle something within her, and she knows their purpose, feels their honour, she bows invisibly towards the gathering. A fire bursts into life and the crowd dance and sing, in step with the drumbeat, cries of joy and celebration soar into the night sky as sheaves of wheat are held high, as honey and milk are poured onto the earth. The woman folk scream and warble, their arms swinging around their heads as their spirits expand to encompass the clearing, the lake and the trees that surround them. The old owl closes her eyes and her body pulsates as she feels the spirits reaching out towards her, and she dances with them as leaf and tree join in the celebration. A shaft of light streams across the sky, extinguished as it hits the surface of the lake, the men folk naked with wild and striking patterns painted upon their flesh bellow as arrow after arrow of fire are shot towards the middle of the lake, the owl watches perplexed and then she sees it. A denser shadow inhabits the centre of the lake and as one flaming arrow collides with it a wall of fire engulfs a man of wicker and wheat and corn that stands upon a wooden raft. The fire licks up his body, quickly consuming him, the corn God is dead, sacrificed. Chunks of flaming wheat and corn fall off him into the water like blood; his time is over, his sacrifice complete. The men cry triumphantly and fall to their knees in gratitude, bowing to the sacrifice of the harvest God. The women continue their rapturous dancing and singing, lost in the frenzy of the season, their spirits at one with nature. And the drumbeats pulse as moon and owl watch silently, their own spirits colliding with those around them.

Fiction, right? Perhaps not, it is simply a depiction of Druid ritual in all its vibrancy and colour, with an intense energy of deep connection that rips the spirit from the body and allows Awen to cascade like a raging waterfall through every molecule and atom. A tribe gathers with one intention and one mind, to loose that mind entirely and become one with the powers of nature, allowing Awen to facilitate that transformation. Modern day Druids coalesce with the ancestors and spirits of place, and spirit to spirit we celebrate that connection to the source, inhibitions vanquished, we dance to the rhythm of the earth and the vast universe around and within us. This is tribal ritual in all its wonder and glory, as a community gathers to express that depth of connection.

The tribe is a community that is defined by a common experience of the world and Druidry celebrates that relationship between the tribe and its land. Our very lives are governed by the ebb and flow of our seasons, the weather and landscape. The crops we grow, the animals we rear, where we live and how we live is dictated by the land of our locality. Establishing a link between the tribe and the land lies at the core of Druid group practise, for it is here that we encounter its spirits, the driving force behind its external reflection, and we celebrate this in ritual. Since time immemorial people have gathered with their priests to honour the earth upon which they lived, to offer gratitude for its abundance, and to plead during famine and failure of crops. This need was partially eliminated after the industrial revolution, and more so in the years since the supermarket revolution. Our need to honour the earth was eliminated; she became a 'thing' to exploit and to own, a commodity. Our reverence for the mother of all life faded, and human society developed an antagonistic relationship with her. Honour and gratitude were replaced by greed and selfishness; humanity began its steady downhill fall from grace, culminating in potential annihilation of our species as the earth shakes her mane and destroys the parasites that ignorantly damage her. And all of this because of disconnection and a sense of apathy that devours humanity, together with an attitude of invincibility fabricated by illusion.

That is not to say that our ancestors were not opportunists. They evidently were, deforesting and destroying, but their inherent sense of gratitude was also present, something we lack to day. Ritual in itself is not capable of bridging this impassiveness within humanity, but by facilitating connection, our assertiveness increases and we reach out into the world, contributing towards the healing of our home world, even if only within a specific locality.

When we gather as a tribe the external expression of ritual differs from our personal rites; we gather as a community to celebrate that sacred relationship between tribe and land, our focus concentrated on intention. The tribe may well meet as a grove or loosely structured group to observe and acknowledge the passing cycles of life, reaching out to honour the spirits of place and the sacredness of land, sea and sky. Our groves or groups evolve into a community of trust, expression and deep affection, akin to an extended family, each individual becoming a sibling in the craft. Although many practise alone, the majority of Druid practitioners enjoy the best of worlds, solitude and company. It is through our groves that we are best able to reach out into the world and facilitate change, affecting our local environment through community projects such as tree planting schemes, or the simple activity of cleaning up a local beach or sacred site. Environmental concerns and political activism are also avenues of expression. Many groups will meet every couple of weeks or once a month, developing new ideas and methods of learning the craft of Druidry, it becomes a support system, emotionally, spiritually and physically.

However advanced we are in our spiritual journey, it is important to acknowledge and comprehend that we are after all human beings and not in any way immune to the tribulations and worries of normal life. We live in the world, and the world affects us, we all have our own problems, whether they be professional or domestic. Druidry does not allow a person to simply float through life unhindered by the world around us, instead we develop the ability to deal with situations that may seem difficult or challenging, emerging out of problematic areas of our lives life a butterfly. Even in difficult times we can find inspiration. The dark night of the soul that we all experience at some point in our lives imbues in us a sense of gratitude and vitality, the problems facing humans in the twenty first century are simply a facet of life. Druidry does not and never can eliminate these trying times, but offers a way of dealing with them adequately, causing us to swim rather than sink beneath the strains of society. Our group, our tribe, are there for us, a human contact and form, someone to lean on when all we want is to cry out in frustration, grief or sadness. The sacred relationship that evolves from group contact offers us counselling and an understanding ear to comfort and assist us in times of great need. Slowly guiding us back to the light of inspiration that floods our spirit and reminding us of the wonder of life. Lucidity and the living of a spiritual life do not automatically eliminate us from the trials of life. There are times when we all succumb to sadness, to sickness, to lethargy and depression. Our groves and our rituals, allow us to celebrate these times as aspects of life, vital to our experience here on earth, facilitating a healing within us, rather than mulling on their significance and effect upon our minds. The tribe offers a support structure for healing, exploration, celebration and acceptance.

Our sense of community in the modern world has vanished, small town life and village communities have evaporated into thin air, and people have become guarded and possessive. We do not share any more. But our groves, that small community of like minded people, provide us with the community spirit that is so lacking in our society. We gather for ritual, for celebration and to reinforce that connection we have to the earth, however simplistic this expression may be.

In the sense that ritual can be any activity that causes the normality of life to fade into the background, we can do so much as a group that moves us ever closer to the essence of soul and the honouring of nature. We may gather to harvest the bounty of nature in the autumn months, to create natural products and food, to decorate our homes as a reminder of the sacredness that inherently exists throughout nature. Making wines and syrups, ointments and salves, delicious puddings and cakes, enable us to honour the sustenance and gifts of the earth. We may gather to support the maturing of a menopausal member of the grove as she embraces the croning. Maturing into wisdom, quenching the hormonal fire within her, we offer our energy and compassion as she slips into cronehood, taking her place in the halls of the wise and knowing ones. We can celebrate the joining together of two spirits, deeply in love with each other, kindred spirits welded together in a celebration of commitment. A group may well facilitate a ritual to embrace adolescence and the consuming flame of puberty, through to the rites of death and dying. A group may organise day trips to the local wood to learn the healing secrets of the plants and lichens, leafs and bark that festoon our landscape, offering their assistance in times of ill health and trauma. Or they may gather with deep intent and dance and sing and scream, loosing their minds through the ecstatic acknowledgement of connection, each individual loosing its identity and sense of self, as the group becomes one. A grove of like minded folk walking the forest path of

Druidry are only limited by their imagination, each event, each ritual strengthens the bond between us and the earth.

The Gorsedd And Eisteddfod

One of the many luxurious and divinely inspirational qualities of a gathering of Druids is the Eisteddfod; an ancient Welsh word which describes a sitting of bards. The Eisteddfod would be governed by a body of Druidic representatives, led by an Archdruid collectively referred to as a Gorsedd, which roughly translates as 'High Throne'. Today many Pagan Gorseddau exist that facilitate Eisteddfodau in various locations throughout the United Kingdom, allowing Awen filled inspiration and creativity to be expressed freely under the eye of the sun. The small Eisteddfodau of Druid groves bear little if no resemblance to the annual Eisteddfod of Wales which takes place at then end of July and the beginning of August. However beautiful and inspiring the Welsh National Eisteddfod is (and I must admit I do enjoy visiting it each time it arrives in North Wales) it does generally lack a degree of spiritual connection to the concept of Awen. However, a grove Eisteddfod offers the expression of creativity within the structure of a spiritual tradition with its roots both in the past and the present. Iolo Morgannwg coined the phrase "Y gwir yn erbyn y byd", (the truth against the world), in reference to the Gorsedd and Eisteddfod. The Eisteddfod focuses on the creative arts, Bardism etc, which all represent the personal, experiential truth of the performer.

I have attended many Eisteddfodau that have moved me beyond articulation, so much wonder, mystery, magic and connection can be relayed during this sacred event. An Eisteddfod may take place at the conclusion of a group or open ritual, grounding those present and offering an opportunity to share experience and spirit. At other times an Eisteddfod may be a stand alone event that attracts folk from near and far. The Eisteddfod is a valued and integral aspect of the wonder of Druidry, an occasion of great joy and sharing.

Your grove should be akin to family, the bonds may even be greater for it is not limited simply by thickness of blood but by intensity of spirit. The more time the grove spends together the more powerful it becomes, enriching each individual within it. Being a member of a grove is also tremendous fun, there is much laughter and joy to be had within a group where each member is comfortable and happy with everyone else. It is a support system both spiritually and physically as we all tread the perilous path of life here on our planet. Although your grove may only meet for ritual and group exploration and development, use it also to enjoy the fun things in life. Day trips out to sacred sites and others areas of interest have an added edge when with the grove. Visit a forest and have each member climb into the branches of a mighty tree and perform your ritual up there, it's quite different! Above all enjoy your grove! There are many groups that are led by egotistical individuals seeking only power over others and serve to boost their ever increasing sense of importance, use your intuition wisely. Although groups do have leaders or rather co-ordinators there should be no ego attached to them, they are simply there to ensure that all goes smoothly, and that the practical, logistical aspect of a group and its dynamics are fulfilled. A co-ordinator or grove leader will arrange the skeletal structure of ritual, ensuring all those present have a specific focus during the rite. It is good practice to share this responsibility with the entire grove, allowing each individual grove member to facilitate and lead a ritual. This enables each person to grow within the grove and increases his/her confidence, especially when faced with a role within a large open ritual. If you venture out to form your own grove, do not fall into the trap of having anyone join you for the sake of increasing the numbers. Many groups admit unsuitable individuals who may have an ulterior motive for being there. Each grove member should be someone that you can trust impeccably, friendships should be forged, and during the growing process your intuition will allow you the privilege to discern who has vision and who is there because they are needy. Modern Paganism has a disturbing affliction, I refer to it as the "Billy-No-Mates" syndrome, where individuals are attracted to the accepting nature of Pagans, but may do so out of neediness rather than a sincere and genuine wish to transform. Be careful when admitting people you know very little about into your grove, they may well undermine its dynamics and destroy it. After all every group that exists has a dynamic, whether they be a witches coven, a Druids grove or the local branch of the Women's Institute, a group's dynamic grows as relationships are formed. Each member of the grove should assume personal responsibility for sensing the wellbeing of this dynamic, voicing any problems he or she may sense, and long before they become difficult issues. Human beings are fickle creatures, treat them all carefully, and use your intuition.

Ritual, in my opinion should not be a set of stringent rules and regulations, pages and pages of script. Ritual only requires the bare necessity of structure, a skeletal frame upon which you put the flesh and decoration. We should never be faced with a situation where a person feels anxious or nervous that they may get something wrong; in ritual we should be comfortable and relaxed. If it does go horribly wrong, laugh it off and carry on, neither the elements nor the spirits will mind, they will laugh with you. Ritual is our connection to Awen and should express that connection however insignificant or simplistic it may seem, or however grand or dramatic. In Druidry we learn that connection is everything, it is our journey, and in ritual the sheer depth of connection moves us to drop the minutiae of our ordinary lives and for a while we come to a complete standstill. In that space we become the world around us and celebrate this wondrous thing we call life. The act of ritual facilitates this expression, allowing us to convey our Awen, our inspiration, whether it be to others who join us during the turning wheel of the year, or simply to the darkness beyond the forest grove, where we sit alone next to the glowing embers of an old fire.

Exercise

What rituals do you perform in your everyday life and what do they signify? What messages are they transmitting to your subconscious? Examine an ordinary day, what do you do each day that follows a pattern, a structure, bleary eyed as you wander to the kitchen in your night clothes, automatically switching on the kettle and reaching for the coffee jar, this is a form of ritual.

What else do you do? Look at each individual aspect of these mundane activities and the ritual we clothe them in. Write each one in a notebook and dissect them, find out what they are saying to you. Most people crumble when they are prevented from performing their daily rituals, they become irritable and bad tempered, why? Seek out the answers and know your mind a little better, understand what makes it tick and what ticks it off! To gain a better understanding of the function of spiritual ritual it is important that we grasp the significance of the simplistic daily rites that we perform automatically. This is the realm of the mind; our daily rituals are performed in a state of almost non-being, a state that is essential for deep ritual. Explore the significance of mundane rituals. Know your own mind, in knowing it you will better understand the dynamics of ritual and their powers of transformation.

CHAPTER 2

THE ELEMENTS OF RITUAL

hen we gather for ritual, whether it is personal or tribal, there are certain structures that we follow. The purpose is twofold, firstly the elements that we employ to construct ritual prepare us psychologically, they instruct the mind that something different is about to take place and act to support a framework for the rite, preventing us from loosing direction and intention. This allows the ritual to dance with fluidity and a sense of gracefulness that allow us to loose the inhibitions of our human minds. We enter a space that is about to be transformed into a mirror representation of the universe, and the elements of ritual provide a focus for this intention, transforming the psyche, allowing us to become susceptible to the subtle energies that surround the circle. Secondly they function as methods of invitation, invocation, evocation and honour; it is here that we face the spirits with which we work, meeting them in a realm of neutrality and inherent beauty. It is here that we sever the illusion of human reality and enter the domain of enchantment, magic and connection, reaffirming our spirituality and place in the universe.

However, when we enter into ritual we must never assume that the elements upon which we call are simply metaphors, the energies we are dealing with are very real! They exist in their own reality; we should never presume that the spirits we are calling will simply come because we choose to call them. Each element of the ritual process must be focused and that focus must stem from a sincere and genuine connective relationship with each individual spirit. It is this sacred relationship and its understanding that allows us to call these elements from the darkest depths of our spirits. Even though our words have power, when those words are presented with an emotional, soul connection the effect is instantaneous and profound. We do not summon anything in our rituals. Each archetype, each spirit is invoked from the memory of connection, it is the calling on something with which we are familiar and have an ongoing relationship. It is not appropriate to arrive at ritual and call on something, expecting it to appear, when the last time you had any dealings with it was during a ritual six weeks ago. The time we spend between rites in our own personal circles, lost in vision and meditation, is the time that we connect to the elements that we honour at ritual. Many people lack confidence in their spiritual path, and develop an ingrained belief that they may be doing it all wrong. Rest assured there is very little you can do wrong if you have the integrity and depth of spirit that you heard within yourself when first drawn to this path. Work with these elements, enjoy their company, and although their expression and life experience may be very different from your own, remember that we all share a common source. So much beauty and wonder lie in the relationships that we form with those of this world and those of the unseen world. Spirituality and the practice of ritual is not a boring, stringent procedure, there is much fun and joy to be had within a sacred circle. Remember to have fun and enjoy the experience, laugh and cry, giggle and be frivolous, be serious and reverent when the situation dictates it, always listen to that wise voice within you that already knows all the answers. I know so many modern Pagans who are so anally retentive; they can't sit down for fear of sucking up the furniture! Enjoy your rituals! The spirits we deal with are themselves not a boring crowd; they also enjoy our company and that connection of deep soul. Work with them, get to know them, it is worth every minute of effort.

Worship Or Reverence

The question of whether or not Druids worship anything can only realistically be defined by the individual practitioner and it would be presumptuous of me to suggest a generic answer on behalf of all Druids. I can only provide my own viewpoint on the matter. First we must examine the definitions of each word. Worship, is perceived as an extravagant admiration to a divine external being of significant supernatural power. A common construct within orthodox religions where the Godhead is perceived as superior to all beings and is somehow in control of all things, and all life is subservient to it. Reverence on the other hand is to honour or respect something that has been accorded as sacred. I prefer the term 'Reverence' in my personal spirituality. I do not worship anything, I revere. There is no omnipotent deity within Druidry! We are an expression of the whole and the whole neither needs nor demands worship. Owing to the animistic nature of Druidry, where we attribute conscious life to nature and to natural objects, all aspects of the universe are seen as holy or sacred, but none require worship. Although we perceive them in their individual physical form, they contain within them an immanency that we also share; to worship them would be akin to worshipping ourselves. We share the same spark, the same source. By revering them, we simply acknowledge their sacredness and the beauty of their expression and the life that courses through their forms. Within each and every aspect of nature we are able to see a reflection of our own nature; it is this that I revere. In ritual, I see no need for worship, I have a relationship with these beings, they are kin, to worship them would be like worshipping my own mother, I don't; I revere her (Sometimes!!). Many may beg to differ with this opinion, and in reality we must honour an individual's relationship whether it is one of worship or reverence, it is their truth and an important aspect of their spirituality. Worship or reverence, perhaps it is too personal a subject to dissect.

The Sacred Circle

In Druidry our rituals take place within a space that has been acknowledged as inherently sacred, within a circle that reflects the cyclic, curving expression of nature. Many Druids have a designated area that is utilised for ritual activities, whether this is in the garden, on the beach or deep within the shadows of a forest, such areas may be inconspicuous or an elaborate glade in a wood or a circle of stones that honour the sacredness of space and its spirits. Our ancestors clearly observed and expressed the concentric cycles of nature within their own ancient temples that lie silently upon our landscape. A space set aside from the humdrum of everyday activities and life. The sequential linear illusion that most humans live within is simply that, an illusion. There is no linearity within nature, all things move in cycles of birth, life, death and rebirth. The circle reflects this philosophy. It is a microcosm of the macrocosm, a miniature representation of the universe contained within a space that has been designated as sacred. It reflects the sacredness of the vast universal force and the facets of that energy apparent on our planet.

A circle cast has ambience, it becomes something that wasn't there just a moment before, the air changes within it, a sense of stillness and peace descends upon those who enter the space. This sensation is easily tested, simply take a long stick and place it upright on the ground, attach to the end of it a long piece of twine or string approximately six feet long. Now stretch the string out until it is straight, the string and stick will act a little like a compass. Walk slowly around the central pole creating as you do a perfect circle, use small stones to mark the circle's perimeter or a stick or staff to mark the circle in sand or bare earth. Sit in this circle and experience it, something magical takes place when we delineate an area as sacred and spend time within its boundary. Sceptics may well comment that we are "Imagining it", my answer to them would be "…and your point is?" Of course we imagine it, but imagination is simply another form of reality, the sensations we feel during the time we spend in our circles are very real, two realities meet, combine and dance together harmoniously.

In modern Paganism where the circle is utilised within the structures of many traditions from Wicca to ritual magic, there is much talk of protection. In Druidry this is not a concept that is adhered to. What in fact do we need protection from? I find the concept absurd, to delineate an area as microcosmically sacred, inviting the spirits of locality and the elements to witness the rite and then sealing off the circle so that only a select few may enter! We do not need protection from the elements of nature, they do not pose a threat to our spiritual wellbeing, they are an aspect of us and we are an aspect of them. Creating a sphere of protection, only facilitates and encourages the fears and anxieties that lie within us, allowing them credence and power over us. To actively seek out nature and venture into her belly to create ritual is to accept her many faces, warts and all, with honour and integrity. There may be times that we may become confused or disorientated by the energies we perceive, for this we cannot blame the entity which we are connecting to, the fault lies with the inadequacy of the relationship we have with them. For instance, we have a river locally which is famed for coercing people to enter the waters many of whom drown as a consequence; the river is seen as evil or malignant. In fact the river's only fault is that of curiosity, it finds an alien being on its shores, whose mind is reaching out to touch it; it does not have the capacity of leaving the body of water, whereas we have legs to carry us to it. The river only wants to know our nature, her intent is neither to harm nor destroy, she is simply curious. We do not require protection from the elements of nature, a deep, resonating relationship with her will provide us with the security that we are safe in her realms, as long as we approach with reverence, respect and integrity.

There is much talk of evil even within the Pagan communities, and in many traditions the circle has evolved into a method of safeguarding its inhabitants. In my opinion evil exists only within the mind of humanity and is socio-cultural in expression. Nature simply acts in accordance to her nature, it is mankind that defines those actions as good or bad, nature does not have the capacity of perceiving things in such a black and white manner. She is neither good nor evil, she simply is, and it is the realm of nature in which Druids work. Considering this fact, it is our duty to establish a relationship with her that does not encourage illusionary concepts of the nature of her spirits. If we sense an alien, unfamiliar spirit we may feel threatened and label it as being evil, but we do so out of ignorance, arrogance and misunderstanding. When we take into account the cyclic nature of the universe we become aware that all things are simply acting within the confines of experience, it is human arrogance that assumes something has an ulterior motive. For example take a piece of blank paper and upon it draw a straight line, a nice thick line that reflects the illusion of linearity, place a cross on either end of this line, and mark each one as being good and evil, opposite extremes, assuming the centre point of this line is perfect balance, where would you place yourself? Where would you place Mother Teressa, Adolf Hitler, an Alder tree, a cat? Most of us would like to think we are somewhere towards the middle, good decent people with the occasional evil thought. Now transform this line to mirror the true nature of the universe as cyclic, i.e. draw a circle. Now it has no beginning, no end, no defined area that is better than another, where are you now?

The circle is a continuation, it is sheer potentiality, everything exists within it, and the concepts of time and space melt away, allowing us to see the true nature and expression of the universe right there in our ritual circle. It is a powerful metaphor for existence and within it sings the great song. In mathematics a

circle is described as "a figure of infinite sides," this is a useful
metaphor for meditation (but please try not to make too much
of a mess on the walls when your head explodes!). If a drawn
circle is magnified, over and over again, the observer will note
that it is indeed made up of infinite straight lines, each one
forming a part of the circle itself, now if you choose one line
and begin to count them, one after the other, by the time you
approach an eighth of the way round every person you will
have ever known will be dead. By the time you get a quarter
of the way round our sun will have burnt itself out and our
solar system vaporised. By the time you reach half way round
the universe will have collapsed in on itself, in fact you will
never be able to count the sides, ever! Irrespective of the size
of the initial circle, it could be drawn as small as a grain of
rice and the same rule would apply. In many ways the circle
is a representation of the infinite nature of the universe and
simultaneously of the soul. Draw a circle and meditate on this
amazing fact, sit within a sacred cast circle and see the entire
universe surrounding you, every aspect of it emblazoned on
the walls of your circle.

Wherever a Druid creates ritual and acknowledges sacred
space the only thing he should leave behind, are traces of
footprints, a silent whisper of something having taken place
there moments before. If an area is frequently used over
periods of years it is quite common to see its effect on the
surroundings, the trees and flowers may be healthier than
others in the vicinity, and it will develop an air of sanctity, a
hushed silence that something sacred has taken place there.

Drawing The Circle

You may hear the circle in Druidry referred to as a "Nemeton",
it is a rather romantic and ancient word that describes a sacred
grove, which in turn can be applied to mean "Circle". The
word nemeton is Gaulish, one of the old languages of the
Celtic people, in Irish the word appears as "Nemed". Both

words share a common root with the Greek "Nemos" and the Latin "Nemus", all meaning a wood, forest or grove or a glade within a wood. In Bath the Goddess "Nemetona" had an altar dedicated to her, the green goddess of the grove. Today a Nemeton may refer either to a circle cast by a tribe, or the personal circle that an individual may cast around him or herself during private rites.

I must stress that we do not "Create" a ritual circle in its literal meaning, we cannot create what is already there, the sacred is around us continuously, we are only acknowledging its existence, the delineation of space by drawing the circle, forming a temple for the focus of ritual, it is not created, it is drawn.

The Personal Circle

To draw the personal circle or nemeton I use a very quick, simple yet effective technique. Sit or stand quietly in your chosen area, and begin by observing your surroundings, embrace the spirit of the place, whispering as you do a greeting to those who inhabit the space. Close your eyes and imagine within you a dull pulsating light, somewhere around your heart, allow this light to grow stronger and brighter with every in breath until it becomes a glowing large ball of light within your chest. Now take one very deep breath, and exhale loudly until no air remains in your lungs and you struggle to keep exhaling. Your body will instinctively want to jerk violently to force you to take an in breath. Use this jerk to project the glowing light within you, draw energy up from the earth and raise some emotional energy deep within your core. Now, abruptly just before you can exhale no more, allow that light to burst from you like the flash of a camera. It should leave you in a split second, as it does open your eyes and imagine the light having exploded from you, and see it surrounding you. As you breathe in, allow the light to vanish from your sight in the knowledge that it is there none the less. To close the circle, simply reverse the procedure, imagine the light's presence again and suck it back into your chest, in a flash. Use your imagination, whatever you create there will exist on many levels. Work with your circle or nemeton, by all means allow my words to inspire, but seek out what works for you, use your inspiration and connection to define and construct the circle, and allow it to become a vital part of your spirituality, a metaphor for unity.

The Group Circle

During a group ritual, all present should be involved in the drawing of the circle, each member contributing to the acknowledgement of sacred space, offering their uniqueness to the ritual itself. I would suggest that the group gathers together 12 stones, they can be as varied or as uniform as the group decides, their choosing should be a group task in itself, perhaps an afternoon spent knee deep in a river hunting for naturally tumbled stones. These stones will eventually mark out the perimeter of your circle and will represent the four elements at the cardinal points, the eight annual festivals and simultaneously represent the ancestral dead. See the next chapter for further details. A staff should stand at the centre of the circle to represent the living tribal community; this can be next to your fire or cauldron. The stones that you have collected should be blessed with intention during a group gathering, each individual in the group will learn in which position each stone should be placed. Each stone is placed in its rightful position with ritual (see following chapter). The group leader will then walk the perimeter of the circle with his wand aimed at the ground; using words of inspiration he draws the first circle. This circle represents the realm of Ceugant, infinity and the primordial darkness. The second circle is drawn a few inches within the first and represents the realm of Gwynfyd, spirit. The third and final circle is drawn around the tribe which gathers within it, and is representative of the realm of Abred, the dimension of physicality, represented here in flesh by the tribe.

The two innermost circles can be drawn in a similar manner to the first, using a wand, however some Druids may prefer to make use of a ritual dagger or sword, the choice is entirely up to the group. When all else fails use your finger! Do not draw the circle using bird seed, although the idea appears romantic, the seeds can contain species of plant unknown to that particular area and may inadvertently be detrimental. If you want to cast something onto the ground for the benefit of the little creatures then use unsalted, un-sugared popcorn. As to the direction in which you should draw the circles, well, the majority will inform you to always cast sunwise, clockwise or deosil, now I am about to be controversial; I draw anticlockwise. Since a child, without ever having read or seen a book on the occult, I used to draw a circle around an old Oak tree that I called "Liz" with dead leaves and twigs, I would then dance anticlockwise around it, just enjoying the moment and being with the tree. When I matured, I stuck to it, the sun may appear to move clockwise, but in actuality it doesn't move at all, we do! The Earth turns anticlockwise on its axis, so I draw my circles in the same pattern as the earth moves, our path around the sun may be clockwise, but the turning planet is not, I tend to go with that. So I draw Widdershins, anticlockwise, and so far it has always worked, in public rituals I tend to go with the norm, use what is comfortable for you and your group.

Ultimately the group circle is something that will evolve with the group, by all means use the ritual in the following chapter as inspiration, but do explore as a group, seeding and growing new ideas together.

The Awen Chant

This chant can often be heard in large open rituals or at camp rituals where there are sometimes hundreds of individuals present; the effect can be spine chilling! When so many voices rise up in harmony, each chanting the sacred word three times or in multiples of three, the sound is amazing. You can almost see the molecules of invisible air begin to move, slowly at first then cascading together in an explosion as they become caught in the sound wave that emanates from happy lungs. The Awen chant spirals through the circle, attuning those present to the inspiring power of the three rays. In a small group or grove, the effect is equally powerful if not more so, especially when people recall their experience of Awen, or if they have explored and experienced the exercise in part 1. A vision of Awen combined with the chant is a powerfully effective manner of preparing the mind for ritual, of settling into the moment.

By splitting the word into three separate syllables, each section is chanted individually yet forms a whole, chant as follows:

"AH – OO – EN"

Within a group setting the effect can be quite dramatic and very beautiful, a cascading symphony of sound pierces the air, each individual will begin and end at different times according to breath, each pitch and tone will vary. The results are normally wonderful, and when the final Awen is chanted, a pronounced silence is present as if the whole area and its spirits have been holding their breath around you, staggered by its beauty. By now the atmosphere of ritual will have been established, with the song of Awen resonating within, we move on to honour the other elements of ritual.

Peace

Many Druids in the modern world feel a deep sense of wanting to change the outside world, of making a difference, but that change must initially occur on the inside. Within a Druid ritual the initial focus is the call for peace, but how can we realistically call for peace in the world or even in ritual for that matter, when so many of us lack that peace within our own lives. How can we possibly hope for global peace when so many of us are in turmoil? Peace is a complicated and subjective concept, something which has differing connotations for all of us. We strive for peace in a complicated world, in societies that can adequately justify atrocities that appal other nations and peoples. The call for peace as used in modern Druid rituals was inspired by the National Gorsedd of Wales and its role within the cultural Eisteddfod movement that has swept the country since the 18th century, works and words inspired by the great and ingenious Iolo Morgannwg. The call for peace is the initial stage of the complicated yet beautiful opening ceremony of the Eisteddfod, performed by the Druids of the National Gorsedd. In modern Druidry aspects of this rite have been adopted for use in our modern Pagan rituals. Generally a pre-selected member of the group will slowly approach each cardinal point and say; "May there be peace in the North, South, East and West." All very well, but without adequate preparation and connection to this concept they are simply empty words. There needs to be an emotional attachment through experience to backup this quite profound statement. Whether we are working as a group or as individuals, working at attaining a degree of peace within our own being must be a fundamental practise for anyone walking the forest path.

How many of us harbour cruel thoughts? How many times do we feel frustrated and angry ready to lash out in moment of frustration? Are we quick to temper, quick to judge? How peaceful are we on the inside? Fair enough, none of us are ever going to be perfect models of humanity, we all want to rip somebody's head off once in a while. But to call for peace within a circle of spirit connection there must be an understanding of the concept itself, and its difficulties. There has never been peace in our world, we have battled with each other since the dawn of time. In Druidry we aspire to inspire peace in others through action and word. The un-peaceful state of our world is a direct result of disconnection, when we are connected, we can only be at peace, and striving every moment to eliminate the illusionary separation that mankind has expertly created, thus creating strife and war.

Before we casually call for peace, without feeling, without conviction, let's work at our own peace, our own inner state and whatever turmoil we find there. By working on ourselves we are effectively working on humanity in its entirety. This is where peace begins, on the inside; with the knowledge that we are all connected as a species we can inspire peace. When each human being perceives every other human as a vital aspect of himself and we see the universe expressing itself through the six billion human eyes that walk this planet, peace will ensue naturally. Find the peace within yourself first, through that connection to spirit and soul; allow that experience to filter through your words, giving them power and the influence to inspire. Watch as your words move the fabric of space, sound waves that travel on a tide of intention, inspiring all who are touched by them to seek a connection that will culminate in peace.

The Spirits Of Place

Personally, the spirits of place are the most enjoyable and fulfilling aspect of my involvement in Druidry, they offer such joy and inspiration that cannot be adequately articulated into words. These are the spirits of locality, of that special place that you travel to, whether to meditate, read a book or to gather for ritual. They are a vital component within our rituals and we must forge a relationship with them before attempting to ritualise and call on them in loud bellowing voices, to hear the reply: "Who the bloody hell are you lot, coming here, shouting and screaming, no I wont come, you can bugger off you rude bastards! Here have some rain!" It does happen!

The spirits of place encompass a multitude of beings that exist on several levels and it is important that we forge relationships with them, getting to know the individual facets before we descend on their territory. Even when we enter a space that we have never visited before, always reach out first with reverence and honour, greeting the spirits of place and asking for a moment's sanctuary in their presence. Then we can settle into their space and into their energy, and the multitude of manners in which they express themselves. But if we have an area that we frequently utilise for ritual it is important to get to know those who live there first, not only will this enhance your rituals, but also enhance your ability to sense these creatures and identify their various forms. When I refer to the spirits of place, I am not simply referring to the unseen world; the spirits of place are also the living, breathing creatures that live there. The hedgehog that scurries through the undergrowth, munching loudly on a slug, who in turn is also a spirit of that place, as worthy of acknowledgement as the hedgehog that eats it. They are the birds that perch in their roosts, nestled up for the night under a feathery wing. The spider that sways gently on her silvery web, gingerly hanging from a bramble leaf waiting for her dinner is also a spirit of place. They are everywhere within our chosen sacred space, from the individual spirit of every tree, shrub and weed, to the ancient echoes of long dead beasts who lived upon that land. They are the fairy folk, and the hidden people, those who journey from beyond the mists to wander through nature's green beauty.

There is much joy and richness to be had from a deep, sacred relationship with the spirits of place, but again it takes work, effort. The craft of Druidry has never been easy, never been a part time course; it takes stamina and hard graft to clear the mind and allow our visions clarity. This lucidity allows us to see the spirits of place when they gather at our rituals. I like to utilise a walking meditation to familiarise myself with the spirits of place, taking a gentle walk through the area that I plan to use or already do. Whilst walking, become aware of each and every footfall, the sound beneath your feet, opening your awareness to your surroundings and the subtle energies that lie hidden within it. A walking meditation is extremely gentle and passive, simply being in a state of mind that is highly receptive to any stimuli the outside world offers. Your actions should be slow, exaggerated, even if you turn your head, do it slowly and gently to prevent your eyes scanning an area too quickly. Allowing yourself to become passive quickly opens your mind, allowing you to perceive things that may not have been initially apparent. Most consider meditation to be the shutting away of the world, not in this case, this is ultimate awareness, the freeing of the mind, using your eyes to see what is really there! During a walking meditation allow a greeting to form in your mind and deep within your spirit, there is absolutely no need to vocalise, simply reach out with your mind passively, and with honour. The spirits of place will respond to you.

I find the walking meditation exercise far more effective during the hours of darkness. Initially in my early Pagan days I was reluctant to venture out in the dark, alone. But I soon discovered that if there was anything scary in the woods, it was me! The sudden inability to see clearly fires the imagination, causing adrenalin to be pumped dramatically from your adrenal glands, the fight or flight response, the emotional reaction that we call fear. What many do not realise is that your body cannot sustain this continuous release of hormones, after several minutes the hormonal tide depletes naturally and settles, the emotion that we incorrectly called fear suddenly vanishes. We find ourselves in another head space, another frame of mind, our vision clears, enabling us to reach out with our spirits into the darkness, where we sense others who reside there, feel their curiosity and the know that they mean us no harm. We are fortunate in the British Isles to have no large predatory animals that may see us as a light snack, which is one less thing to worry about. It is amazing how quickly our eyes adjust to the dark, textures and colours seem new and exciting, different and surreal, a normal coniferous forest can become a magical world of enchantment and spirit during the night time hours. With humanity settling down for the evening or tumbling into their beds, the night offers an unique psychic quiet time where a solitary Druid in the woods can reach out unhindered, touching and communing with the spirits of place, with little or no disturbances. Once we adjust to the nocturnal world, lost in the delicious velvet texture of darkness and shadows, submitting ourselves to our true senses, ignoring and inhibiting any hormonal response our body may unleash against us, our awareness increases immeasurably. Meeting the spirits of place, under their terms, is not only a test of dedication and commitment to the development of sacred relationships, but a method of increasing our psychic response and ability to control the sometimes irritating subconscious mind that insists on keeping us irrationally safe. After all that is one of its primary functions, to keep us safe and secure, but sometimes we have to ram it into a box, shut the lid and carry on regardless. In a situation where you are hyper aware, the flood gates to your psychic abilities open wide, any real physical danger you may be in will become instantly apparent, even before you are at any great risk of harm. Attuning to the spirits of place expands your awareness to the very edges of the forest if not beyond; you will be adequately forewarned of any danger.

It's all very well meeting the spirits of place on a warm sunny day, with buttercups tickling your toes and white fluffy clouds decorating the sky, when suddenly a kid on a pink Barbie bike rams into you and runs off screaming "Mum! There's a nutter over there!" it can be rather distracting! The truth is; that many modern Pagans will assume the safe route, the nice and easy way, willing to neither try nor compromise. Sometimes we need to confront our insecurities and fears, to journey and meet the spirits of place when it is uncomfortable for us to do so, the night offers such an opportunity.

The Gods

Most people involved in Druidry or Paganism in general will have come across the concept of God's, the myriad of deities, male and female that form a pantheon of mysterious and sometimes little understood entities. In truth, few truly understand the concept whatsoever, again due solely to a lack of inter relationship. In general there are three differing opinions of whom or what the gods are. First they are perceived by many to be individual spirits, older than humanity, who have developed an interest in mankind and offer guidance and help to those who sense them. Secondly they can be the creative thought forms of humanity, created over thousands of years, each individual facet given an identity and an attribution that benefits or represents an aspect of the tribe. Constantly nourished by the tribe and its reverence or worship the thought form develops a life of its own, and begins to act independently of the people, a God is born. The third option is the belief that they are beyond any form of simple human comprehension and will never be understood whilst we live in corporeal form. I believe the answer lies somewhere between the three differing opinions, a blend of all three, depending of course on the deity itself, its mythology and historical interaction.

In many of the Pagan pantheons, it is apparent that several gods were not initially deities, but assumed the role of, or were exalted to the rank of deity by man. Many of the British Gods fit this category, originally they were seemingly ordinary human beings with the occasional extraordinary ability or power. We have no evidence to suggest that certain deities such as Pwyll, Branwen, Bran etc were worshipped or revered at all in ancient times, they are modern deities, having been honoured with their status by twentieth century Pagans. Does this nullify or render their deification void? Probably not, I believe that a deity is, any being that an individual connects to and forms a relationship with, and is very subjective in nature. I doubt anyone has the right to claim that someone is not a deity if an individual has experienced otherwise.

The Gods are elusive, intriguing, confusing and complicated entities; I have no doubt, through personal experience that these deities exist as spirits just beyond the veil. I do not believe that they require or need our acknowledgement, but when we do and subsequently begin to work with them, growing with them, they can enrich our path dramatically, offering a concrete foundation to our spiritual quest. A God is whatever you want it to be, and your relationship with it should not be dictated by the words of another. It is quite common to see the attributions of a deity written in a book, and there are several available on the market, but bear in mind that these attributions, some of which are very modern, are simply the opinions of one individual, and are in no way an indication of deep connection to that particular deity. The attributions are extremely subjective, to objectively understand and discover the true nature of a deity, one must form a relationship with it. Their mythologies will offer clues to their nature, as long as you bear in mind that even the mythologies are opinionated to a degree. The scribe who finally rendered the myth into written form will have contributed to the tale, which is particularly true of the old Celtic tales written by Christian scribes between the 6th and 12th centuries. These have a definite Christian overtone to them, yet some of the esoteric mysteries remain intact, owing primarily to the scribes' ignorance of Pagan esoteric truths. The Gods are a vast and complex set of archetypical personas; they are not simply constructs that can be called to on a whim. In Celtic Britain alone we have over 400 deities that have at some point or another interacted with humanity. Some of these deities may not be anthropomorphic, in other words they may not assume human form or bear any resemblance to a known life form. The form a deity appears to any individual will be dependent on the interaction. The visual format will be projected by the worker onto the energy matrix of that deity, which in turn will appear in a manner that the human mind can grasp and understand. Our relationship with deity is not a one way thing, it is dependent on many factors, and any interaction occurs primarily due to relational experience. However we view deity it is a truth that an aspect of that force exists within us, each of us share that same dark origination, and ultimately the same soul. It is our experience that differs and facilitates that unique interrelation that humanity deems enriching and fulfilling, spirit connects to spirit. A deity's spirit is only different because it has experienced the reverence or worship mankind has offered it, culminating in a rich history of interaction which can assist us on our own paths through the forests. The Gods are not just out there somewhere, in a distant dimension or world. They exist within our molecules, they are an integral part of our culture and heritage, and the language of ritual allows us to converse with these beings and listen to their songs. After all it is not just us who benefit from this relationship, the deities also benefit for they experience an aspect of our spirit and its interaction with the realities of this incarnation. Together we are all learning and growing, discovering the wonders of the universe, enriching the great soul as we journey.

Who are the deities of your locality, and what are their tales? In many regions of Britain they reside in abundance, in other areas they hide their faces from the glare of the people, seek them out, speak to them, they are still there, some may be sleeping soundly, rouse them and sing their songs to the world.

The Ancestors

Wherever we gather for ritual we step upon ground that has been walked upon for countless centuries, generation after generation of individuals who have each contributed to their tribe and reacted to the influences of their environment. Some of these individuals may have lived and died over six thousand years ago or more, some may still be living, old and reflective, lost in memory and recollection. These are the ancestors; the echoes of their lives are imbued in the very Earth. Traditionally any stones or rocks either within the ritual area or placed there by the modern tribe, represent the spirit of the ancestors and their eternal nature. The trees and living plants reflect the lives and nature of those living. Our ancestors have influenced our lives, dictated the way in which we live and react to the Earth, the place in which we are born may be a place that our ancestors of blood have lived upon for centuries. Our great Island of Britain keeps within it the memory and experience of the ancestors of heritage, reaching back millennia. Their lives had value, and their memory lives on, each footfall, each whisper and action locked into the land, there to be listened to. An aspect of them lives within us, within our racial memory, our species communicates with itself, and the experience of our ancestors speak to us from beyond the mists of time, tied into the land and the molecules of our DNA. They speak to us, and in ritual we honour them. We honour their memory, those that we remember who have passed into the halls of the dead and those who have long since been assigned to the corridors of heritage. They are the folk who shaped our landscape, and developed the skills which we now possess, and the knowledge by which we survive. The ancestors are a vital aspect of our lives, the shapers of our society, by connecting to their memory we honour them. By reaching out with our senses we gain wisdom and knowledge from their experiences upon this Earth and their interaction with us from the world of Spirit.

What do you know of your own family, your own ancestors of blood? The mole you have on the back of your hand or the nape of your neck that your family have all shared for generations, the bump on your nose, the colour of your hair and eyes, are all attributions that you have inherited from your ancestors. Even your name reflects this connection, your surname in particular honours your ancestors, and can normally be traced back centuries, connecting us to faceless individuals who lived hundreds of years ago, who are responsible for our being, for our experience. Our surnames identify our tribe, the tribe of blood, and still we carry it today. I am often asked why I do not have a Druidic name; the truth is I do not regard it necessary. My name honours those who gave me this life and shaped this land, those whose genes swim within my body. The ones who determined that my hair would be brown, my chest hairy, my legs long, my name honours them with each voicing of it, with every signature I honour my ancestors of blood. My language honours my ancestors of Heritage, my birth place, my present home, throughout all these things exist the echoes and spirits of our ancestors, and in ritual we acknowledge them and their influences and effects upon our lives and the world around us. They were and are the Awen filled inspiration of our past, and we will one day fall into the ranks of the ancestors taking our place within the halls of the dead, listening to the words of our descendents calling our memory, acknowledging our legacy. The ancestors connect us to tribal memory and to the essence of the Druids of old, those who inspire this modern expression of that ancient spirituality. We honour them in ritual, with gratitude and celebration, sure in the knowledge that their spirits join our circles to sing the great song. Rock and tree, blood and spirit, the ancestors are within us and around us, a constant influence on our lives and our developing spirituality. Listen to their voices on the gentle breeze, one day those voices will welcome our own as the solid outline of our human form dies and allows our spirits to become ancestors.

The Cardinal Points

At the four cardinal points of the circle we traditionally find the four elements of life, Earth, Air, Fire and Water. As the basic elements that support life here on Earth they are acknowledged and honoured, they support our circle, witness our rites and dance with us as we sing the great song. But what are they, who are they? Are they really there? What does it mean to "Call on the Elements!"? Who are we invoking, are we indeed invoking or being invoked ourselves by a presence that is everywhere?

In the majority of Pagan rites the four elements are called upon at the beginning of every rite, and then dismissed at its conclusion. The normal routine requires a person to approach each cardinal point, whilst the remaining circle attendees face the same direction. With a physical and vocal gesture of greeting the elemental power is called upon to attend the rite, taking its place at the appropriate quarter and remaining there until it is no longer required. But what does this achieve, in fact what happens here at all? Do the elements simply come on demand, and where do they come from? Pagan ritual is in grave danger of becoming sanitised, of simply relaying a message that keeps those present firmly rooted in the outer mysteries of the craft, that nice, safe place where we don't have to give too much of ourselves. The pleasant thing that we do eight times a year with some friends! Ritual can so easily become an hour of empty gestures, of going through the motions with no connection to that which the ritual represents. We end up being 'Muggles' dressed as Pagans, and nowhere do we see evidence of this as strong as with the calling of the four elements. They become words devoid of any emotion that do not express an intense relationship and understanding with the elements and their role, not only in our lives but on everything that exists in our world. The four elements of Earth, Air, Fire and Water are not out there somewhere, waiting for a bunch of Druids to call them, they are an integral part of us, and they exist within our cells as well as the outside world. We need to develop an understanding of these elements and their roles.

Air

Let's begin with Air, traditionally this is the first element to be acknowledged, and normally resides in the East. The East also being the portion of the morning sky in which the sun will rise, and therefore represents dawn, new beginnings and a hoard of other attributions that you can find in many Pagan books. Air also exists within us, and again as previously stated all the elements of ritual should be worked upon prior to any ritual activity, ensuring that we know what we are doing, who we are honouring and why. Our words become passion filled rather than empty, and each word that falls from our lips is conveyed with an emotional attachment that betrays the relationship we have with each element. Our words give our story away if you like. When you stand in circle and listen to the words of someone calling air, someone who has sailed through the air on gossamer wings with the sylphs, and danced with the mighty hurricane, you can feel it, you can feel the power of attachment that individual has with the element they call upon. So when we call on air, begin on the inside, allow air to invoke you.

When meditating with Air, begin by focusing on your breath, feel the steady rise and fall of your chest with each in and out breath, focus your attention on the air in your nasopharynx (the part that lies behind your nostrils joining your nose to your throat), as you breath in you will instantly become aware of a cooling sensation cascading down your airways, this happens all the time, we just pay it no heed. As the air enters your bronchi it is warmed and you become unaware of the coolness, the air that leaves your body is warm and moist, feel it for a while, sense it. Now draw your attention to your lungs, expand your awareness, tell your mind that you are going to look inside your body, watch the air as it floods the main corridors of your lungs, until finally it arrives at that magical junction where blood and air meet. A single molecule of air attaches itself to a red blood cell, and at terrifying speeds travels headlong through the body's waterways, enriching every cell, organism and molecule with life-giving air. When it has expired, the blood transports the waste in the form of carbon dioxide back to the lungs, back through the airways and into the wide world outside. Air travels through us every single second that we live, and its acknowledgement should begin on the inside, the sylphs do not just exist in the gentle breeze that tickles your face in early spring, they swim within you also. When you call on Air, begin by focusing on the inside of your body; allow the images to call you. Air is everywhere; evoke the images and project them onto the outside world, see the molecules of hydrogen, oxygen and nitrogen interacting with everything around them, then call them. Invoke them when you have acknowledged their essence within you, being a part of you as they are a part of the fluttering of bee's wings on a distant shore. But, Air is also destructive, it can kill mercilessly, being a part of Air means we have an awareness of all it powers, nice and ugly. A hurricane can destroy a town in minutes, killing anyone that dares to stand in its way, and an aspect of this destructive force exists within the air that traverses our bodies. Our anger and frustration expresses this destructive force as we dispel air in large quantities and at great speed, when we shout, when we scream helplessly, it is air that we expel, the same air that kills so many every year, the same air that gives life.

Fire

When we move to the southern quarter of the circle we encounter Fire, and its spirits the Salamanders. Metaphorically, the Southern quarter represent growth, the midday sun is here, it is the path to maturity, the development and integration of intelligence. The warm southern winds bring comfort and heat from the furthest regions of the globe, caressing our land during the summer months, comforting us, burning away the cold residue of winter and spring. In the same manner as calling on Air, we begin on the inside with Fire, drawing it out from deep within our bodies, allowing it to coalesce with the fiery ball of the sun, or his light as he burns the moon. Look inwardly once more and allow a state of gentle contemplation to wash over you, as you search for the fire that lies within your own body. Find it within the tissue of you brain, as neural transmitters fire over and over again, sending messages down nerve pathways, that travel in perpetual darkness at the speed of light. See the fire within your cells as their nuclei transmit information, opening gates for chemical messages to interact with your body, watch the fiery consumption of foreign cells as your body's defences seek them out and destroy them. In your gut, feel the engulfing flames of digestion, the burning of acid as it breakdowns foodstuff, destroying and transforming.

Have you ever had indigestion? Do you remember the sensation, the fire that erupts from your stomach to burn your oesophagus? Our bodies may not have flames within them but the power of fire is there nonetheless, the potentiality of destruction and transformation. Although fire can relentlessly and totally destroy anything in its way, it also transforms, fire allows for new growth, new habitation, and that which it touches is never the same again. Fire and its heat teach us that death and destruction matter not, nothing is ever truly destroyed or annihilated; they are simply transformed. Intense heat and pressure from the fires within the earth transform carbon into precious, glittering diamonds; a thing of beauty emerges from simple carbon. The gift of fire warms the spirit and provides us with the fire of inspiration.

Water

Moving to the Western quarter of our circle we acknowledge the powers and life-giving properties of water. This is the traditional realm of the spirits of water, the nymphs or naiads. Here we see the sun set at the end of the day, and metaphorically the west is symbolic of maturity, growing old and wise. Water is perhaps the easiest element to form a sacred relationship with, owing to its immense presence within our very bodies, but it also instils great fear in many who suffer from hydrophobia. Water hides many secrets, displaying only its surface to those who would gaze upon it, beneath the glimmering, shiny surface hides a secret world. As we gaze upon water we instantly see another reality in the reflections that shimmer upon its surface, the distorted images of trees and landscape on the rippling surface of a wind blown lake, or the near perfect mirror image on a calm pond. Yet beneath the images lies a vast and hidden world, full of life in abundance, from the tiny creatures that swim gently through its body to those who live upon its floor, in mud and rock and clay. Our ancestors believed that bodies of water had deep mystical qualities, in particular those with islands within them. They were perceived as doorways to the otherworld, that realm of the gods and the spirits. Offerings were cast into them, after being purposefully damaged to render them useless in this world and fit only for sacrifice, sure in the knowledge that they were received by the Gods.

Water still holds the same intrigue and mystery to the people in the twenty first century, its calming properties call to us, the mystery of its beauty and the world hid beneath it, speaks to us. The majority of folk, except those who fear water find peace, and serenity gazing out to sea, or sitting beside the still waters of a lake at dawn. Water is immensely powerful, life giving and destructive, it only takes one single drop of water to create a ripple, yet every drop of water must work together as one entity to create a flood. Water is attracted to itself; it senses itself in another form and is drawn towards it. In esoteric metaphor water is seen to represent the emotions, owing to its fluidity, its rising and flowing, ebb and flow, the great tides that crash upon our shores twice a day, reflecting the movement of our emotions, and their effect upon the world around us.

When we connect with water, we first sense it within our bodies, it exists everywhere; our bodies being over 90 per cent water; we are almost entirely made of this miraculous substance. When you break us down into our chemical constituents we are simply a little hydrogen with some oxygen attached to it, throw in some carbon and you have a human, but not necessarily a human being. Something else provides the "being", that is the spirit, the drive behind the chemicals and molecules that make up the ordinary human. Yet water has its own spirit, and that spirit resides within us equally as it dwells within a babbling brook or gentle stream. It is there for us to tap into its wealth and wisdom at any time.

To connect with water we need only focus on the blood crashing through our arteries and veins, nourishing our bodies, hydrating every cell, every tissue, carrying the vitality of this element to every single part of our being. When we consciously allow our minds to travel the vast waterways of our own inner world, we develop an acute sense of the amount of water that exists within us and its qualities. Without it we are nothing, without it, like most things on earth, we would wither and die. Have you ever been thirsty, parched to the point of madness, where the water inside your body is screaming for its kin? Thirst is a terrible state of being, it is in thirst that we truly sense the magnetic quality of water as it forces the mind to seek it out, to quench the burning fire in our cells that would consume us and render us mere carbon without the dampness of water. As individuals in tune with water we can summon tears and feel the wonder of its power as it rises to the corners of our eyes and trickles in endless streams down our cheeks. How peculiar that when we display emotion we shed water, it is no great surprise therefore that we acquaint it to emotion. In times of need, distress, pain, grief, anguish and joy, we cry, the floodgates open and water pours from us, as salty as the sea, displaying the tide that constantly rises and falls within us. Where was that water seconds before, where did it come from?

Are you aware of pure briny water flowing inside your body? Probably not, yet summon your own tears and the proof is there, water, pure, clear and flowing from your own body. It is quite difficult to connect to a large body of water when you have no familiarity with its spirit, before you approach a lake and call upon its spirit, or call upon the vast qualities of water in ritual, call upon the water within you, this way you will instantly attract the waters of the world to you.

When we work with water it is important to remember and recall the emotional attributions that we have given it. When we focus on our own emotions and the water that carries hormones and chemicals through the avenues of our bodies we can easily perceive and sense the power of water and its spirits, for they are right there inside us. When you face the West, as the sun sets into the western sea, allow your own emotional tide to rise, summon the water within you and bring the tears and spirit of water to your eyes, and then call, with a quivering voice, full of emotion and feeling. Sense the waters of the world reaching out to you as water streams from your being, attracting the spirit of water that resides everywhere, in the air around you and the frozen mass of the arctic ice. Remember water is attracted to itself, it will not respond to words of dry air that spill from your lips, but it will respond to the floodgates of your emotions. Before approaching water in ritual sit with it in the quiet of your own space or sanctuary and call it, acknowledge its presence within you and allow it to rise. Feel the deep emotions that lie quietly inside you, give it permission to rise slowly through your body until it chokes you, causing your breath to gasp, rising until that water is set free as you break down into tears. Cry until you feel your heart will tear under the strain, observe the flowing of water. You have initiated these tears and this emotion it is not a reaction to an external stimuli. Control it. Experience the emotional power of water, and recall it every time you acknowledge it in ritual.

Earth

Finally we move to the North to form relations with the power of Earth, our Mother. Here the sun has well set and we stand at the witching hour, the depth of night, at the border of two days, it is neither yesterday, tomorrow nor today. The darkness of the North calls to us through the element of Earth and her spirits, and she sings to us of mystery and truth. The metaphors for earth are akin to Death, which in itself is only another border, another portal to cross where one finds oneself not of any time or any place, but simply in a state of being. The stability that Earth offers is obviously perceived, by observing our landscapes and the support system the earth provides each individual location on this planet. Moving closer to the subtle energy of Earth and her moods we are able more clearly to see her effects and how those energies affect our own bodies and the element of Earth that exists within us. What does the mother provide in your locality, what relationship do you have with her. Think of the soil of your home territory, what colour is it, have you smelt it, taken it in your hands and inhaled the delicate aroma of life and decay simultaneously dancing within its structure. Are you aware of the plant life and other vegetation that Earth allows to develop in your area? Do you watch her through the season, her changing face as the colours of her flesh dull and brighten during the year, as the trees she supports gently fall asleep leaving skeletal frames to delicately decorate her skin? What about the Earth within your flesh, what connection do you have there?

Whilst reading these words, stop for a moment, reach over with one hand and feel the bony ridge that protrudes on your opposite hand, then the firmness of your knuckles. Feel their contours and their firmness, solid bone lying hidden beneath your skin, an earthy framework of various elements that can be found in the Earth. How aware are you of the earthy structure that supports the organs and water, the skin and tissue of your body, the frame that dictated the shape you took at birth, the contours of your face, and the length of your fingers? Our bones provide the stability of Earth; they provide for us an opportunity to connect to the integrative quality of the Earth that lies within us. We came from her, reached up from her depths as micro organisms, to see the light of the sun and to eventually evolve into the animal that we are today. Meditate on the aspect of Earth that lives within you. What are your bones, do you know their composition, their names and their function? Many are strangers to their own bodies, strangers to the elements that invoke us from the depths of our own being. By attuning to it and understanding the ebb and flow of our own make up, we gain a better understanding of our Earth, of her fragility and changing cycles, of the delicate ecology of which we are a part. The Earth does not need our healing or magic, neither does she require our help; all she needs is for us to live in balance with her, in a non parasitic manner, in harmony with her moods, behaving as creatures that are an integral part of her, not entities that are able to and do control her mostly to her detriment. We are the ones in need of healing, and that healing will bring us closer to the energy of Earth as that energy is reflected within us. That balance will consequently affect our Mother, harmony would prevail and the Earth and her inhabitants may live together in peace.

For this to happen we must not only have a cerebral understanding of the nature of Earth but a deep and mutual relationship with her. She birthed us and she will consume us upon our deaths, as our bodies slowly dissolve back into the security and warmth of her flesh, assimilating us into that which we initially sprang from. We once again become Earth. To know that we are an aspect of her in life will enrich our societies and benefit our planet and all life upon her. By connecting to her we find balance and that balance brings harmony and honour. The Earth is our Mother and she exists within us, we are an integral aspect of her as she is an aspect of us, there is no real separation only that which man has invented through greed and pride. Feel the Earth coursing through you and the stability of the Earth beneath your feet, drawing on both sources, which are one and the same whenever you approach the North in your rituals.

There are many practical applications for experiencing Earth, caves and other subterranean structures such as fogous offer us a unique opportunity to delve into the very heart of Earth, where we are surrounded by her flesh, in the moist darkness of her being. Spending a night in a cave (ensuring that it is safe to do so beforehand), is a rewarding and moving method of connecting to Earth, submerged in that womb, in the very being that provides our bodies with the environment it needs to survive, with the fuel and air that we depend upon utterly. Within that darkness we find ourselves in that place out of place, in a time out of time, where we stand at the border of all things. The ordinary world feels a million miles away as we sit or lie there with our *Mum*, locked in a tight embrace of connection. She is also found in more frivolous manners, a patch of mud in the garden, the delicious liquid Earth that just begs for you take your clothes off and writhe in her fluidity! The compost heap that smoulders with intense heat that tempts you to sink your hand into the tickling warmth of its being, to feel the warmth of Earth reacting with Earth, the bounty and life giving property of death and decay. Earth teaches us many lessons; one of the most poignant is the mystery of death and its effects upon life, for the Earth to manifest any beauty any fruit, aspects of her must die and decay to provide the nourishment for life. She is life and death inexorably linked together in an eternal dance, singing the song of Awen as her faces and moods change to fit each cycle.

Elements, Invoke.

Each element of ritual is a ritual in itself, and the preparation and connective qualities we have with these elements should be daily integrative acts, sacred in their own rights. They are the manner in which we live the tradition, the daily acts that affirm our spiritual truths. The elements of ritual are never summoned, nor are they invoked, I believe that they invoke us. They are constantly calling us to join the chorus, like water is attracted to water, each element of ritual is attracted to the other, each one calling the other to join the song, it is only our ears that need retraining, our senses fine tuning to re-hear the calling. They call to us from within our bodies, from the echoes of ancestors on this wild land, the hedgehog and wren, the oak and the larch, they are all calling us. We need to stop simply hearing and begin to listen! When we do, that song that we celebrate and connect to in ritual begins to resonate through our lives. Waves emanate from us, joining the song of the world, in harmony and with clear intent, knowing we are the Earth and finding the lyrics to express those three shining rays of Awen that radiate like a beacon from our brows. The elements invoke, they are forever a part of us, not concepts that we indiscriminately summon, stir and call thee up! Without sacred relationship, our words are meaningless and have no impact, they may be pretty and oh so poetic, metered to perfection, but without relationship they are dead, it is this interaction that makes Druidry the unique spiritual tradition that it is, and our rituals reflect this quality.

Our rituals should have clear intent, and that intention made clear to all present, so that we work in harmony, knowing the purpose of that ritual and its relevance to the tribe. Ritual enriches and expands the experience of the tribe, grove or group, bringing us closer to each other and to the sacred relationship that we share with our own species and the world of spirit.

Chapter 3
A Modern Druid Ritual

have included the following ritual for the purpose of dissection, allowing you, the reader to eviscerate it and take from it the elements which you connect to, or simply just like the sound of. My intention is not to preach a framework for ritual that must be adhered to, I offer a ritual basis that I use alone and in group. Many people who are new to Druidry find the structural preparation of ritual, especially when it involves others, to be rather daunting, and will often look to books for ideas and inspiration. Those who have been walking the path for many years may also seek inspiration every now and then. By sharing my own personal ritual construct within the context of my Druidry, I hope to inspire you to seek out new avenues of expression in your rituals, personal and tribal. Please bear in mind that the following ritual outline is a construct of my spirituality and of its expression in ritual, I do not claim any antiquity or succession, other than that which is inspired from spirit. The ritual and any concept within it do not represent a definitive version of Druid ritual, it is my version, it is my Druidry, the way by which I work with Awen and the spirits of this tradition.

I am always interested in reading someone's idea and constructs of ritual; some are absolutely dire, others new and refreshing. One of the most magical aspects of Druidry is that it evolves, it does not fall stagnant. With daily inspiration the outward expression of our spiritual path can change from day to day, our rituals differing each time we gather, each situation, each circumstance evolving with our development and experience of Druidry. With no stringent rules and regulations, we have the freedom to express such joy and wonder of the universe and the world upon which we live, and the deep connection of soul. Druid ritual really is a joy, and when we take just the eight cycles of the year, they have such diversity and variation, each one applicable to the energies of that season, each one reflecting the song of nature during that time, the mood of the practitioners change in accordance with the ritual and the celebration. When we attune to nature and the nature of spirit and soul, we move with the faces of the cycles of life, our bodies realign themselves to the natural rhythm of the earth as we move closer to her energies, and see them reflected within our own physical forms, our rituals facilitate this relationship.

But, back to the ritual, take from it what you like and leave out the things that either does not resonate with you or you simply just don't like! Incorporate aspects of it into your own rituals if you like, or use the entire ritual. Explore your own rituals, have they become unchanging, the format the same as usual, do they need a little more inspiration and some spicing up? I have no doubt that if I was to rewrite this ritual again next year it would be slightly different, inspired by the coming year and the interactions and experiences that I will have during the year. But that's OK, they should evolve, change their mood and structure, keeping us inspired and honestly displaying the changing, evolving nature of our spirituality. Be free in your rituals, and above all enjoy them! The day they adopt that same feeling you had when you were dragged to church or Sunday school is the day they need revaluating!

The following ritual example has been written for group or grove use, with some modifications it can be utilised for large open rites and individual, personal rituals. Please remember the words I use are from my own heart, they are not inscribed in stone, use your own inspiration to connect to each element or by all means use the words that follow.

The Ritual

All participants arrive at the specified ritual area and prepare the site. The ritual coordinator or leader should have pre-assigned each individual element of the rite to the group members who will be active during the proceedings.

Leader:

> *"To know truth, to love truth, to maintain truth. Let us arrive fully in this place with honour and integrity, respect and reverence."*

All present recite the Druid prayer three times:

> *"We swear by peace and love to stand, heart to heart and hand to hand, mark oh spirits and hear us now concerning this our sacred vow!"*

Now we chant the Awen, calling for inspiration to flood into the grove and the circle, by intoning the word three times, each time for as long as the breath will last.

> *"AH-OO-EN"*

All present focus on the environment that surround them, opening their senses to become acutely aware of the subtle energies that surround them, grounding themselves in this place and this time. The leader then proceeds to declare the intention of the rite and asks that the sacred circle be drawn.

The circle is drawn as mentioned in the previous chapter by the placing of twelve stones; a single individual may well be responsible for this task, or indeed twelve different people who have been assigned a stone each. The placing of each stone should be accompanied by words which describe the attribution assigned to each. Some groves may well decorate their stones to represent their chosen attribution, spending time painting them or carving symbols or images onto their surface. This act integrates the stones into the group or individuals' spiritual practise and expression, clearly displaying a sacred working relationship with their given attribution. The stones also represent the relationship between the living tribe and the ancestral dead.

The stones are placed in a circle in the following order:
1. East, Air. 2. Winter Solstice, *Alban Arthan*. 3. Imbolc, *Gwyl Ffraid*. 4. South, Fire. 5. Vernal Equinox, *Alban Eilir*. 6. Beltane, *Calan Mai*. 7. West, Water. 8. Summer Solstice, *Alban Hefin*. 9. Lughnassadh, *Gwyl Awst*. 10. North, Earth. 11. Autumn Equinox, *Alban Elfed*. 12. Samhain, *Calan Gaeaf*.

Begin by placing the stones with the following or similar words.

1. East, Air. *"Blessings of the dawn upon this circle, as the light of a new day brings clarity and wisdom, may we be blessed with clear thought and intention. Winds of the East that bring the breath of inspiration, and the clear air that we breath, bless this circle and all present."*

2. Alban Arthan, Winter Solstice. *"Blessings of new birth and new beginnings be upon this circle, and the warmth of inspiration and new light. Wisdom of the bear and innocence of the child be upon all who gather here."*

3. Gwyl Ffraid, Imbolc. *"Blessings of the stirring fields be upon this circle, of life that stirs and raises its head to greet the warmth of the sun. May the beauty of cold and frost and the call of spring bless this circle and all who gather here."*

4. South, Fire. *"We call upon the blessings of the Southern winds, the spark of life and the fire within the head. May the burning heat of passion and intelligence bless this circle and all who gather here."*

5. Alban Eilir, Vernal Equinox. *"We call upon the blessings of the time of balance upon this circle, to guide us through our rite. May the mystery of the egg and dancing hare be bestowed upon this gathering."*

6.   Calan Mai, Beltane. *"Blessings of fruition and fertility be upon this circle, may all concepts and intentions fruit from this rite. May the passion of sexuality and the wonder of sensuousness be upon this circle and all who gather here."*

7.   West, Water. *"We call upon the blessings of the Western winds, the cool and changing winds of emotion and feeling to bless this circle and all those present."*

8.   Alban Hefin, Summer Solstice. *"Blessings of the mighty sun be upon our circle, of power and strength. Sun that burns bright, giver of life, bless this circle and all who gather here."*

9.   Gwyl Awst, Lughnassadh. *"Blessings of the harvest be upon this circle, may we who gather here reap the benefits of our crop. Powers of the harvest, of blood and gold, sacrifice and understanding bless this circle."*

10.   North, Earth. *"Blessings of the earth our mother be upon this circle. May the stability and security of our earth provide this rite with integrity and honour."*

11.   Alban Elfed, Autumn Equinox. *"Blessings of maturity and the last breath be upon this circle. May the bounty of the second harvest be upon us as we reflect, contemplate and accept the gifts of life and death."*

12.   Calan Gaeaf, Samhain. *"Blessings of the dying time be upon this circle, of death and decay and the mystery of the grave. May the gift of stillness and potentiality be bestowed upon this circle and those who gather here."*

At the conclusion of the laying of stones, the mindset of the grove will have adjusted to the mentality of the ritual intention, the bonds of earthly life numbed slightly. At this time it is traditional to call for peace. A chosen member of the grove approaches the eastern quarter and speaks.

"Creatures and people of the East, lands of the rising sun, may you strive for peace, may you grow from peace. May there be peace throughout the east."

Moving to the southern quarter:

"Creatures and people of the South, land of the midday sun, may you strive for peace, may you grow from peace. May there be peace throughout the south."

Moving to the western quarter:

"Creatures and people of the west, land of the setting sun, may you strive for peace, may you grow from peace. May there be peace throughout the west."

Moving to the northern quarter:

"Creatures and people of the north, land of the night and cold, may you strive for peace, may you grow from peace. May there be peace throughout the north."

Moving to the centre of the circle:

"May there be peace above and peace below, and peace throughout all the worlds."

The speaker then asks the grove if there is peace three times, *"Is there peace?"* to which they respond, *"There is peace!"*

The leader now approaches the eastern quarter, the remaining grove should form a circle close to the centre of the space. With his wand or chosen tool the leader begins to draw the first of the three circles. The circle of Ceugant.

"From the depth of darkness do we draw this circle round, from the cauldron of the Gods and the darkness before the shining pillars of life."

Moving a few inches inwards he draws the second circle of *Gwynfyd.*

"From the darkness shines the light of spirit. We draw this circle in honour of our ancestors and those who assist us from beyond the veil, spirits of Gwynfyd, you within the halls of the dead witness our rite."

The third circle is drawn around the grove itself and represents the here and now, the realm of *Abred*.

"We draw the circle of life, of stone of mud and clay, of leaf and bark. Circle of Abred, circle of the tribe, circle of our community. May the darkness and shining rays of Awen permeate this space."

In my experience the atmosphere of drawing the circles may be enhanced if the remaining grove whispers a chant, this chant can be as complex or as simple as the grove requires. From the intoning of a single word to entire verses, allow your imagination to inspire you. Whilst chanting the grove should hold the image of the circles within their minds, watching as each one is drawn, contributing their own energy and creative force to their drawing.

At the centre of the circle or within close proximity to the central cauldron or fire, we place a staff upright in the ground to represent the living tribe, those who gather at the ritual. The staff represents the spirit of the tribe working in conjunction with the stones which represent the ancestral dead.

"Spirit of the tribe, the flowing waters of our community, we honour you. Spirit of connection and sharing, we honour you. As this living tribe gathers here upon this earth, we do so with honour and integrity, reaching out to you of our blood and our heritage that have passed into the halls of the dead. With honour we come."

Now we honour the spirits of place, with each grove member turning to face the perimeter of the circle, arms outstretched to embrace the spirits of the land, sea and sky.

"Spirits of this place, you of the hidden places and the shadows, hear our call. Shapers of this place, shapers of bark and crystal, of earth and rock, hear us. Know that we come with honour into your kingdom. You of wing and hoof and claw, hear us, creatures and spirits of this place witness and share in our rite."

Next we call upon the spirits of our ancestors that echo to us from the trees and hills, from the soft gentle breeze that tantalises our skin, and awaken within us ancient memories and songs that stir the spirit.

"Ancestors, you of the hills and the wind, you who walked the fertile plains of our land hear our call. You of memory and heritage and of the recent dead we honour you in our rite. Whisper to us your songs of ancient moonlight through the mists of time, blessed be the ancestors."

Calling upon the gods of the tribe and the gods of the land is a deeply personal process, unique to each grove and individual. Many groves revere a token god or goddess that may have been revered within their locality for centuries, acknowledged as an integral aspect of that place and that tribe. I here offer an example of a typical calling to the gods of my locality, the words and emotional attachment would differ according to each grove and gathering.

"Modron, great goddess of this land, you of the shining stars and the silver moonlight, hear us. Milk of the mother; bless this tribe as we honour you in our rite. You who stands at the gates of life and death, great mother of the bounty of our land, hear us now. Witness our rite. Blessed be the mother."

"Llyr, our Lord of the waters that lap at our island hear our call. You of the waves and of the wild and forlorn places hear us. You who guards the doorways to the west and opens the portals of death hear us. Mighty Lord of this place, we come with honour and reverence, witness our rite. Blessed be the father."

Now we turn our attention to the four cardinal points and the elemental energies of Air and fire, water and earth. Tokens to physically represent them may be placed at each point. Incense for air, a candle for fire, mead for water and a stone for earth. Those chosen to perform this task move to their appropriate quarter.

East, Air.

"Creatures and spirits of the East, powers of Air and inspiration, hear us. You of the breath of life from the first to the last, gentle breeze and hurricane hear us. Flowing spirit of inspiration that calls to us through the breeze, voices of our ancestors hear us through the winds of the east. Hail and welcome!"

South, Fire.

"Creatures and spirits of the South, powers of fire and intelligence hear us. You of the burning midday sun and warmth of the hearth, flickering salamanders of candlelight and molten core of our mother hear us. Spirits of transformation and destruction hear us, join us at our rite, be here with us now, Hail and welcome!"

West, Water.

"Creatures and spirits of the West, powers of water and emotion hear us. Spirits of bubbling brooks, our wells and sacred springs, hear us, you of the rivers and lakes and oceans hear us, flowing waters of life we honour you here in our rite, from the blood that courses our bodies to the droplets that escape our lungs. Witness this rite, we bid you hail and welcome!"

North, Earth.

"Creatures and spirits of the north, powers of earth and stability, strength of the mother, hear us. Mighty spirits that move and transform our land, raising mountains and hills hear us. You of the hidden places that lie deep within the womb of the mother hear us; know that we gather to honour you. Witness this rite, we bid you hail and welcome!"

We now focus on the intention of the rite, having honoured the spirits and elements that Druids deem sacred and an integral aspect of the tradition we can move on to the work at hand. Obviously this section of the ritual depends entirely on the nature and focus of the rite; it may well be a seasonal celebration focusing on the festivals of the wheel of the year, or a ritual for healing or inspiration. This is the heart of the ritual and may be planned well in advance or allowed to flow like the rays of Awen, becoming an entity in its own right, developing a life and momentum of its own. Within a group rite it is vitally important that the intention of the ritual is made clear to those who willingly gather there, ensuring the intent is held in the heart and focused in the mind. This section of any rite develops inertia, a fluidity that normally gains momentum, knowing when it will or should conclude will occur naturally as the energy within the group peaks, plateaus and decreases naturally. Allow this section of the rite to be what it needs to be, whilst simultaneously maintaining the awareness of the circle itself, holding the space and the energy contained within it. However, delineating a place as sacred and honouring the spirits as demonstrated in this ritual example does not necessarily mean that you need to immerse yourself or your grove in intense ritual practise. Sometimes it is enough to acknowledge the sanctity of nature and simply be in a space with the spirits surrounding you, ears pricked and spirits open to the inspiration that can be found in such a place.

At the conclusion of the ritual intention many groves will hold an eisteddfod allowing the creative force of the grove to express itself, inspiring the grove and relaying messages from the world beyond the visible. Traditionally we conclude the ritual events with the recital of the Gorsedd prayer, which is as follows.

"Grant o Spirits thy inspiration,
And in inspiration, strength,
And in strength, knowledge,

And in knowledge, understanding,
And in understanding the knowledge of Awen,
And in the knowledge of Awen, the love of it,
And in the love of it, the love of the universe and all existence."

As the ritual draws naturally to a close, each element that was honoured and called upon to witness it must be dismissed with honour and respect, finding words inspired by the rite to offer gratitude to those who gathered with us. Normally the same individuals who initially called each aspect of the ritual will close. As the last remaining stone is thanked and dismissed and removed from the circle the rite is over and complete. All that should remain behind is the echo of something having taken place there, a vibrancy of reverence and inspiration that seeps into the landscape.

Let us now turn and examine the underlying energies and significance of the eight cycles that form the wheel of the year. Our year is conveniently broken down to bite-size pieces each one parading along the stage of moon of sun, each one applicable to a cycle of human life and development. The wheel of the year not only offers periods of intense spiritual experience and expression but also offers the joyous practise of celebration as we tread the wheel, dancing and moving to the subtle rhythms of the earth. When we incorporate our experience of working with Awen and the natural energies of the universe, integrating them with ritual practise, we develop a stable framework for the expression of our spirituality. The wheel of the Pagan year allows us to move ever closer to the energies with which we have formed a sacred relationship with, permitting us to express ourselves in conjunction with the cycle of life and death and rebirth. I shall begin at the beginning and take you on a journey through the drama of our yearly cycle, starting at the point where the new sun heralds the arrival of the new year at Alban Arthan; the Winter Solstice. Please bear in mind that the reflections I offer on the passing wheel of the year are based on my experiences of it, and its applicability to my personal spiritual development, they are the thoughts and muses that enter my mind during each phase. They are not necessarily the view and experience of other Pagan Druids; they are my own, journey with me through the cycle of life with the rays of Awen providing a spectacular backdrop to the drama of life.

PART FOUR

CHAPTER 1

ALBAN ARTHAN/WINTER SOLSTICE

'Twas the dawning of solstice, when all through the night,
The people were stirring to the call of the light.
When darkness runs fleeing in fear of the sun,
We know a new year has already begun.
We rise from our graves to greet a new morn,
And watch as the mother's new child is born.
Bathed in his light we answer his call,
Hope has now come, happy solstice to all!

(K. Hughes. Inspired by the poem "A visit from St.Nicolas, by
Clement. C. Moore)

The Owl in the old Oak Tree waits and the tree waits with her, as he has every Solstice morning for the last six hundred years, and that silence is familiar, a disconcerting kind of silence as the entire world holds its breath. A shrew scarpers across the forest floor and joins more of its kind, the Owl glances once, but she's not interested, she nuzzles against the tree, as if seeking comfort, solace, confirmation. But the tree simply sighs, deep within his darkness he feels it, feels the dawn tugging at his roots, his bare and skeletal branches reach towards his mother in the night sky, and she smiles a knowing smile, her brightness casting long shadows through the frosty forest, as she reflects the light of the coming Sun. She too feels his strength. And then it happens, the old and wise Oak trembles as the sun bursts above the horizon, a tiny sliver of bright orange, and the rays flood the landscape, caressing everything in its path, a glow of pink illuminates the world as sunlight and frost *mingle, meld and blend with each other. Suddenly the forest erupts; birds soar into the sky with a great cry of triumph and of joy, the little creatures dance and caper among the decaying leaves. And silently a lone figure clad in a dark woollen cloak moves from the shadows and with arms outstretched in a welcoming gesture greets the first rays as they trickle across his smiling face. He pulls down his hood and laughs, laughs in joy and in relief. The light has come. "Happy Solstice!" the lone Druid cries into the pink forest, and the forest replies. It is Solstice morning for sure!*

The beginning, the silence before the sigh, sheer anticipation, this is the true beginning of the Celtic year, the period of greatest darkness, yet it harbours the promise of light, the promise of hope, of new life and growth. Difficult to comprehend, understandably when the whole of nature slumbers, protected against the merciless energy of winter, the cold, frost, ice and snow. The old standing stones upon the moor wait in expectation of a new dawn. The hum of energy streams through the sacred landscape as the Sun begins its journey once more towards the north. This is the beginning; for upon the dawn of the Winter Solstice it all happens, light is victorious, and death and darkness flee before the tiny bright ball that rises on the distant horizon. This is the birth, the birth of our very source of life, the Sun. Slowly we emerge from the womb and tomb of Calan Gaeaf, blinking in the new light that struggles to gain a foothold on the distant horizon, turning our faces to greet the dawn and embark upon the journey of birthing.

I am intoxicated by the sheer energy of this season, its contrasting and enlightening energies, its complexities and paradoxically its simplicity. Innocence underlies this festival of welcoming. I get completely caught up in the drama of winter, and oh what a drama it is…where to begin, how on earth do you articulate the meaning and connection one feels to this season, a season that is so misunderstood by the trivial nature of humanity.

This is the shortest day and longest night, we truly feel ninety three million miles away from our Sun, yet surprisingly we are three million miles closer to the glowing orb at this point of year than at any other. However it is the angle of the Earth on its axis, which dictates our seasons and their wondrous drama. In technical terms the Earth is twenty three degrees and twenty seven minutes off the perpendicular to the plane of orbit! In simplistic terms the axis of the earth causes the northern hemisphere to tilt away from the sun during our winter, the sun appears lower on the horizon for this reason. Immediately after the solstice the earth slowly begins to turn her face towards the sun once more.

Alban Arthan marks the beginning of the season, the initiation of the period of light and growth. It begins at dawn, normally on or around the 21st of December each year as the sun enters the astrological sign of Capricorn. This is the day of Alban Arthan or Winter Solstice (I rather like the term Mistletide which expresses the mystery and magic of that elusive Druidic herb, the Mistletoe). The word Solstice is derived from two Latin words, "Sol" and "Stice", this is literally translated as "Sun stands still", which is in fact what seems to happen. Slowly but surely throughout the season of Samhain the sun moves ever further southwards, rising later setting earlier in the frozen winter skies. And suddenly it seems to stop dead in its tracks, and the world holds its breath, will it ever move, will it ever grow strong? Of course in the twenty first century we know it will eventually begin its journey northwards once more, to bring light and heat on its journey towards the Summer Solstice, but was it as clear to our ancestors? No. They did not have our technology, they didn't have the ability to shut out the world and cuddle up in front of a gas fire in a centrally heated home, full of food transported from the furthest corners of the planet to sustain themselves. Food rich in nutrients to keep us fat and well through the winter days, until the arrival of spring, they had none of the comforts we have now. But their lives were simpler, and utterly dependent upon the Earth for sustenance and nourishment, and they appealed to her and her God's, to keep them safe. Many would perish; the weak would die of consumption and cold. The weakest animals would be slaughtered to provide food for the tribe. The dawning of Solstice gave them hope, it foretold the demise of winter and that all would be well.

The Neolithic peoples built chambers and cromlechs to mark this time, a time when they knew that everything would be OK. Unlike us, they depended entirely upon knowing, if they got it wrong the lambs would be born too early and die on the frosty hillsides, they would miss the valuable windows for sowing the seeds that would be harvested later the following year.

We have it easy, our refrigerators full of goodies from an almost endless supply of foodstuff from the local supermarkets. But where did it all come from, our ancestors relied upon that which they harvested during the autumn months, they couldn't realistically provide sustenance for the animal stock during the winter, so the weakest were slaughtered to provide food for the tribe. This wasn't cruel or in any way detrimental or unethical, it was a necessity. Unlike the present, where aggressive agriculture provides us with what we want when we want it. We all try and be good, try and be ethical, try and eat positively, but, in all honesty, how ethical is our eating? Whether we are omnivorous, vegetarian or vegan, where does our food come from? The chicken that lived a deformed and painful life in a battery farm, the salmon fed with pellets of disease inducing chemicals, the bananas from South America where those who pick them cannot afford to eat them. The Soya from distant shores where people are abused and mistreated, killed and kept in poverty; we are all at fault. Regardless of what you eat and how you eat it, the fact is that the ecological footprint we contribute towards on a daily basis is destroying our relationship with the natural world. Consider the amount of poisoned vapour that every one of the planes that land or take off at Heathrow Airport every 90 seconds leave behind, and how many of those planes carry what we consider to be ethically produced foodstuffs from other lands, thousands of miles away. No, we are all part of the society that is destroying our planet, convenience has overtaken compassion. None of us are blameless. An essential part and process of development within Druidry is the understanding and acceptance of personal responsibility, and our role within the world. During this time of new light a new form of thinking should arise, questions asked to be pondered over during the coming cold months, and allowed to bloom into positive fruition during the growing time.

In Druidry we take personal responsibility for ourselves and our decisions, and if we can ethically and positively justify our actions then we can't go far wrong. The small things make a difference, but the danger of this being invalidated by fundamental fanaticism and obsessive non-creative behaviour is a real threat to the positive and transformative actions we could be pursuing. Fanaticism is neither healthy nor conducive to transformation; passion on the other hand will move mountains. Fanaticism in any field whether it be religion, food, politics etc is dangerous however you look at it, and ultimately comes from anger, anger caused by frustration which eventually leads to a sense of helplessness. The resulting outcome becomes rage, and fanatics are full of it! This doesn't help ourselves or the cause for which we felt such passion. Taking action doesn't necessarily have to be on a grand scale, sometimes it cannot realistically happen. We have no illusions in Druidry, no unrealistic ideals, we accept the truth, we may not understand it and we may not like it, but we acknowledge the existence of the truth however grim, and strive to change it, to make a difference. A little bit goes a long way.

It seems that our society has become overly complicated, and this seems to have seeped over into spirituality, modern

Druidry being no exception. I find myself wondering why this has happened, why this has occurred in the first place, this over complication of a natural spiritual tradition, a tradition of the land and of the moonlit places. What has happened to the simplicity? We seem to have forgotten how simple this Druidry, this spirituality is, and have become lost and confused in its invented complexities. The new born sun teaches us the simplicity and true essence of life, of making our own decisions here in this world of physical density, and accepting responsibility for our actions. Like a new born child whose early months and years are crucial in the forming of personality the beginning of this new cycle can infuse within us new concepts and new ideals that will fruit in later months. What we have reflected upon during the dying time of Samhain is now illuminated by the light of the newborn sun, how we use it will affect the rest of the year and our lives. People become blind to the natural and instinctive aspect of spirituality and become lost in vastly over complicated systems, which lend very little to the spirit of connection. The message of the new born sun is to allow it to illuminate the grains of truth and their expression within our own lives and the practical applicability of our spirituality upon life in general.

At this time of year, we can almost see those three rays of light illuminating the earth's deep blue skies as the sun grows stronger, the days grow longer and the shadows shorter. And Awen gives birth to our creativity after weeks asleep in the cauldron, in the tomb, beneath the breath of death. Solstice dawns and we are inspired. We have withdrawn, deep into ourselves, deep into the sanctity and stillness of our grove but now it is time to stir, to slowly stretch tired, stiff limbs and anticipate the light. But, our groves are still, dark, forbidding, scary, there is little movement here, only the cold breeze that causes dead leaves to suddenly seem animated, if only for seconds, casting shadows in the moonlit grove, shadows that we may not want to see, and shadows that cause us to smile with a deeper understanding. Like the earth, she who has withdrawn into herself, and seeks solace and inspiration within cold mud and clay, we feel and sense a stirring, the stirring of life beneath the surface, for the earth is aware, something has aroused. Change is taking place; a change that can be felt deep, deep within the earth herself; hope has reached the depths of Annwn and the depths of our beloved Mother. The light stirs, yet darkness clings, and clings, reluctant to let go, but it has to, it has no choice, with a frustrated frown and a surrendering grunt, the darkness gives up its crown. And the stirrings begin, the tiniest growth within bulbs and seeds, minute fractures appear on the surface of buried treasure, treasure that will soon emerge as green stems, ready to bloom during the springtime, as the Goddess of the earth leaps in joy and caresses sensually her lover the sun. But for now they only stir, for the winter still demands respect, it does not ask, it demands, the harshest days are ahead. Days lacking in mercy as the tempest stirs and summons the winds of change and of birth. But deep, in the silence of the earth, we feel it, the first awakening of the earth and of ourselves.

These changes, paradoxically subtle yet immensely powerful can cause changes to be felt beneath tons of earth and soil. Are we so naive and stupid to believe that our very bodies do not feel these changes, of course they do. We feel them, we sense them, but we fight, fight to the bitter end, and what do we achieve, nothing, instead of giving into the energies and flowing with it as nature intended, we think we can shut it out. How very foolish we are. Is it no surprise that we suffer strange and bizarre afflictions in the twenty first century? Take SAD for instance, Seasonal Affective Disorder, fair enough we live in a society so affected by stresses and pressures, but we have distanced ourselves so much from our Mother the Earth, that we become ill, lacking the natural vitamins from the Sun's rays. Even in winter he still offers some sustenance, but we shut ourselves away, and suffer as a consequence.

Within Druidry we embrace the seasons and accept the energies of the earth and how they are reflected within our own bodies, how they change us and alter us, what secrets they are telling us. In the cold of December and the merciless nights of frost and storms, we find a place of comfort and consolation deep within our psyche, a place where we as humans have been for countless thousands of years, a place of stillness and of new ideas, and a place of birthing. Accepting the seasons and their mysteries bring us that little bit closer to an understanding of our nature, and nowhere is that acceptance more vital than during this time of birthing which will have ramifications throughout the rest of the year.

But this path is fraught with difficulties, and one which seems most poignant at this time of year is that which has stricken so many of us on the forest road: loneliness. With the coming of the light and the resurrection from the grave, the cold light of that first morning can sometimes leave us feeling isolated and alone. In truth we are, we are born from singularity and are programmed to accept duality, yet our earthly experience is inherently a lonely one. We may understand within our spirits that we are connected by invisible strands of spirit and soul to each other, yet we embark upon life as individuals, each experience different and unique. Loneliness however cannot be equated with separation, for within it there is a message that teaches connection. *'Because of the loneliness';* these were words written in a book and presented to me by a friend, and with those words came such feeling. I could feel her loneliness as much as she could feel mine, and in those few moments of understanding and connection the sheer weight of that loneliness eased and slipped away. And holding hands across a crowded restaurant in central London, the trees burst through the concrete jungle and enveloped us in their branches, new buds burst into the brightest green I had ever seen, and acorns and holly berries danced for us, danced in sheer joy. And in those brief moments loneliness seemed an impossible concept, how could one be lonely when we are so much a part of nature that surely we are never alone! But those branches slowly vanished, and the tremendous oppression of the city returned, and once again we found ourselves in the same place as we were before, lonely. And as our hands slipped apart we smiled, and within that smile was an understanding, an understanding of two spirits, like all spirits inexplicably connected forever, yet incomprehensibly separated through sheer volume of mass and matter, each of us striving to hear that song of home, to somehow feel that connection to the source and our home within it.

This loneliness is something that's essential to the growth of a Pagan, that the connection we feel can be shared, music and poetry, art and song shared is simply beautiful, but none of us can truly experience what another sees in his vision, hears in her soul quest. This is our journey, and we face it alone, the celebration of the wheel and that joyous feasting as we trance the wheel is wondrous and precious. In an age of spiritual tourism, where so many assume spirituality and the experience of the spiritual can be bought for a few hundred pounds. Many believe that the right mantras recited over the right crystals that have been ravished from the body of our mother at huge cost to the environment, they can attain enlightenment! But what is enlightenment? Surely true enlightenment equates to true loneliness on this plane of existence. And if in all honesty we acquired enlightenment then surely we would be consumed by its power and understanding, and die, having no need for our human form any longer.

We are alone, and the path through the forest is a lonely one. Something calls us, something in the shadows; and it feels familiar, and we understand that this loneliness is part and parcel of this experience. Ultimately on a physical level we are all alone, we journey alone, and we die alone, this is our journey and the vehicle is this body. Loneliness makes us feel even more human, for that is obviously what we are. The experience of this loneliness with its contradictory nature must be comprehended in order to transmute the spirit. It transforms us, our bodies dense with molecules and atoms seem separate from the rest of the world, yet through our loneliness we achieve an understanding of the connection we have to the all. Loneliness sets us free; it is the first vital wound that is dealt to us on the embarkation of our spiritual journey. Through it we gain an understanding of contradiction and paradox, but discover the vitality and truth hidden within their message to us. Loneliness forces us to experience the esoteric and spiritual for ourselves without taking someone else's experience as concrete truth and through that experience we discover our truths. Ultimately we realise that they bear a strong resemblance to the truths of others who have also travelled through loneliness, to the fount of spirit.

Think of Humanity in general, how we gel, meld and blend with each other, seeking companionship, friendships, relationships, at no other time of year is this more obvious than during the Yuletide season. We move towards others of similar interests and opinions, world view and vision, we seek our tribe, attempt to find our siblings in this vast world which we inhabit, we feel a part of something more, something bigger, but are we? The danger here is the gelling together of tribes to ease the sense of loneliness, to dispel it, to be within a tight knit group of people where we need not be alone. We wander then into the realms of other people's vision, of someone else's experience, not our own. Loneliness and the exploration of spirituality as individuals, unleashes something deep within our subconsciousness, we find that we are not alone after all, but completely connected. But to find this we must travel that dappled path alone, no one can take us there, to the hidden places, we must and can only go alone.

And the value of this loneliness is understood, appreciated as something integral to spiritual growth and development, and enriches our sharing, our inspiration and its message becomes clear and filled with vision and sincerity. People know when they meet someone who has traversed those inner roads, stumbled, fallen, picked themselves up and carried on. We can see a certain spark in the eyes of those who have seen, communed and shared with those of the hills and of the wild and dark places. We know that they were there alone, with no hand to guide them, no voice of reason to influence them other than the shining rays that shine from within their core.

Loneliness leads to inspiration, and the realisation of connection. But so many shun the lonely path, immersing themselves in activities and exhausting workloads, evading the call of the green, shutting their ears to the voice that calls from the darkness of the grove, leaves which rustle and move. The voice of the Green Man and those of leaf and bark, call us to join, to play for a while. But no, we shut our ears, *'It's scary in there!', 'I'll go when I am with a bunch of people!', 'Not now! I'm busy! Go away, leave me alone!'* And we ignore the call that will take us to the threshold of mystery, shutting our ears to the call of the lonely path.

Have you ever been out there on a dark and moonless Solstice eve, the eve of the shortest day and longest night? Have you ever stood in the deepest darkness of a wild and forlorn place and felt this night, been there with it, danced with it, your body moving to the subtle rhythms of the earth. Felt that energy, that anticipation that only occurs upon this night, anticipation that most of us will recall feeling as children three days later on Christmas Eve. This night has a hunger, a hunger for new life, the world grows weary of the depth of dreams and sleep, and it calls for sunshine, for the warming rays to caress the voluptuous curves and folds of our green and sleeping earth. And we feel it too. It is here within us, this wonder and sense of expectation that we feel at this time of year, the crackle of energy sparks and flows through us as we sense a shift to the normal pattern of things.

This excitement and sense of apprehensive expectation is masked by the fact that we are aware that the merciless nature of winter is not over, for the worst is almost certainly to come. We must face the storms, the plummeting temperatures, the death and diseases of winter. Promise is there none the less, and although this season stretches from the edge of Solstice to the very beginning of February we are aware of how long this season feels. But why, why is winter so hard, and why do we dislike it so much?

The answer to this question is surprisingly simple; we resist. We resent the fact that winter is upon us, that the nights draw close and the cold seeps into our bones and affects our minds, our rationality, our common sense, and we fight it as if our lives were in danger, but why? This constant antagonistic approach we have towards life in general as inhabitants of the twenty first century is extremely destructive. Why do we fight what is natural, what is the norm, why do we not understand that it is us that have become abnormal? We have become so far removed from nature that it activates some self destruct mechanism within us, rather than achieving an understanding of the mechanisms behind and throughout the season, we ignore it, shut ourselves away from it and deny its essence. No surprise really that the suicide rate elevates to dramatic heights during winter!

Alban Arthan, the Welsh, Druidic term for this season as coined by the legendary Iolo Morgannwg in his collection of bardic wonders, "Barddas", is now commonly used throughout the Druidic movement to denote this festival. The term itself is split into two components, Alban, meaning high point, regal or supreme, suggesting that the four Albans are the peaks or top most section of any season. They are the crescendo of energy, and the orgasmic climax of a particular cycle. It is also interesting to note that the term Alban is also Welsh for Scotland, is this sheer coincidence, after all Scotland is the highest point of the British Isles? Arthan refers to a Bear, a great bear that many equate to King Arthur and his attributions of strength and stability.

This is Yuletide, Mistletide, Christmastide, the season of hope, regardless of where we are in the Northern Hemisphere. This is a time of great joy, and one that has been celebrated for probably the entire time that man has lived upon this earth. We are all familiar with the season and the preparation for it; I doubt unless one lived on a remote island in the Outer Hebrides, one could avoid the tacky tinsel and Christmas cards that hit the shops in September. But the origins of what we know as Christmas, that festival that we all loved as children, has its roots in our ancient Pagan past, it is true to say that Christmas has Pagan DNA!

The history and truth behind the season we commonly refer to as Christmas is fascinating and one that every Pagan should be familiar with. It is a thrilling ride into ancient times, an adventurous roller coaster into our Pagan past, and one of the only remaining Christianised festivals that still retains blatantly Pagan ornamentation and symbology. It is as Pagan as it can be. Consider the main symbols of this season, and what the general populace know about them. In truth very little, the entire season and its celebrations are taken on face value, rarely do folk question or contemplate the symbolic significance of Yuletide with its glitter and lights. Within this season we have magic, myth and legend, and these touch some primal and ancient part of us. Throughout the mists of time the legends and myths surrounding the winter solstice have changed, initially they were the vessels our ancestors used to describe what they could not comprehend, to make that which seemed impossible, possible. These legends offered an explanation, an explanation that was to become religion. When legends and myths are stripped of their allegorical meaning, and taken as literalism, they become dogmatic and oppressive religious systems which prevent the individual from seeking their own path and embarking upon their own journey to the source. They are an extremely ingenious method of controlling the masses.

Legends tell us so much during this cycle of the year, not only do they attempt to explain the solar and agricultural systems and phenomena, but they tell us something about ourselves, something we have forgotten. Over the centuries these tales have been externalised, become fantastical reflections of the external worlds, voyages into the unknown, to the land of dreams and of children. Surely as we grow older we learn to discard these myths and face the void and desolate emptiness of the adult mind. What we have failed to realise is that legends tell us more about humanity than we give them credit for. Myth and legend are the history of the heart, the history of the tribe, not the history of books and academia, with the bias of the conqueror; they are the history of our people, of the land, sea and sky. They teach us about ourselves and our place in the world, how we interact with it, and more importantly how we treat it.

What are these legends? Obviously the one that springs to most people's minds during the festivities of Yuletide is Santa Claus. The virgin birth of Jesus Christ comes a poor second. It never fails to amuse me that generally that is the order of it. The rituals of Yuletide are something we are all actively involved in, whether we enjoy the season or not. Most of us have to go through the motions, if only for the sake of the children, but none can deny the fact that something within these rituals feels familiar. Every year we go through the same rituals concerning the Midwinter feast, and it stirs something, something moves within us, and makes us feel good. The only problem is we are not sure why we feel good, or why it all feels so familiar. This is the magic of the season, the hum of energy crackling through the winter night; this is the true magic that lies hidden behind the plastic and tacky tinsel. It is the strange and mysterious cloaked figure in red that soars through the air on a magical sleigh. This is magic as we never see it during any other time of the year; we are all joined within some global collective consciousness of good

will. It is at this time we realise that peace is inherently missing
in our modern and busy lives, and that peace is something we
all hope. Look to the streets and to the public houses, even
their inhabitants feel certain joyousness and display overtly
intimate expressions of human emotions, towards each
other!! People want to touch you, kiss you, hug you and wish
you well, why? The answer is surprisingly simple, they are
remembering something, and it makes them feel wonderful,
makes life taste of something. Every wish and blessing relays
a message; they are expressions and blessings of hope. This
after all is the true message of Alban Arthan, hope. We have
simply forgotten why there is so much joy, and why we have
reason to celebrate.

So often I hear Pagans expressing distaste for the season,
I find this sad and very upsetting, after all this is a Pagan
celebration. I have heard so many Pagans voice their dislike
for the lights and glitter of the season, but hang on a minute;
it was us who invented them! They belong to us, none of
the decorative attributions of Mid Winter belong to the
Christians, they belong to us, they are our spells, song spells,
blessings and charms, they are a manifestation of our magic,
and of the magic of the world around us. They are our way
of reaching out in hope as the whole of nature reaches out
in hope, the hope and expectation of light and of warmth.
For days prior to the feast of Alban Arthan our ancestors and
we in the present world call upon the blessings of the sun,
decorating our homes with fine greenery and foliage from the
evergreens, lighting candles in the hope of new light, affirming
to ourselves the birthing of new life and hope. It is said that
the our ancestors brought in the foliage of the evergreens for
they believed that they contained within them the spirits of
the forests, thus ensuring they were safe from the harshness
of winter, a reciprocal form of protection resulted through
reverence and respect. Our present decorating trends have
within them the same truth; we need only open our eyes

and see it. Dismissing the commercialism of the season and returning to the true essence of its celebration, we reclaim it from the Christian church.

The festival of Alban Arthan, is one of the oldest celebrations in human history, and reaches back into the deepest shadows of the past, a festival that has been celebrated by humanity for the best part of 30,000 years. Our landscape is marked by countless temples and monuments that mark this season, actively displaying the precise moment of the Solstice. But deep at the root of this festival is something we all once possessed and that something is the essence of the season and the true magic behind and throughout it, a something so powerful that it effects us all to an extent. This something is wonder and awe at the magic and potentiality available to all mankind upon this most sacred night. But, the most magical aspect of this wonder is that we have all been there, tasted it, felt that anticipation and excitement that caused sleep to flee before it, fought against the night and dreamt of Dawn, that marvellous dawning of gift filled stockings, and the rich aromas of festive food and drink. We have all been there, one thing we all have in common with one another, a shared magic, and a shared belief in magical and wondrous creatures that brought hope and caused smiles to erupt on the faces of children. Do you remember that feeling of realizing that Santa Claus was in fact Granddad in a red costume, and having had one too many whiskeys! Do you remember the sense of utter pain and disbelief, your whole world turned upside down! Santa Claus does not exist. To that I say, Bollocks!! Of course he exists, he has always existed, he is the magic of the season, and the hope of the new born sun.

It's quite irrelevant that Santa Claus has mutated over the centuries into the jolly old elf we know today. For beneath the white beard and the Coca Cola inspired red outfit lurks an older and darker Santa, the real symbol of the season. He is the shaman, the wild huntsman. He is Odin, he is Cernunnos, he is Gwyn ap Nudd, he is the God! He is the embodiment of the season of hope, the bringer of warmth and the gift of life, perhaps the oldest surviving God that exists, revered by mankind for millennia and he is still here, the God of winter, the spirit and magic of new life.

To those who no longer believe, to those who can no longer see beyond the commercialism, and see the season for what it truly is, I feel a sense of sympathy, for in a way they have lost the magic of the season, a magic which is so difficult to regain. In one way we are particularly fortunate that our culture has never lost this link, a link to our Pagan past, and of all the Christianised festivals it is the one that's most blatantly and obviously stolen, they couldn't get rid of its symbology, couldn't destroy its magic, no matter how hard they tried.

Yuletide and its relevance to the so called messiah of the Christian Church is a pure fabrication of the Church of Rome and its attempt to cloud and murk the waters and traditions of ancient Pagan practises. They superimposed the birth of the Christ child onto the older Pagan Roman festivals of Sol Invictus and Saturnalia, and for countless centuries they have succeeded.

What do our rituals convey at this time of year? What are we connecting to, and how do we achieve this? What relevance do these rituals have in the lives of people in the twenty first century? The acts of ritual during Alban Arthan connect us to the underlying energies of this season to the subtle flow of energy pulsing through our land and through our veins. We acknowledge the awakening of ourselves but bear in mind that we still need time to adjust to focus on this process of birthing. Ritual helps us achieve this, it is the acknowledgement of the energies and the utilisation of them to create transformation within ourselves, and we take stock of our lives, and reassess our situations and circumstances. We discover what needs to change, what can remain the same and how we implement any change that need to occur.

During this time I practise numerous rituals, all them
relevant to myself and my family, and how we celebrate the
season. I start with the feast and ritual of sunset on the eve
of the Winter Solstice, *Nosweith Alban Arthan*. We know that
the Celts measured their days by nights, and we retain an echo
of this tradition in our modern term 'Fortnight', which refers
to the passage of fourteen nights, rather than the typical day.
The setting of the sun on the eve of Solstice, heralds the true
death of the Sun, the final battle has been fought as he sets in
the yawning of the southern skies. Will he ever return to bring
hope to the land? And so we descend into the uncertainty of
the longest night, and we wait in that silence, in the seemingly
endless hours of absolute darkness before the coming of the
new dawn. Of course we know that tomorrow the sun will
rise and will remain in the sky a minute longer than he did
yesterday, and slowly begin the cumbersome climb towards
the northern stars. We spend this time in vision and depth of
meditation. Lost in our song spells and inner music we connect
to the energy of winter and offer thanks to the darkness of
Samhain and those weeks of imprisonment in the tomb, the
womb of our mother. Within our vision we set in motion that
deeper understanding of the implications and necessities of
the winter period and we honour it, embracing the dawning
of new life and hope. And in that honouring we pay homage
to ourselves and our place in this world, how we interact with
our environment and those who share our lives.

On the night of Solstice, spend time in silence lost in your
visions of the year ahead and allow ideas of transformation
to be conceived within you and slowly seep out, like the roots
and tubules deep within the earth; reach towards the growing
light, and realize your ideals. Honour the sun for the gift of life
that he provides this planet and his light that warms our soil
and enriches this earth. But also understand the power of the
sun and his physical aspects, his rays are deadly and it is the
silk thin veil that we call our atmosphere that protects us from

this deadly force. He is a force that is the gift of life and also that of death.

Towards dawn we light fires to honour the sun, offering encouragement, singing our praises to the Orb of life that will rise and bring hope to the world. In my grove we use carols with the words altered to reflect our tradition, after all we are all familiar with the traditional carols and they speak to a childlike aspect of ourselves which continues to love this season. When we hear them, they cause us to smile, and its difficult not to hum along to them, even if outwardly we express dislike towards them.

In my grove the carols and hymns that we sing have been given another title, rather than the overtly Christian overtones of the words Carols and Hymns, we have chosen to call them "Helens and Hers" instead, which always brings a smile to the faces of those who hear this term for the first time.

There is something quite magical about being on a frost ridden beach with a fire burning in honour of the sun and the sound of seasonal songs echoing around the coastline, with the smell of mulled wines and ciders floating into the dark and moonless night. Gather around the Yule log with those whom you love and care for and share this season together, celebrate together, ritualise the lighting of the candles on your Yule tree in honour of the coming sun, share the warmth and inspiration of new light. Don't worry if you feel you are not ready to give up the darkness and that tomb of potentiality, the darkness still has hold, maybe not as prevalent as it was, but it continues to act as medium between the un-manifest and the manifest, allow your creativity to take advantage of this. Let the song of the season resonate deep within your soul.

We know the true meaning and significance of the festivals and the turning year, and have a responsibility to share that knowledge and transform these feasts into occasions of true joy and celebration and fight the façade that has been forced upon the world by the industries who benefit from them. At

Alban Arthan we can make a difference by celebrating the
season as it should be, naturally and holistically, others may
learn by observation.

The eve of the solstice itself and leading up to dawn is
an ideal time for the banishing of unwanted energies, either
within your life or within the world around you. Spend some
time looking within and discovering that which you really
could do without, work with it, meditate on your problems,
your worries and anxieties, your irritating habits, addictions
that you find lurking in the deepest corners of your mind.
Why do these things bother you? What place do they have
in your life, and how do they affect your life and the lives of
others? If you find that they affect your life negatively then
work on banishing them, cast them into your Yule fire and be
rid of them once and for all. This act of banishing is simply
a key, an affirmation to your subconscious and conscious
mind to actively work at changing that which can no longer be
the status quo. Be assured that as dawn approaches that you
have made positive changes to your life and realise that work,
sometimes hard work is needed to ensure the success of the
banishing.

Welcome the dawn and the light of the newborn sun, and
visualise its bright orange glow permeating your entire soul,
reaching into hidden shadows of your subconscious and sowing
seeds of light and hope and of transformation. What to most
is known as Christmas Day is a fantastic opportunity to take
advantage of the energies present within the world. This day
is not only a joyous time of coming together of celebrating
the warmth and light with those we love, but is also an ideal
opportunity for the working of magic. For one single day a
year, the majority of the western world is embraced in a spirit
of goodwill and peace, of make believe, fantasy and joy. It is
palpable, we only need to step outside the door and we can
feel the shift in energy, the peacefulness and stillness of the
world, the sighing of nature as she realises that those irritating

humans will leave her alone all day! This year we were lucky enough to be gifted with a White Yuletide, where the snow really lay crisp and deep and even, blanketing the entire world in its soft, freezing cloak, dampening sound, creating that unique dullness that only snow can bring. Make the most of these energies, use them to create change and transformation within the world. Isn't it criminal that we only have a spirit of peace once a year! When the whole of humanity comes together and celebrates within the same consciousness, all the secret wishes and desires we have are realised, each of us secretly hoping that a God like figure will climb down the chimney with a large sack of goodies. We can use this day to work on the peace we lack in our own lives, and as a consequence work on having peace infect this world we live in.

Oh I hear the comments of the hardened Druids through the ether already, those who deplore the fact that any Pagan could have anything whatsoever to do with the feast of the 25th of December. To those amongst you I say 'Lighten up', we are not the Jehovah's Witnesses of the Pagan world, and this after all is a celebration sacred to the Pagan past and only stolen by the Christians. OK, the consumerism is a problem for most people, but think of it this way, the result of all that consumerism is a day when the whole of nature can be at peace and people are brought together in a spirit of that peace and love for each other, sharing and giving of themselves. We should be working to encourage that same peace to infiltrate every other day of the year, the consumerism would deplete naturally! Simply because the feast of Christmas as the world knows it, is obsessed with spending ridiculous amounts of money on tat that will more than likely be shoved into a drawer and forgotten by the time January comes along, doesn't mean we have to comply. As Pagans we really should know a little better, with the understanding and connection we have to this season surely we have more to celebrate and come together for. Knowing the message of nature and the planet, we cannot help but be moved, touched and in awe of that joyous wonder and miraculous thing we call life! None of us have to succumb to the efforts of the manufacturers, the hardened advertising campaigns of the high street stores, we can share so much more, and it needn't cost us a penny. We can influence and by example teach our communities the hidden message behind the glitter and fairy lights. The gifts we share during this season should be those of inspiration and joy, Awen filled we can bring back the true message of the season to a world obsessed by its commercial programming.

Together we can ensure that our children grow mature knowing the true meaning of the season and its message, and allow them to forever hear those sleigh bells that pierce the dark nights as the God of light illuminates the sky. Why succumb to the propaganda and marketing skills of industry when there is real magic and transformation afoot? Listen to the running of the deer and see the rising of the sun as nature intended us to see it, as a symbol of warmth and light, and the precious gift of birth.

CHAPTER 2
GWYL FFRAID/IMBOLC

lowly but surely the wheel turns, bringing us to another season. We sit deep within the cold of winter's grasp, in the shadows of a cave blinking as the approaching light strengthens, shining daggers of light onto the walls of our spirit. The light calls us, yawning at first we stretch, reluctant to let go of the sanctuary of winters contemplation, yet aware of the subtle calling that sings to us from the crisp, frost ridden skies of late January and early February. Alban Arthan brought us the promise of light and warmth, yet still we wait, patient, anticipating the coming of spring. We feel the gentle movements deep within the earth as bulbs crack and tear. Hidden life lying beneath tons of soil slowly send their tendrils and stems through the dark, cold soil, their timing impeccable, ready to burst forth as the sun smiles his warmth upon the land. As we sit in the sanctuary of the cave of winter we become aware of subtle movements within our own bodies, a crackling hum of energy stings the spirit. Our bodies prepare for that satisfying stretch, as if waking in the morning after a long and well needed sleep; we extend our rested limbs and welcome a new day, a new season. With the dawning of the first day of spring comes the realisation that we must move forth, the period of reflection and introversion is nearing its conclusion. The time is ripe to embark upon the journey into the growing time, allowing the light of the burgeoning sun to illuminate new ideas and hopes for the future, which slowly develop into tangibility.

This growing light and the renewal of life is, however not an easy time for many Pagans; reluctantly at first, struggling with the blinding light, we begin to surrender to the calling of the earth. Many of us remain sluggish, out spirits traumatised by the birthing that was heralded at Alban Arthan, shocking us into existence. During this time of year a part of me would like nothing better than to hide under the duvet devouring as many boxes of chocolates as I can lay my hands on! To languish in the last dregs of darkness is much easier than struggling to one's feet, complaining and moaning like a child awoken for the bus to school. Yet the young goddess of the earth calls to us. Here on Anglesey it is *Ffraid*, the young maiden goddess in her infant form that prances across the landscape, beckoning the summer greens that lie hidden beneath the earth. But I often find myself objecting to this rude awakening, preferring to bask in the sacred art of listening, being and resting before the onslaught of summer. But there comes a point where we can no longer deny the call of the light and we must go forwards, embracing the new season, walking on childlike feet that carry us towards the coming summer.

This is Gwyl Ffraid, the feast of Brigit, otherwise known as Imbolc, meaning "In the belly", or "Oimelc" referring to the lactation of the ewes as their young reach out from the womb to prance innocently through the moist, pale green fields of our land. Ffraid is the Welsh name of the Goddess Brigit later canonised by the Christian church to become Saint Bridget. On the island of Anglesey where I live we have a river that runs from the eastern quadrant of the island to the south western corner, it is called Afon Fraint, the River of Ffraid (Brigit). This sacred river takes on a life of its own during the season of Gwyl Ffraid as its banks burst with the heavy winter rainfall that has finally filtered through the landscape. Its perilous journey to the west is a wonder to behold, one day in early February I found myself meditating near the river, close to the sacred chamber and ritual enclosure of Bryn Celli Ddu. I reached out to the Goddess of the river and asked that she speak to me of the relevance of the season. The fast flowing river bubbled and whispered as I sat on the damp bank, my bum steadily numbing with the cold bite of February. Directly opposite a lamb came gambling across the field towards me, kicking its back legs in joy, lost in the blissfulness of its young life. The sunlight shone like a million diamonds on the wet grass as it abruptly stopped opposite my soggy seat. It stared at me, its ears flapping backwards and forwards, the vapour of its breath rising into a column that vanished in the crisp, cool air. There was no fear or anxiety in its eyes, only curiosity, I gazed at it in wonder and suddenly found myself saying *"My Goddess?"* I shrugged myself and chastised myself for asking such an idiotic question, when deep in the recesses of my freezing brain a voice whispered:

"Why would you consider it unlikely that I would appear to you in the guise of a newborn lamb? I am the innocence of this island, the lamb included. Why do you sit it here and rationalise me?" Embarrassed I replied,

"Goddess I apologise…" Before I could continue her voice resonated deep within my skull.

"Do not apologise to me! Do not succumb to the pacifying nature of an adult who has lost the ability to see my innocence. You should know better! Get off your arse and see my season for what it truly represents, only then may you know me!" With that, her voice vanished from my perception, she had left me, cold and confused with soaking wet underpants and snot running uncontrollably from my nostrils. Slowly I rose to my feet, the sudden bleating of the lamb shocking me back into the realisation of its presence, it rose onto its hind legs and darted back across the field towards the herd, gambolling joyfully. Darting to its mother, who casually sniffed its wagging tail and permitting it to violently clamp its mouth onto her swollen nipple; I became aware of other lambs, just to my left, obscured by the bare branches of a hawthorn. There were three in total, one stood on the very edge of the river, its head bowed, its eyes darting from left to right as it watched its own reflection in the tumultuous

water. The second, jumped in joy, over and over, teasing a
blackbird that struggled with a large worm it was dragging
from the ground. Whilst the third took pride of place on a
small mound of earth that rose two or three feet from the
ground, its bleating cries seemed to say: *"I am king of the castle,
I am king of the castle!"*

The playful nature of the lambs, suddenly brought to mind
the message of the Goddess in her guise as the child of early
spring, it was there as clear as the pristine blue skies above me.
Her message was that of innocence and wonder, the accepting
nature of a child's perception. Its applicability to my Druidry
struck my mind with such obviousness that I could not believe
I had not previously perceived it!

To effectively live as pagans in the twenty first century,
we must retain the attributions of children, of infancy and
frivolity, wonder, acceptance and above all magic! The main
attribute that separates a child from the rational mindset of
an adult is its complete acceptance of things magical and
wondrous, I am not referring here to the magic of conjuration
or spell casting; although no doubt they are inexorably linked
to the magic to which I now refer. Magic, the ability to see the
wonder and life force that exists within and around everything
our eyes can see and our brains sense. And here at this time
of Gwyl Ffraid, Imbolc, when the lambs suckle at the white
milk of the mother, lost in innocence, we learn the lessons
of childhood. One of the primary lessons of the child is
the ability not only to see the wonder in the blue crocus that
greets us on a February morning, or the magic of interacting
with a robin, but that we are able to retain that wonder and
transport it into our adult lives. We occupy a space in time
that has become increasingly cynical and caught up in the
hateful tendencies that rule the major part of our lives, greed,
capital gain, destruction, manipulation etc! Without a return to
innocence and wonder we are doomed to live a life dominated
by fear and doubt.

Gwyl Ffraid and the message of the playful lambs in the greening fields teach us to become like children once more, to embrace the innocence we all had; to perceive the magic that naturally exists in our universe. When we see the world through the eyes of a child, our perspective alters dramatically and an element of awe enters our spiritual life. As pagans in the new century we are in danger of complacency, of falling into the trap that has caught so many world religions, where we take for granted the wondrous nature of Nature! As we grow and loose the innocent wonder and magical qualities of a child our eyes close to the possibilities of magic, it becomes a quaint memory, a portion of our lives that we forget and place within the sphere of fairy tales. I do not believe that any individual can successfully transform spiritually and awaken to the wonders of nature without reopening their eyes to magic and the awe inspiring moments within the practise of our spirituality that shake the foundations of logic. Druidry is a tradition based on the wonder and connection of magic, our focus is the natural world, our rites take place beneath the skies, where we honour the spirits of place and fairy folk. Without this wonder, magic is destroyed and we become lost to it, and plummet to a life dominated by doubt based on rationality. Without this awe and magic, our spiritual lives become dull and cerebral. When all we have is our conceptual minds, we enter the world of the armchair philosopher, and our spirituality devolves and coagulates in the trappings of the skull. Once we loose sight of the magic of the natural world and the connection of spirit and soul we may as well put a gun to our heads, it's over. We become like the starling that Branwen trained to relay her message to her brother Bran. Years later her innocent heart broke and she died lonely and in pain on the banks of the river Alaw on Anglesey. It is said locally that since that day the starlings fly in their thousands in search of the innocent Branwen with whom they shared such a sacred relationship with, hoping to find her and comfort her. To this day they fly and congregate on our river banks, searching desperately for the loss of innocence. How many folk today fly from one thing to another hoping to find the key to their spirituality, when that key lies within the innocent nature of their spirit?

Within Druidry, this is not an option. At Imbolc we venture out into the world and learn the qualities of a child, and the attributions of innocence and wonder. Like the lambs in the field, it is a time of year for learning new skills, developing and interacting with our environment and communities naturally and instinctively. We have spent the previous dark months lost in the blissful nature of darkness and its transforming qualities, now we awaken with the innocence of a child seeing the world for what it is, a place of infinite possibilities and potential. We have found ourselves at the threshold of programming, when we are at our most vulnerable. In Druidry we seek to reclaim the power of our previous programmers and venture out into the world and into the dappled groves of our Druidry with clear sight and integrity. We empower our lives through clear intention and a behavioural pattern based on experience and wonder, rather on how we should behave or interact with the world. When we learn from nature and allow ourselves to become inspired by her, the Goddess in her youthful demeanour teaches us to fall into balance, forming a positive morality through connection. When this occurs, the child programmes itself in accordance to the laws of nature and the ever shining rays of Awen.

How many of us become entrapped in our problems and shortfalls, secure in our insecurities, steadily loosing the ability and perceptive notion to realise that we are not alone in our quest. We are an integral part of this wondrous world that is slowly awakening to the harsh cold light of spring, imbuing us with the transformative quality of Awen. Since Alban Arthan the three rays of Awen have increased in brilliance and radiance, now their light begins to burn at the spirit, prompting us to put into action those ideas and actions that were seeded during the previous growing time, and slept in the incubatory silence of the earth during the darkness of Calan Gaeaf. We begin to discover the voice of the bard within us, as a song, silent at first rises from the spirit, articulating itself in response to the wonder it perceives in the natural world. As life stirs and the land transforms during late February and early march, bringing vitality and hope to the land our songs gains momentum and the bard within captures this awe through words and music, art and creativity. We begin to find our voice, laughing now at our inability to motivate ourselves during the cold months, and accepting the fact that the resting period is finally over. Yet, unlike the majority of society who still yearn for the coming summer, we find ourselves in a unique position of understanding, life is good and there is much to learn between now and the turbulence of puberty that waits around the corner. Through the innocence of a child and in a wondrous manner we are more able to inspire those around us. When one sees so much beauty and awe in the world that surrounds us, and hears the voices of the unseen ones calling to us from behind trees, that magic is reflected outwards, we begin to project the shining rays of Awen onto the world around us. Our voices join the singing of the trees as they awake, yawning innocently and wondrously perceiving the world around them and their place within it.

The loss of innocence that afflicts modern man has been an allegorical teaching within many spiritual traditions and world religions. Within Christianity we see the tale of Adam and Eve and their fall from innocence, before they ate the apple of knowledge, innocence prevailed. They were naked and not ashamed. In our own native tales we have examples of the fall from innocence, in the fourth branch of the Mabinogi, we are introduced to the most beautiful maiden the world had ever seen, Blodeuwedd. Created from the flowers of Oak, Meadowsweet and broom, her eyes opened onto the wonders of the world and her heart loved all things instantly, yet as her experience of the world increased, the magic waned, and her wonder turned to malice and eventually murder. The magician Math transformed her into an owl and cursed her to a life hunting the shadows at night. Ironically she became an animal famed for its attributions of wisdom, which may suggest that wisdom alone is not enough to sustain a spiritual life, one must have wisdom nurtured by wonder and magic. Even J.R.R. Tolkien in his Lord of the Rings trilogy exemplifies the qualities of innocence and wonder, it is his hobbits that eventually conquer the negative forces of his Middle Earth, owing to their innate ability to see the world through innocent eyes, thus preventing their corruption.

Technically Gwyl Ffraid is the first day of spring, yet the landscape may contradict this assumption. However, to those that spent the previous season listening to the voice of the coming light, watching the land for subtle signs of life the evidence is quite apparent. Our land may still be frost ridden and prone to deep and heavy snowfalls, yet beneath our feet we can feel the gentle vibrancy of new life as it struggles through the frozen earth to greet the sun. Snowdrops announce the beginning of the season and the first signs of growth, their arrival heralding the promise of fertility and fruition. With their tiny bent heads, bowed as if in reverence, their spirits sing of gratitude and joy, listening as they do to the whispers of the Goddess as she gently breathes upon the earth.

The cold and snowy landscape of February offers so much in the way of exploration, it is spring, the time to go forth into the world and interact with the energies that slowly wake up, yawning. Stumbling from cave of winter we find ourselves bare footed in the snow, adoring the crunch that announces each footfall. Have you noticed how different the world seems when covered in a thick delicious blanket of brilliant white snow? How each footstep sounds so exquisitely different than at any other time of year? Whenever you are fortunate enough to find the land draped in snow, use this time to escape into the countryside and allow yourself the luxury of simply being there, listening to the voices that speak to you from beneath the earth. The anticipation of spring and summer lies just beneath our feet.

chapter 3
alban eilir/vernal equinox

G wyl Ffraid has long since passed, the sun gains momentum as he travels ever northwards, calling for the earth to blossom and into the colours of the approaching summer. Our eyes become accustomed to the growing light and we no longer blink and shelter them from his brilliance. Our voices, the song of the bard within join harmoniously with the blossoming buds as they sing the song of the coming summer. Colours deepen as life returns to the land, leaves festoon the forests and the young god awakens to bless the land with fertility and fruition, the promise of summer is tangible. This is Alban Eilir, the high point of spring, the time of awakening. However the spring equinox can easily lure us into a false of security, the air will not have warmed significantly as yet, and the whisper of winter remains on the spring winds, reminding us of its sting and its sanctuary.

How have we programmed ourselves since Gwyl Ffraid, what decisions will be further implemented during late spring? Have we succumbed to the pressures and conforming nature of humanity and modern society, or have we developed a view of the world that mirrors our spirituality? The danger of Alban Eilir is complacency, of falling into the trap of duality, as we grow with the cycle of life we risk plummeting from the cliffs of singularity and enter the world of illusion presented by modern society. Today night and day are in balance. It is imperative that we ourselves and as a community retain the balance that is necessary for spiritual growth and development. Having come from birth and encountered the first steps of infancy we begin to groan with the growing pains of summer, our bodies aching as tired limbs stretch, embracing the new light and the balance that this season holds. We are growing up, experiencing and reacting to stimuli that bombard us from the natural world and from our communities. The wheel of the year offers a unique method of naturally acclimatising to a new spiritual path, allowing the natural, underlying energies of each season to permeate the spirit, teaching us the secret ways of nature that mirror the essence of our spiritual tradition. As we tread the wheel of the year, falling from one season to another the spirit learns with each cycle, and sees itself reflected in the singular nature of the natural world as it sings the song of Awen. With each coming year the process repeats itself and we find a familiarity with each season as the dance of sun and moon parades before us. Yet with each year we learn more, each season and its applicability to human life teaches us something new; no two seasons are ever the same, Alban Eilir this year may well be very different from the next. We grow with each passing year, each cycle imbuing in us a sense of growth and development and the liberty that comes from simply allowing ourselves the decadent experience of living life.

As we grow, our experiences form the major part of our programming, how we react with the world around us and those who inhabit it. How we treat others and indeed ourselves, reflect the lessons that we have learnt through growth and development. A normal human child, growing up in the twenty first century faces the tumultuous storm of puberty, the flowering of the body and the first stirrings of sexuality appear. Within our Druidry we are able to explore this emotional storm each Alban Eilir as the earth enters her own puberty, screaming with her first menstruation and the growing pains that stretch and tear at her flesh as new growth takes over. We find ourselves caught up in the drama of her puberty as our own bodies react to the stirrings of the earth.

There is fickleness to this time of year, we are presented with the risks of falling, tumbling from our paths into complacency, unable or unwilling to face the challenges of life and the cycles of growth and maturity, and the secrets they teach the spirit. After today the darkness is conquered by the growing sun, banished into the underworld to wait the declining that will naturally occur at midsummer, when the sun tires of his journey and begins his descent into the southern skies. But for now, we stand at the threshold of balance, night and day sharing an equal amount of time on their thrones. As the dawn approaches the light is victorious, the sun's rays appear brighter, stronger, and the darkness flees in fear of its intensity.

The scales of balance are shifted, we find ourselves initially confused and disorientated by the starkness of the spring sunshine, our breaths stolen from our lungs as an array of green suddenly bursts across the landscape. It is late spring, the time for resting is over, and we must begin on the journey of our own lives and allow ourselves the opportunity of becoming caught in the drama of summer. It is time for creating the myth that becomes our lives during the coming year, as we respond to the call of nature that stirs deep in the recesses of our spirits, calling us to react to the earth's moods and ebb and flow.

What are the myths of our lives, and is it important to have one? We are born into this world with a clean slate, an empty book with only the potential number of chapters contained within. However we are not born with a handbook, no-one can tell us how we live our lives; it is up to us, it is by our conscious interaction with the world and with the shadows of our spirits that we grow and mature, both in life and in our spirituality.

What we write within the pages of our own book ultimately dictates how we react to the world around us and if we are capable of opening to the whispers of soul that cascade through our spirits, tickling the body and stimulating the mind to venture out into the realms of connection and transformation.

During Alban Eilir, it is important to study the myths that surround our people and communities, learning from the lives of those who have gone before us, our ancient ancestors and the recently departed. The myths of our people teach us the history of the heart, not the blood filled pages of history as written by the victorious, but the myths that developed within communities who worked closely with the land and the cycles of life. These myths teach us more about ourselves and the nature of the spirit than those written by the conquerors, they provide us with a key to our own social consciousness and the spirit of the tribe, the spirit that continues to course through our bodies. What are the myths of your locality and what can they teach you during this most impressionable part of the year, when we are vulnerable to the growing pains of life and of the earth? What can they teach you in relation to your own life and the life of your tribe? Why are we not creating our own myths that will teach our children and our children's children the deep connection that we have experienced through our Druidry and the wonder of the rays of Awen? Exploring the myths of our ancestors is a unique form of learning. Many are old words written in ancient manuscripts, or the tales that fall from the lips of our elders, but they provide us with a key to our imagination, the first port of call on the way to our spirits.

When we hear the myths of our people or read them, especially when they speak of peoples that we can identify with, they ignite the visual portion of our imagination. Images and symbols, names and faces, castles and dreams, kings and queens and ordinary folk of the land, flood into our minds, stirring an echo of their lives and the allegorical attribution of the myths into being. We begin to interact with the myths, and learn about the spirits and natural forces that our ancestors revered. Through them many of us encounter our first experience of active visualisation, of seeing in the mind's eye images of the past, images that stir something primal within us, they speak to our spirits and our hearts, they speak of the connection we have to our ancestors and the land upon which we live. Here at this time of balance when darkness teeters on the cliff of light, about to plummet over into the underworld we learn much from the myths that surround us. They can act to focus the mind, and allow us the luxury of opening the door into the infinite mind, and the potential that lies beyond where we discover the essence of our spirits. In fact many individuals have found their spirits through the myths of their people, having never thought about it previously, they suddenly feel and sense a stirring within, in a place unfamiliar to their conceptual minds, and suddenly "Bang!" the doors open and the pathway of spirit and connection becomes clear.

By exploring the myths of our people and of our localities we develop an understanding of their connection to the earth, and their reverence for it. But we stand at a fragile threshold, I see Alban Eilir as akin to the early years of high school, where we struggle with the hormonal storm that rages within us, and the inability to control an erection which seems to raise its head at any given opportunity! We also find ourselves unable or unwilling to succumb to those older and seemingly wiser than ourselves. We become rebellious, and this rebelliousness can potentially lead to disaster; we are at a point in life where listening is imperative to development and ultimate transformation. The earth must listen to the call of nature to bloom and burst into fruition, we are not excluded. The art of listening is perhaps the most difficult of all our tasks when we are trapped in the throes of growing pains, where every joint aches in response to the call of the earth, but we must listen, not only to those who have become wise in the arts of understanding Awen but to nature herself. It is here that we discover our own myths and how we proceed to write them, we are impressionable. With each passing Alban Eilir we become susceptible to more input, more inspiration all of which provide us with the stable ground that we need for our development within Druidry. However to listen is not quite enough, we must also question in order to develop fully. By questioning the call of nature we listen more deeply for its response, by questioning our teachers and elders we challenge them to reach deeper into their experiences to fully articulate their teachings, enriching their own experiences as they are forced to re-live their own path through the forest.

By listening and challenging, we begin to find the words to our own book, the book that will ultimately become the story of our lives, and the myth by which our descendants will know us by. The balance of Alban Eilir has within it the potentiality of the egg that is synonymous with the season, the symbol of the great goddess in her innocent form, within it lies the potential for new life and growth and untold development and transformation, but it also has the potential of being rotten, having festered for too long in the darkness it has gone bad, gone off. Alban Eilir teaches us the vitality of balance, of living in accordance to the season, of being pro active rather than submissively observing the passing cycles of life. The egg is symbolic of empowerment; it is during this cycle of fertility and fruition that we can decide whether to be empowered or disempowered, be worshipper or celebrant. We embrace the challenges of life and allow them to be integrated into our lives, and empower that life and the life of the tribe. It is at Alban Eilir where we consciously decide to either succumb to the illusion of life as modern society dictates or decide to see beyond that illusion and see the strands of spirit and soul that connect all life on this earth, seen and unseen; the choice is ours. By perceiving the illusion as simply a veil that covers the eyes of the sleeping, we are able to enjoy this experience with a profundity unseen in the non magical world. Life is wonderful, the wonder that the young chick of the Goddess sees as it breaks through the shell of the seasonal egg; is a quality that we should all retain within our Druidry in order to fully experience its majesty. The good times and the bad are integral to this experience; the happiness and depression that we all encounter should be embraced and allowed to empower our lives, adding to our myth, creating the story of our lives, and the connection we have to the unseen places.

The beauty of the Druid path lies in its experience, and here at this season we develop our truths in relation to that experience, moving from the realms of simple belief into the wonder of knowing. We experience therefore we know, we do not need to rely on blind faith or simplistic belief. At this time of balance, many will fall into the trap of the arm chair philosopher, the 'Carpet Druid', where the exploration of spirituality becomes a mental exercise rather than a profound experience through connection. Druidry is a living tradition, experiential in nature. It cannot be over analysed or intellectualised, those who do so pose a threat to the tradition by stagnating its heart and its spirit. It becomes cerebral, and ever so quaint a thing, to strip apart and analyse, criticise and rationalise. Of course developing the mind is a vital aspect of any spiritual path, yet many become lost in its cerebral exploration, and fail to experience it through connection. Unfortunately Paganism and Druidry are afflicted by what I term the "Billy no mates", those who feel they do not fit into any mainstream group of society and find an acceptance within the liberated and accepting nature of Paganism, they may have read a few books and may even be able to recite the entire works of Ross Nichols, yet their eyes betray a lack of connection to spirit and to the experience of the three rays. The connection that lies at the heart of modern Druidry, inspired by our past can only be experienced through spirit, it does not lie in any book, books seek to inspire - they cannot teach the tradition. We are all at risk of becoming "Carpet Druids", and at Alban Eilir this risk is tangible, we stand at the borders of creation, do we create an illusion of connection that allow us to 'play' in the Druid community or do we create a reality of deep connection that enriches the tribe?

Through the sacred art of creation, creating the myths that encompass our own life within this mortal experience, we create the story of our lives, and how our lives integrate with the continuous cycles of life that surround us on our beautiful planet. Through connection to the hidden energies that lie just beyond human perception, attuning ourselves to their ebb and flow, we begin to integrate the truths of spirit and soul into our everyday lives. It is at this season we learn the truth of deep integration, where the physical and the spiritual work in tandem, together, un-separated, the cogs of life and spirit moving in unison, balance is achieved. Within Druidry and bathed in the ever glowing lights of the three rays, we gain an understanding of our unique position, and many of life's questions, worries and anxieties are nullified as a consequence. How many times do folk cry into the darkness, the heart and mind screaming the question "Why?"

In Druidry we realise through our experience of the universe and our position within it, that this question is futile. In Druidry there is no 'why', we already know the answers, they may not have clarity or reason, but we learn acceptance. Each and every experience and circumstance we encounter results as a ripple that cascade from the splash of existence. We affect the world around us and each and every living thing that occupies it, we are a billion realities all occurring and living at the same moment. Each reality affects other realities, adding to experience, enriching the cycles of life that every being encounters. Through the creation of our own unique story we gain an understanding of the process of creating our own realities, and how that reality not only mirrors the universe, but is an integral aspect of its development and experience. We are after all the universe experiencing itself through limitless realities. We learn through our Druidry that none of us are victims. Each of us are living in accordance to our own personal truths that develop through connection, and create the realities that we choose to live in, there is no 'Why' in Druidry, everything simply 'Is'.

Yet this perilous position is riddled with dangers and contradictions, balance is a fragile state and we can fall from the state of balance easily by succumbing to illusion. Each Vernal Equinox we learn the truth of balance, and of its frailty, as we perceive the different realities that surround us, it is easy to learn the illusion of antagonism and duality. We may perceive ourselves to be separate from the world and the realities that we see within it, yet the message of the Equinox is that we are all standing in the same boat; it is simply the view that is different. Some may see land, others a gull that graces the vast blue skies, another may be focused on the cascading waves, whilst others simply dream of a life beneath the water. Yet all who stand within the same boat are aware on some level, of the life force that pulses in unison through all who stand there.

The perception of reality is a complex and paradoxical issue, one which is highlighted during this phase of balance. Many questions arise focused on our paths through life and the reasons why some of us choose to become aware of the music that pulses beyond the conceptual world.

Yet the reasons become clear through the experience of our chosen spiritual paths, we learn balance, and when that balance is achieved, however fragile it is, we discover the secret and mystery of truth that emanate from the rays of Awen. We no longer need to ask 'why', moving in balance means that we have a deeper non-conceptual understanding of the processes of life and the experience of living. The beauty of Druidry is knowledge, accepting the myriad of life's experience as an expression of our connection and learning from that connection. In order to achieve balance and an understanding of the realities which we create, we need to retain some of the wonder that we encountered during the previous season, and allow the inertia of that wondrous state to carry us through the coming year and infiltrate our lives.

Our perception of reality and the cause and effect ripples that emanates from that perception can either hinder or enhance our development both as human beings and as spirits. We are able to choose, and during this time of balance we activate our abilities to either succumb to general programming, or develop our own in relation to our connection through spirit and soul.

Look around you during this time, analyse the world that you live in and the reality which you have created. How does your reality reflect the connection you have through your Druidry? What choices will you make during this time that will impact the rest of the year and your development?

The Season of Alban Eilir feels immensely feminine, the divine female dances across our landscape imbuing it with life and fertility, and although we aware of the masculine energy of the sun, the earth upon which we stand reflects the beauty of the feminine, it is the time of the Goddess. Eostre the Germanic Goddess synonymous with the season is integrally tied in with the Christian rites of Easter, from whom it takes its name. Even the feast itself, which moves each year, is dictated by her festival, the Vernal Equinox.

The Christian re-birthing feast of Easter is dictated by the cycle of moon and sun, falling on the first Sunday after the first full moon immediately following the Vernal Equinox. Even the word Oestrogen is taken from the name of the Goddess, forever associating it with the divine feminine. There are countless books available which explore the associations of the Goddess Eostre and the season. However Druidry is the exploration of our spirituality in conjunction with our locality, tribe and land, therefore I will not dwell on the associations of Eostra but rather elaborate on the Goddess which I connect to during this time, the Goddess of my locality.

Sometimes I feel it is too easy to rely on the words of others to connect to the Gods and Goddesses with whom we forge relationships, it can make us lazy, preventing us from developing rich connection to our deities which walk with us on the forest path. During this fragile time of growth and development we begin the courting relationships with our Gods and Goddesses, learning their ways and how they enrich our spiritual practise. We are all in danger of intellectualising deities, of knowing them only on a cerebral, conceptual level, where they exist as simple metaphors, however the Gods are much more, and only a deep and lasting relationship can elaborate on their function and applicability to our lives. How we interact with these forces is dependent on our ability to know them on a truly personal level. Who are the Gods of your tribe and your locality? Do you know of Gods who have been revered in your area for centuries? Here on the Island of Anglesey where I live, the Goddess of spring comes in the form of the bee. My partner is a beekeeper, the caretaker for a matriarchal society that lives at the bottom of the garden; our lives are linked to theirs. We respond to their reaction to the natural world, to the call of the sun and moon, which speaks to them, reaches into their hive, awakening the spirit that lies within it, summoning them to dance the dance of sunlight and fertility.

Our bees represent our relationship with the land; they are a bridge that links the denseness of our physicality with the subtle energies of nature that they feel within every molecule of their tiny bodies. However they differ greatly from us in that they respond and act upon the calling of nature, they feel the pull of the sun and the song of the greening earth more than our physical bodies do. But they provide us with a key to understand the message of connection by inspiring us to listen deeper to the moods and cycles of nature. As they arise in late spring to forage among the early blossoms, feeding on the remnants of honey that remain in the hive, their queen begins her cycle of birthing the new workers for the coming year. Life bursts into fruition and the skies around our field is filled with the blissful music of a million tiny wings. But deep within the hive, surrounded by the last remnants of golden honey that mirrors the colour of the strengthening sun the Queen, the Goddess of the hive, bursts into life and activity. It is here that I feel the presence of the spring Goddess reflected by the lives of the bees. Divinely feminine, intelligent and focused, living in complete and utter balance with the cycles of life, they respond to the pull of the sun that draws them from the sanctuary of the hive. Others may see their Goddess in the leaping March hare that epitomises the season, or in the birds busying themselves for the breeding season, but I see the Goddess in the swarm of bees. It is the sign of spring melting into early summer, it is tangible, and you can see it and feel it. Bees have always been associated with divinity and magic; from the old Greek myths to ancient shamanistic practises and traditions. I see them as the symbol of late spring and the creatures that herald the coming of summer, they are the epitome of hope, yet within them they carry the message of death. The bee carries a sting, fatal to some, incredibly painful to most; and even within the honey we find properties of healing and transformation, yet it also carries the risk of death, honey can be quite toxic to young human babies. Bees are symbols of balance.

Even the relationship between bee and keeper is a fine balance, one of respect and honour, without the keeper the bees would have no home and would die, would starve through the long resting period of winter, yet without the bee, there would be no harvest of honey. They are, to me, the symbol of the great mother that our ancestors and our people have revered for millennia, they are the method by which my partner and I connect to the cycles of life in our locality. They are non anthropomorphic, and so is the Goddess that I associate with them, her name is *Melynen*, "She of the honey", she is the spirit of the hive and of the bees that live within it; she is the first tangible symbol of spring in my locality, in my home. It is here that I connect with my Gods and my ancestors, and it is within the spirits and physical dance of the bees that I meet the Goddess of Spring, she is my Eostra.

During this season, we learn to identify and further learn about the nature of our Gods, each Alban Eilir I reaffirm my connection to my personal Gods and the spirits of this place I call home. Druidry is a spiritual tradition firmly focused on the relationship between tribe and land and the Gods that dwell there. As spring gradually turns to summer, we go forward; further enhancing our relationship with our deities, integrating them into our spiritual lives. Alban Eilir provides us with the natural, underlying energies to pursue this task of discovery.

But the wheel turns, onwards and forwards taking us from this season and swiftly into another, where beauty and sexuality burns the earth with passion and fervour.

chapter 4
CALAN MAI/BELTANE

"I live in the deepest forest,
Rest in the sweetest glades,
I am friend of Oak,
Lover of Yew,
But look to the smallest pimpernel and I am there,
My breath is the wind,
Fear me not for I am kind,
But know terror in my presence,
The Owl sits on my shoulders and whispers the
sweetest songs in the night,
But even her eyes see me not, yet know me she does.
I am keeper of secrets and giver of truth,
I hide not, but no eyes see me,
I am seen through the heart,
Darkness and light are my clothes,
I walk in the shadows of all things,
Yet it is my light that illuminates the darkest recesses of your soul.
I am rare and strange, yet all know me,
I am mystery, yet the youngest infant walks arm in arm with me.
All who know me carry my mark,
A small green bud within their heart,
Revere me not, for I am all,
I am there when the trees dance by moonlight,
I nursed the souls of those who danced on ropes end,
My laughter joins those of the children as they swing on
branches of the mighty Oak,
Come walk with me,
We will listen to the song of the universe, together.
(Ian Gibbs, 2005)

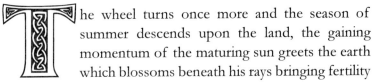he wheel turns once more and the season of summer descends upon the land, the gaining momentum of the maturing sun greets the earth which blossoms beneath his rays bringing fertility and growth. The Green Man, the spirit of the forest and the hidden places, sighs into the arms of the great mother, his lover, and through their union of sex and passion, vibrancy and colour, paints the land with brush strokes of power and sensuality. It is at this season that we perceive the great spirit of nature, as he reigns with the Goddess, he is mystery and intrigue, fear and joy all wrapped up in leaves of fresh green and the blossoming flowers of the cherry, apple and hawthorn. We catch glimpses of his face as we walk the forest path, through woodland groves and hedgerows we see him, if only for a second, a blink and a smile that tells us he is there, warming under the breath of his brother the sun; that shines upon him from the blue and clear heavens of late April and early May. He is life and he is also death, he is all things but it is the green; and our connection to the green, that enable us to sense his presence. He stirs our groins and our hormones dance erotically for him, as the Orgasmic texture of wood, bark and sap sing to us whilst he penetrates our minds, his union divinely delicious and sublime. We join with him in passion and sensuality lost in his embrace, the Goddess stroking and tickling our feet and legs, the Green Man caressing our very being, arousing us to the wonder and fruition of summer. And yet there in Ian's delicious poem we sense more than one face, life blooms in the Green Man's domain, and yet the message of death continues to prevail. From clothes of shadow, to the subtle and gentle nursing of those who have taken their lives, hanging by ropes from his branches, he is the harbinger of life yet has the power to open the gates of death and nurse those who use his domain to pass from this life to the next. The Green Man is always there, and at Calan Mai he is tangible, alive and vibrant, yet invisible to those who do not have the ability

to perceive him. Active perception and observation are to me, the gifts of Calan Mai; it is a time for opening the eyes to the wonder of nature and the embrace of the natural world.

When we become active observers of the seasons; silently watching the turning years' influence on the land, we hear also the secrets of nature that whisper to us from the trees. The blossoms of summer seem to surprise the passive observer, arriving abruptly, branches that once were bare and fruitless suddenly burst into green, festooning the land with colour and vibrancy. To the priest of nature the descent into summer is anticipated and noticed, every bud and every leaf witnessed and felt. The true priest of nature is not an individual that simply perceives the greening of the earth but is an active participant of its development, sensing the greening that rises deep from the spirit in response to the call of nature. As priests of Druidry we do not passively succumb to the seasons but work with them, responding to the underlying energies of each season and their inherent inspiration, we see the glowing rays of Awen throughout each season.

Calan Mai, the true beginning of the summer season, blesses the land with warmth and fertility. Traditionally the festival of Calan Mai, or Beltane, is a Celtic fire festival, possibly named after the Celtic father God Beli, large bonfires would be lit across the land in honour of the sun and the greening. Traditionally a time of frivolity and sensuality, sexuality and celebration, the people rejoiced with the earth beneath the warming sun, leaping over the flames to invoke the powers of fertility that infect the land beneath them. The calendar date for the celebration of Calan Mai occurs on the last day of April from sunset to sunrise on the first day of May, yet this date may not herald the true coming of Calan Mai. To know of its precise arrival we must observe and listen to the land. Calan Mai may occur here on the Island of Anglesey two weeks before it appears in the lowlands of Scotland, and possibly a week later than the fertile fields of Wiltshire. The celebration of the festivals are not cosmetic occasions that fit into our busy, normal lives, they are fickle and independent of the human obsession with organisation. They happen when they are ready, when nature dictates a set time and date. The dawning of any season is a powerful and inspirational time, when we feel the heart beat of nature deep within our spirits because of our close relationship with her. However the signs that herald the dawning of Beltane will not succumb to humanity, it will happen as a result of the land's response to the movement of sun and moon. For us to feel, sense and observe the coming of a season we too must be in tune with the dance of the cosmic bodies and their effect on our planet. It is all too well to be aware of the coming of a full moon simply because your diary informs you of its arrival, it another thing to be able to sense the force and power of our satellite upon our bodies as she pulls the oceans of our planet. The seasons allow us to fall back in tune with the planet; we have distanced ourselves from the cycle of life over the centuries, deafened our ears to the whispers of the trees and silenced our empathic ability to sense the dawning and sunset of a season, the rise and fall of the moon and sun.

Here on Anglesey long before the blooming of the hawthorn flower, which is to me the true arrival of Calan Mai, the air begins to change, an anticipation fills the air and those who inhabit it. The birds that feast on the myriad of feeders in my garden act differently, their friskiness, the fact that they can no longer hide how horny they feel makes me smile as they loose themselves in their mating rituals. The males puff up their feathers and partake of strange, ancient and exotic dances that most females look perfectly bored with, until even their hormones can no longer abstain from a bit of 'nookie'. Suddenly with a frantic struggle and a lot of squirming and chirping the jobs done, and the female takes herself off to the fat balls for a well deserved snack as the male flies off to boast to the other lads in the vicinity.

Yet others have been through the process and fly backwards and forwards with beaks full of flies and worms to feed their young who hide in camouflaged nests deep within the hedgerows. At Calan Mai I am always reminded of the troubles of Branwen, the daughter of Llyr and the sister of Bran, who during her cruel confinement in the kitchens of King Matholwch of Ireland, befriends an injured starling. She begins a sacred and trusting relationship with this bird that eventually flies the great divide of the Irish Sea carrying news of Branwen's predicament to her Brother. Eventually she is rescued and a great war erupts between the land of the mighty and the emerald Isle. Yet it is Branwen's relationship with the starling, a creature of nature and of instinct that intrigues and touches me. It relays a message of one spirit reaching out to another, two very different species who respond to each other through connection. It teaches us the mystery of connection and sacred relationships between humanity and the natural world.

I find myself lost for hours sitting on damp grass watching the spectacle that occurs right here in my own garden, as each and every creature reacts to the coming season, and the fact that Calan Mai is just around the corner. Their lives become hectic and full, their feeding fast and furious and their nest building skills outdoing our most adept human engineers. At the end of the garden I have my friend Rowan, a young mountain ash of about nine feet in height and quite thin, she has been with us a few years now since her arrival as a little sapling. Yet she is strong and graceful and she too reacts to the coming summer. Each morning I rise and greet her, but just before Calan Mai, she is different, no longer does she yawn, I sense an anticipation within her, her buds are now milky white as the flowers that lie within prepare to burst forth in all their glory. She knows that the season is coming, the season of her flowering and ultimately the time when her berries of scarlet decorate her branches like a Yule tree. She senses the

coming of summer, through bark and bud and root. Are we
so different with our advanced brains and neural pathways to
believe that we are too dense to feel the changes around us, or
do we simply ignore them?

   The signs of the coming summer are everywhere, and on
some subconscious level we are all aware of it, the gardeners
who long for the fruiting of their works and those who loose
themselves hiking through dale and glen, to the witches and
Druids that sit each morning on wet grass watching and
listening to the land around them. It is here that we learn from
the wonders of nature and see the rays of Awen that shine
from each bud and early flower. This is our classroom and our
reason for being; this is the heart of the priesthood of Druidry,
the very essence of our tradition, Nature. Within her we can
see ourselves and the heart of the universe shining from every
living being within her domain, within every object animate
or inanimate. She is a reflection of Awen and of its radiant
light; it is here that we connect to the wonders of life and
the inspiration that lies at the heart of Druidry. By becoming
active participants of nature, natural priests of the tradition,
relying on the message of nature and her inspiration to teach
us of our tradition, we are able to inspire the world around us
and begin to change things for the better, starting small in our
own localities before going global! It is within the realm of
nature and attuning to her ebb and flow that we can perceive
the coming of the seasons, and each year we get better at it,
more adept at knowing, feeling and listening. But listening is
no easy task; we all hear the voice of the land, but how many
of us actually listen to it? By listening to it on a deep spiritual
level, we listen to ourselves and to the song of the universe
that pulses through it all, but that requires work. To become
true priests of nature requires effort, it's being out there in
the wide world listening to nature as she invokes us from the
slumber of illusion. We all read books, but how many of us
read nature? Out there in the domain of the natural world lie

a billion tales, each one relaying the message of connection and ancestry, we only need to stop and listen, with heart and spirit.

The birds who become lost in their mating rituals, respond to a tradition that links them to their ancestors of a thousand generations past. The cat and her greeting trill as she meets you home from work, mimicking her mother's trill and her grandmother's as she returns to the familiarity of the nest. The small creatures of nature and the plants and trees right there in your own back yard, respond to a millennia of connection, a connection that humanity has distanced itself through years of literal obsession and the seeking of truth in complex and sometimes costly methods. We are in danger of becoming spiritual tourists, of gaining only a superficial understanding of the metaphors of life as seen in nature, which obscure us from the truth that develops from connection. In Druidry we become adept priests of nature; able to see the inspiration and hear the whispers that sing to us from river and rock, the closer we get to understanding nature the closer we get to understanding human nature as an aspect of it. Since the sunset of Alban Eilir and the decisions that were made during that period, we have established who and what we are in respect to our human lives and the continuation of our spiritualities. We have begun to forge the relationships and ideals that will flower during the coming summer months, expressing our inherent qualities as priests of nature and inspiration. Having realised that none of us are victims and each and every human individual has the freedom of choice, we now begin to implement those choices and reap the benefits or consequences of those decisions. The art of achieving balance during the previous season now becomes apparent. Have we successfully managed to achieve a healthy balance between our physical and spiritual lives? Are we able to learn from the mysteries of nature and apply that learning to our lives as priests within the tradition?

What of learning? we know from the classical authors that our Druid ancestors were masters of knowledge and learning, what are we learning today that help transform our lives and enrich our communities and tribes? Each Calan Mai I always set myself a task, something new to learn that will span the next year. Normally it involves the natural world or the world of the Ovate, learning new skills of healing or divination; which can be linked closely to the study of natural science. During the coming months the earth blesses us with an abundance of plant materials for both food and Ovatic use; these can assist our development within Druidry and contribute to the wellbeing of the tribe. How aware are we of the natural materials in our own localities? Do we know, and are we able to identify the other creatures who share this space with us? Druidry is not an airy-fairy, fluffy ever so nice tradition, it's about getting our hands, dirty by connecting to the land, by getting to know it like the back of our hands, and that way we learn so much about ourselves and the nature of spirit and soul. Each of us will perceive the mysteries and teachings of nature in differing manners through our own unique relationship with it, yet these experiences form parts of a jigsaw that contribute to a larger picture, bringing an abundance of knowledge and wisdom into our tribe. Some Druids may find themselves drawn to the teachings of the trees and the plants that grace our landscape whilst others will be drawn to the continuous cycles and powers of the moon and sun and their effect on nature. However we interact with nature, and whichever methods we feel an attraction towards, will ultimately meld and conjoin into one, bringing a wealth of wisdom and inspiration to the tribe. We are all teachers and pupils, and we all have the ability to inspire others and develop into vessels of inspiration and priests of nature. But again this requires sincere effort and an ability to learn from nature. This season provides us with an abundance of opportunities to forge sacred relationships with the world around us and those who inhabit it.

As priests of nature and guardians of the natural world it is imperative that we learn from her and apply that learning into our every day lives. It is not enough to simply watch nature, we must interact with her, learn of her moods and temperaments, her ebb and flow, watching her closely and seeing ourselves and our underlying energies reflected within her. Nature has much to teach us, there are obvious practical reasons like getting out of the house or the city for a while, enjoying the company of the natural world, but it is also great fun! When was the last time your grove spent a day foraging and learning in the local woodland or forest? When was the last time that your kitchen looked like a bomb exploded in it, because you and your grove had been busy creating herbal preparations? When was the last time your grove had fun? The Druid path is highly rewarding both spiritually and physically. The process of learning should be enjoyable, we have moments when we are reverent and serious, but we still need to enjoy this process and the tradition which we have chosen to identify with and grow within.

Make an effort, meet the plants, trees and creatures of your locality, get to know them and allow them the opportunity of getting to know you. We are priests of nature and we walk arm in arm with the trees and plants that grow and live around us and the spirits that inhabit their corporeal forms, they are our friends and allies. During the warm season of Beltane we have ample opportunities to venture out and learn from the kingdom of nature, as the Green Man watches us from the foliage, learn to identify the trees of your neighbourhood. Who are they, what properties do they hold and how can we use them to benefit our communities? One should also be prepared to care for their wellbeing. The many plants that grow along our hedgerows and on the woodland floor can be appreciated not only for the tendrils of spirit that reach out from them to touch our hearts, but their physical properties can be used for the arts of healing and soothing. You can find dozens of books that will describe the properties of plants and their healing qualities, but this alone is insufficient. We must get to know them, form a relationship with them. Take time out not only to have the ability to adequately identify them but to listen to their own song that sings through their stalks, leaves and buds. If a book tells you that the bramble is good for healing open wounds, go out and find out for yourself, connect with the essence of the plant, with its spirit and ask to be shown its qualities, it will respond to the ears that are willing to hear it. Our plant brethren are able to communicate with us, but on a level unfamiliar to the majority of humans. They speak to our hearts and spirits, they have no need for words or symbols, but communicate with us as our spirits coalesce with theirs, conjoining for a period. Then and only then, during that deep reciprocal connection do we sense the heart of a plant or tree, flower or fungus. We can learn so much more than a book is capable of teaching us by deep, personal communication.

Take for instance the common stinging nettle, we have an abundance of them that grow on the other side of the wall at the bottom of our garden, they are friends, allies in combating ordinary human ailments, not pests or weeds to be destroyed. Next time you see a nettle lifting its head towards the sky in May, pay it a little attention, learn from it. I remember clearly the time I spent with some nettles, I had unfortunately slipped on a pile of cow shit in the field and landed rather heavily amongst a few nettles, instantaneously they attacked me with their rather ferocious venom, painful and sore, embarrassed and defeated I remained there in the cow shit, thinking, "Right you little bastards, talk to me or I'm gonna eat you!" At first I noticed their heart shaped leaves covered in fine hair, that danced in the breeze, and the spiky venomous needles that protruded from their stalks, it was late May and the nettles had begun to flower, their flowers reminded me of the tiny alveoli that line our lungs, and immediately the impression that they would be useful for respiratory disorders came to mind. I leaned on one elbow and stared closely at this group of herbs that I had barely given any attention to earlier, my elbow already stinging from the venom crushed another nettle, and without caution I squeezed the stem with my fingers. A soothing juice emitted from its body and to my amazement I found that it helped soothe the sting. Suddenly the nettles became more than just weeds, more than just inconvenient pests in the garden, but a thing of beauty. I could see their spirits cavorting beneath and around each leaf and stalk, their non-linguistic method of communication subtly penetrating my mind. I decided to learn more about the infamous nettle, today they are my favourite herb. Not only are they delicious to eat (but only the young plants and well before they have begun to flower), they also contain Iron and formic acid which act well as a boosting tonic for the body after the onslaught of winter and spring. They are also beneficial for asthma sufferers, simply take a handful of young nettles and extract from them their fine green juice; the same juice can be found in their roots, then in the same quantity of honey add some brown sugar and heat slowly until warm, but not hot, sip this delicious concoction to aid with respiratory problems. It turns out that the nettle is a wonderfully resourceful herb; it can be made into paper or cloth, used as an effective shampoo to combat dandruff and poor hair condition. Its uses are boundless. Had it not been for that accidental encounter all those years ago, I might never have got to know the old nettle and learnt so much, not only about its qualities but of myself and the ground upon which it grows.

Learning and developing a relationship with plants is a simple yet effective task, which brings us closer to the natural world and to the world of the Ovate of the Druid tradition. It is here in the natural world that we learn balance, of the physical and magic, mundane and extraordinary, and learn how to apply these aspects of nature into our everyday lives, naturally and organically. The green world is a bridge that moves us closer to truth and to the very heart of our spirituality. By studying nature and natural science we begin to see the rays of Awen shining within all things, moving us closer to true inspiration that teaches by example rather than influence.

This Calan Mai, I would highly recommend that you spend days roaming free in your locality, speaking and communicating with nature, learn about the joys of potions and lotions, creams and ointments, using your friends the plants, to heal and soothe illnesses and pains. One task that I find highly enjoyable and a great deal of fun is to provide food for the table for an entire weekend using only what you can harvest from the natural world, not so easy this early on in summer, but achievable with a little effort and ability to identify edible plants. There is something magical about identifying, gathering and preparing wholesome foods from the natural world, free and organic, connecting with them as you go along with honour and reverence, thanking them for their contribution. Create sumptuous and soothing balms and creams by harvesting herbs from your garden and the local hedgerows and heating them in your favourite organic oil. Steep the ingredients for just over an hour, add a little natural beeswax, whip or whisk into a fine texture whilst the product cools, bottle and store in your medicine cabinet. Creating natural products is enjoyable and highly rewarding, conducive to the skills of the Ovate and a powerful method for learning the attributions of plants and trees. Your imagination is your only restriction.

Fire plays an important role at the feast of Calan Mai, representing the passion and power of sexuality and relationships, and the transformative qualities of the natural world that seep fertility into the land. It is a time when we honour our sexuality and those whom we share our passion and intimacy with. In the olden days it is said that after the Beltane rituals couples would dart into the forest to copulate beneath the green canopy, lost in lust and passion, reflecting the sexual potency of the land around them. Times change, but people do not, we may not partake of orgies as the general public would like to believe, but sexuality and its expression is still an important aspect of our spirituality. The conjoining of two people lost in lust, love and passion, exploring the sensuousness of each other's bodies, revering and appreciating beauty and wonder that another human body holds. The burning flames of sexual passion are accentuated during Calan Mai with its message of sexuality and fertility hidden within the old folk customs of the May pole and garland, becoming a microcosmic representation of the great union of sun and earth.

Regardless of our sexual orientation, sex is a vital component of our experience of life and within a loving and caring relationship has the potential of moving us on a deeply spiritual level. Two people locked in deep sexual union, their bodies entwined; the pulse of each individual pumping deep within each other's bodies is an exquisite and moving experience, we become one. However, sex and its expression can be a problem for many, whether due to issues of insecurity or inexperience, preventing them from engaging in meaningful and inspiring sexual relations. When we join with another person and kneel at their temple, we revere ourselves and our own sexuality. Sex magic has been used for centuries, where the act of sex is used as a method of heightening our connection and shifting the consciousness to another level. We cannot deny that we are also lustful and carnal, and however special and spiritual the art of lovemaking can be, we also enjoy a 'good hard shag'! Our sexuality and the exploration of our bodies and those of other human beings are acts in which we develop a relationship with our own physiology; we get to know the tidal flow of our physical forms. Our brains burst in to a heightened state, flooding with activity as hormones and chemicals are released into the bloodstream to affect the erogenous zones of our bodies, increasing sensitivity and reaction. Our heart rate doubles, the breath becomes quick. Sex creates changes within the body similar to those we experience in deep vision and trance. To actively observe the changes in your body during sex brings an awareness of the wonder of the human body. Sex is also an opportunity to truly appreciate the beauty of the human body as an aspect of nature, we all see the beauty of the trees and the mountains, but we also need to be aware and appreciative of the bodies we have and their inherent beauty. They are a part of nature, and although the matter of vain beauty and what defines a person as ugly or unattractive are subjective issues, we are all truly beautiful, we are a part of nature; we can be nothing else but beauty.

Our bodies are amazing machines, and sex allows us to explore aspects of our machinery with honour and respect. Think of the last time you had sex, do you remember the blissfulness of climax, the sheer emptiness of thought? Can you recall any actual thoughts whatsoever other than the surrendering to a moment, to a physical and spiritual experience, where both heart and mind, join and burn in the passion of orgasm, to the exclusion of the mundane and trivial? The blissfulness of climax is akin to the experience of being the three rays; it is a shift of consciousness where we simply 'are', lost in a moment, where the restraints of the conceptual mind are shattered into a billion pieces. We have been having sex since the beginning of our species' time on earth, it is natural and intrinsically wonderful, and we probably don't do it enough!

This Calan Mai, be radical and a little crazy with your grove or group and try this experiment of connection! Announce that this season the members of the grove are to get to know each other better, on a deeper level, a more appreciative level, not so much sexually, but rather sensuously. I shall recount the time that I experienced this rite with a male only grove to give you an example. We arrived at the ritual site, settled and created sacred space; the day was warm and sunny, one of those unusually summer like Beltane's. As the sun smiled upon us the leader of the grove removed his robe, his body glistened as the sun caught the beads of sweat that ran across his shoulders and chest, and he stood there proud and unashamed in his nakedness. I looked at him, my eyes unavoidably sliding towards his genitals, and then snapping back, embarrassed to his face! I realised what was to follow, and although forewarned I was far from prepared, I felt a tinge of horror as the grove followed suit. I slowly removed my robe, my hands shaking nervously and soon we all stood there naked. Some, like me were unsure of the experience and felt a little awkward, hands shuffled to discreetly hide their genitals. The grove leader spoke: *"Do not avert your eyes from each other's bodies, see them, touch them, take these paints and create upon the canvas of the body, see your bodies as the vessels of beauty that they are, as carriers of spirit, as gifts of our ancestors and a reflection of the wonder and beauty of the universe and the gods."*

The assembly consisted of a wide spectrum of men from all walks of life, many who had never been openly naked with other 'guys' before. We were thin, fat, tall, short, toned and un-toned, but we were all men in the same position. Soon the tension eased and we took paint and brush and began to adorn each other's bodies, stroking flesh and hair, touching, sensing. Spirals and lozenges adorned our bodies, trees and nymphs and landscapes decorated legs and backs. As three painted men drummed, we danced and celebrated nature's reflection in our own bodies. There was no arousal, no embarrassing erections to conceal, we were men, gay and straight, lost in sheer connection with each other, celebrating the wonder of the human body and its inherent beauty. It was sheer and pure sensuality without being erotic or sexual; we were all 'one' sharing our bodies, sharing each other. In the aftermath of the rite, we sat on the hot grass beneath the baking sun, sharing food and wine, admiring the elaborate artwork that decorated our bodies. All sense of self consciousness and awkwardness had long since passed; we had seen beyond the vanity of human society and perceived the spirit that resided within our mortal shell and the wonder of the shell itself, its beauty and strength, its fragility and inspiration. The rite transformed me, removed my sense of image and vanity from the bondage of the image stricken world we live in and into a place of simplicity and inspiration. We were human beings simply being, together in a place of beauty yet in the presence of the immanent beauty of our own bodies, not in a vain sense but in truth, with honour and reverence.

Try it out, with those with whom you work closely, see beyond self consciousness and loose yourselves in sensuality, appreciating nature in your own bodies. We are incredible machines, and sometimes we need reminding of that. Be brave and cast caution to the wind whilst the sun shines upon you this Calan Mai. *"Cast not a clout, till May be out?"* Well the May is out, cast off your clothes and celebrate the marvellous and magnificent human body, see it for what is, be free and shameless in our most natural state. And then if you fancy it, grab the one you love and carry them off to the depth of the woods, as our ancestors did, for a bloody good bit of 'how's your father!'"

CHAPTER 5
ALBAN HEFIN/MIDSUMMER

e sit patiently upon the hilltop, our cloaks cast aside, our bodies absorbing the last rays of sunlight that have bathed the earth in balmy warmth. In the distance the calming voice of the sea whispers to us as her waves crash upon the shores, decorating the coastline with froth and debris. It is midsummer's night, the day before the dawning of the waning sun, the sun has shone strong and mighty upon us these past weeks, our land responding to his call, greening and fruiting into the bounty of the approaching harvest. Steadily the sun vanishes behind the horizon; the skies redden as if bloodstained, in grief at his departure. We wait, our bonfire lies still and silent awaiting the embrace of the flame, upon its body lie objects of sacrifice and blessings, offerings to the gods of the land and the power of the sun. As darkness looms over the land, a drum beat begins, all eyes look beyond the island to the range of mountains that gracefully step into the Irish Sea. The time is nearing; a silence descends upon the land as each creature holds its breath in anticipation.

Suddenly in the distance, glowing on the summit of a mountain we see the first flickers of light from a mighty bonfire, we sense our brothers and sisters from another tribe dancing and whirling around the sacred flames, made of nine different woods. A cry escapes the lips of a priestess as she lights the torch that will engulf our bonfire, with a burst of life the bonfire transforms into a raging beast of smoke and fire, and the crackling of wood that screams as it releases its water to the power of flame. The dancing begins, with libation and chanting, cries and screams. The sun *has reached its peak of power and we stand at the border of the longest day and shortest night, magic fills the air as smoke carries our offerings to the gods. Suddenly the third and final bonfire of our sacred landscape bursts into life, 6 miles away as the crow flies on the summit of Mount Cybi, we see the flickering light from their celebratory pyre. Three tribes gather, each aware of the other as our fires greet the night sky in praise of the power of the sun, yet carrying the message of the impending death of summer. Figures leap through the flames hoping to be blessed by the blackening, to be touched and marked by the sacred flames, cleansed and endowed with the fruits of summer. This is the culmination of nearly twenty four hours of celebration and ritual, dancing with the peaking power of the mighty sun, partying through the short night time hours, and engaging in rites of passage and celebration under the midday sun. Now we arrive at the threshold of his waning, the death warrant of summer, as we burn the gifts of summertime on its own funeral pyre. Exhausted by the coming dawn of the waning sun the fires burn out, their ash collected and kept until the following year, the celebrants return home to sleep through the daylight.*

We have arrived at the peak of the sun's power, in direct opposition to the Winter Solstice and the birthing that was encountered there; this is Alban Hefin, the high point of summer. *Hefin* is derived from the welsh words *Cyntefin* and *Mehefin* which are titles for the month of June, within each word we see the root word '*hef*' which is subsequently derived from *haf* meaning Summer. Alban Hefin, according to Iolo Morgannwg is the high point, the peak of the power of summer, where immediately after, we reap the benefits of summer's harvest yet also accept the demise of the summer season. The mighty sun looses his reign and hold over the earth and succumbs to the power of the coming darkness. Commonly the season is incorrectly described as the first day of summer, especially if you observe the information found on our modern calendars. This error clearly demonstrates modern man's alienation from the powers of nature and of the cycles of life, it is not the beginning of summer, that occurred during Calan Mai, it is Midsummer. Alban Hefin however is not a depressing festival, it is one of celebration and gratitude, many warm weeks and the abundance of nature's larder lie before us, yet we steadily gain awareness of the sun's decline. The nights draw closer, the evenings, turn cooler, the grass damper, all subtly informing us of a change, the sun is declining, he grows weak and weary. The sun has journeyed as far north as he is capable of going and now begins his steady decline into the southern skies. It is difficult to imagine that the power of the sun wanes during the height of summer, yet wane he does and on a deep connective level we are aware of his degeneration and the effects that it has upon our bodies and spirits.

Traditionally it is a time for magic and transformation, the peak of power, not only of the sun but also of us. We are reminded during this time of the nature of power, personal and planetary and of its uses and misuse. We have reached adulthood, the peak of existence, and all around us we see the abundance of growth that responds to the song of life as moon and sun parade across the stage of the heavens. As we mature within our spiritual lives we develop an understanding of the applicability of that path and how it affects the realities that surround us. It is now, at the brink of adulthood and wise maturity that we apply the inspiration that we have learnt through walking the path of spirit, and how we use that to enrich the tribe. There are many teachers within the tradition, and it is true that to some extent we are all teachers, but what of those who actively embark on the path of the teacher? Here at the peak of the sun's power I am reminded of the responsibilities of the teacher and of the path of the Awenydd, he or she who inspires. Not all are comfortable with the calling of the teacher; many choose to walk the forest path wrapped in loneliness and solitude, seeking no communion with a tribe or grove. Others may well join a grove or group but not have the desire to reach out and teach, preferring to remain a seed of inspiration within that tribe. However others within the tradition respond to a deeper, irresistible calling to become a teacher of the tradition. Whether this be through the writing of books, giving talks or workshops is irrelevant, what is important is the responsibility that stems from accepting the path of the teacher.

There comes a point within any spiritual practise where one has developed to an extent where we can reach out and offer some of that inspiration, formally or informally to guide others who may stumble at first to find their feet. It is then that the responsibility of the teacher to bring about an awareness of the philosophies and experiential nature of the tradition becomes apparent. The Druids of the Iron Age were teachers; those who mingled among the community, yet on some level existed externally of it, standing on the outside and able to objectively observe the nature of the tribe and the nature of human society. The path of the teacher is fraught with pitfalls, the most prominent being that of ego. We cannot always assume that a teacher's intent is entirely positive; there are many teachers who take that position simply because it fulfils a need within them and satisfies some egotistical corner of their minds. By adopting the role of teacher we adopt an aura of power and responsibility; however it is a precarious role where the abuse of that power can be seen throughout the world of the teacher. There should be no gurus in Druidry, those who have absolved themselves of responsibility and take to an elevated station above the community and offer keys to enlightenment, there should only be those who teach through inspiration. We may well refer to them as teachers of the tradition, but above all they are there to inspire, not to dictate. When we are faced with the calling to inspire the world around us and take to the position of the elder or teacher, we must carefully analyse that impulse and what drives. We must understand the nature of responsibility, or rather our ability to respond. A grove leader or teacher of the tradition has a responsibility for the wellbeing of those who come under their wing; many who first come to the tradition are vulnerable and sometimes gullible. The true nature of the teacher is to inspire and guide without coercion, and to have an understanding of the nature of vulnerability and suggestibility.

We no longer find ourselves in the enviable position of our ancestors, where those who were perceived as possessing metaphysical gifts were sent to the Druids to be trained in the arts of magic. Today those who gain an interest in the tradition do so from information available on the internet or from countless books. After a while they may well meet up with others who share a common interest eventually leading them to an established or newly formed grove, either way they will eventually come across those whom they perceive as teachers. It is a sad and upsetting fact that many teachers, even within Druidry have an ulterior motive, where their position satisfies a need within themselves that they may not have accepted or dealt with during the course of their own progression. We all need to be wary of those who are on so called 'power trips'. As an elder or teacher of the tradition of Druidry we are still priests of Awen, constantly learning and developing our own connection with the universe and must have an understanding of the nature of responsibility and power, and the true essence of inspiration. The gift of discernment is essential for those embarking upon the role of the teacher, to have the ability to adequately discern the intention of another and guide them appropriately. We cannot deny that many needy and vulnerable folk enter the world of Pagan spirituality for the simple reason that Pagans are generally accepting, understanding and non judgemental. Yet we must also be aware of people's intention for joining such a sub culture, their expressed intention may be far from truthful. Druidry has a strong basis in truth and the expression of truth, sometimes the truth is uncomfortable and occasionally cruel, but absolutely necessary. We have all met those who have embarked on power trips and those who enter our tradition out of sheer loneliness, simply because they cannot find acceptance in another sub culture of our modern society. A teacher of the tradition is also a counsellor, an advisor, someone who has the inherent ability to listen, after all the primary skill of Druidry is the ability to listen to the land and the song of Awen. A teacher must himself learn how to listen, and then through developing the skills required of the Ovate, that of the sight and discernment, reach out to the vulnerable and gullible and guide them towards inspiration that will eventually speak to them on a deep and connective level. A teacher is not there to proselytize or seek converts to the tradition, they are there to guide through inspiration and experience those who are new to the path and those who may need a gentle hand to guide them through the initial shadows that adorn the forest.

Since the dawning of Alban Eilir, we have learnt the power of balance and intention, and have found ourselves a place in the world, found our feet and our ability to inspire and to listen fully and responsibly, we must also learn to discern the intention of others. Human beings can be cruel, greedy and manipulative; simply because we move within a placid and gentle sub culture does not signify that we are immune to these aspects of humanity, or that we should tolerate it. They affect us and can destroy the dynamic and relationship that a tribe or grove has developed over the years. Learning to discern intention from another may alert us to a problem long before it raises its head to bite us. Being a teacher of the tradition requires us to be active within the community yet have the skill to step away from it and observe it from the shadows, objectively. Learning to perceive the wonders and dangers of assuming a teaching role is the first hurdle for a perspective teacher and it is here that they are likely to fall. Standing at the peak of power with the summer solstice sun shining over us we are reminded of the responsibility that comes with maturity and the peaking of power, it has the ability to adorn the land with a lush and valuable harvest, yet also has the potentiality to scorch the land and destroy the crop. The choice is ours entirely.

Over the last six months we have travelled inwards and also explored our relationship with the natural world, and how we react to its ebb and flow. We have delved deep into the darkness to find our truth, and from that truth we have constructed the skeleton, the framework for our spirituality. Throughout the season of late spring and early summer we began to adorn that framework with the flesh of our spiritual practise and experience, creating the parameters of our belief structure, what we know and what we are open to explore. We have added to that skeleton the experience and knowledge that comes from the immanency of our practise and the relationships we have forged with deity, nature and the ancestors. We all share the same skeleton, the same framework; it is the decoration that differs, providing the tradition with the uniqueness that it embraces, with the different skills and talents that those on the path bring to enrich the tribe and our communities. And now that skeleton is almost clothed, as we stand beside the funeral pyre of summer, and look ahead to the golden, glowing bounty of the harvest.

Traditionally we leap over fire to cleanse ourselves of those attributions that may not be conducive to the expression of our Druidry. None of us are perfect, we carry the flaws of humanity; we can be fickle and stubborn. Do our lives adequately and sincerely reflect the nature of our spiritual practise? How does our Druidry change the outward expression of the persona we created before our embarkation on the forest path? We must think and listen to the inner voice that sings to us from the universe and our connection to it. We attempt to live by a positive morality that mirrors the conviction we gain through our experience of the spiritual.

The magical transformation of summer becoming autumn is about to settle across our land, and we change with it, slowly, relaxing into the balminess of late June and July. We learn to be still and merely watch the passing summer, occasionally venturing into the wild to garner the gifts of nature for the larder and medicine cabinet, and we also learn the gift of magic, of transformation. Magic, personally, plays an important and vital role within Druidry, many may argue the point, but I disagree. Magic has always been an aspect of Druidry. When we look back over the centuries to the tales and chronicles of our ancestors; we see the magicians and spell casters that existed there, those who had the ability and skills to transform anything. Those who could walk between the worlds, entering the otherworld at will, interacting with those who live there before returning to this reality. I wonder why this is no longer a reality for us, have we become so densely locked into our craniums that we have lost the ability to extend the mind and open the doorways that existed for our ancestors? Have we become so trapped by the density of our bodies that we may never experience the otherworldly interaction of our forefathers?

The Trials Of Blodeuwedd

Not of mother nor of father, was my making, was my creation,
From the ninefold elements was I made,
From fruit and fruit trees of the initiator,
From the hillside primrose,
From the buds of the trees and woods,
From the earth and soil was I created,
From the blossom of nettle,
From the water of the ninth wave,
I was enchanted by math before being animated,
From the wand of magic Gwydion created me.

(Extract from the song of "Cad Goddeu", the Book of Taliesin)

The night was still and calm, the forest whispered to me as I walked silently into the darkness of its sanctuary. The rustling of undergrowth alerted me to the presence of other nocturnal creatures that shared the woodland with the silent, majestic trees. Ahead stood the yew I had come to visit, her dark branches reaching to the vaults of the heavens, her presence seemingly deflecting the growth of other trees, she stands alone in her own grove of birch and Oak, watching, listening. From the small cotton bag at my side I take two candles and set them upon the stone tablet that rests upon her roots. The flicker of flame blinds me for a second and I glance away quickly to prevent my night vision from faltering completely. Eventually the candles accept the flame and a warm, yellow glow envelops me and the base of the yew, her snake like roots peer from the moist, clay rich soil. I breathe deeply and begin to absorb the beauty of the nocturnal woodland, smelling the richness of old leaf and new growth, of nocturnal scented flowers and the aroma of life hidden in decomposition. The songspell burns in my head, the words I have written dance to my lips, and I prepare myself for the task ahead.

Suddenly a cry startles me, and there within the lowest branches of the yew, that drape like arms towards the ground, sits a barn owl. Her ghostly aspect only emphasises the mysterious wisdom that lies behind her powerful eyes.

"Greetings Blodeuwedd." I offer. She looks at me, into my very soul, and further settles herself onto her branch, observing the strange creature on two legs that watches her from the ground. "Well, I have work to do, just ignore me." I inform her. Her cry deafens me, and in its wake a strange dizziness falls upon me, I stumble to the ground and seek stability in the yew's roots. My vision blurs, and a voice filters slowly into my consciousness.

"I am innocent." It says gently.

I look to the owl and answer, sarcastically. "Innocent? Well you did shag Gronw sweetie when you were wedded to Lleu, then tried to kill him, you can kinda see why Gwydion was a little pissed off!"

"Then you have failed to understand the truth of my tale, failed to understand the nature of my being." The voice replied. I *look to the owl, she simply stares at me, yet the dizziness continues, the woodland around me blurs into incomprehensible shapes and shadows.*

"I'm sorry I don't get your drift." I state confusingly.

"You sit there with magic in your mind, brandishing your wand like the great Math himself, yet you fail to comprehend the meaning of magic. Magic is balance, it is not control or manipulation it is the act of balanced transformation." The owl ruffles her feathers and the voice continues to haunt me. "I was created, forced into this world by a man of power, but I am essentially spirit, the misuse of magic has cursed me for all time. I am now a billion birds that haunt the night sky, each one imbued with my spirit, with my curse."

"But that magic was different, it was older and more powerful than the magic I'm about to use." I reply.

"Was it? Is it? Be careful with your magic Kris, use it only when necessary, do not abuse its power and take advantage of it, do not assume that the spirits you ask for assistance share your convictions and morality, do not allow it to prevent you from attempting to transform through balance and connection. My curse is a message to you. Take heed!" The owl pierced the night again with its cry and took to wing; a spectre of light against the prevailing darkness. The dizziness lifted leaving me confused and perplexed.

"Blodeuwedd…" I whisper into the night.

* * *

The mythological figure of Blodeuwedd is associated with the feast of the summer solstice, a creature that was created by the magical powers of two magicians, Math, son of Mathonwy and Gwydion. They took the flowers of the woodland glades and barren hillsides and from them fashioned the beautiful body of a maiden whom they named 'flower face'. Somehow her story reminds me of Mary Shelley's Frankenstein, a creature created by magic yet naturally flawed according to human standards, teaching us that we do not have the ability to control the forces of nature, we can only work in balance with it. Blodeuwedd existed prior to the creation of her human form, she existed as a force of nature, a spirit of the unseen world, bound into alien form she should not have been expected to assume the morality of a human being, yet she was and then wrongfully condemned for eternity. We may possess the skills to manipulate nature to our own advantage, but ultimately it has the freedom of will and choice. Blodeuwedd eventually betrayed her makers and her new husband and fell into an adulterous affair with another man; together they attempted to kill her husband Lleu. Blodeuwedd was cursed by her creator and sentenced to live as an Owl, forever a creature of the night and scorned by other birds. The story of Blodeuwedd and Lleu teaches the lessons of magic, of its use and misuse. The story is too complex to provide us with a candidate for blame, and that is not its intention. Its purpose is to teach of the properties of magic and of the dangers of its misuse. Blodeuwedd is a force of nature, a creature of another world; she represents the wonder and beauty of nature, yet of its inability to conform to the illusions of the human mind. What we want and what we get are definitely not one and same thing, demonstrated clearly in this tale.

She is torn between two men, a man who she had no choice but to love and another whom she falls naturally in love with. I see the two men as representative of the waning and waxing sun, of winter and summer, Lleu being the Lord of the waxing, growing sun, and Gronw, the hunter Lord of the waning, decreasing sun. We find Blodeuwedd sandwiched between the two, in a state of flux, lost in the twilight of the summer solstice between two men that represent the balance of summer and winter. Man's inability to understand the nature of magic caused him to wrongfully judge the misunderstood Blodeuwedd and curse her to the night, to the realm of darkness represented as the waning year. Ironically it is the realm of the man she loved, the hunter Gronw.

Today the Welsh still refer to the Owl as Blodeuwedd, the bird is eternally linked to the creature of nature that was forced into human form and then punished for her inability to conform to human standards. She has since been transformed into a Goddess, yet is still largely misunderstood. She represents the fine balance of nature and the dangers of magic, she stands pivoted in the dark hours of the summer solstice, trapped between two worlds and two loves. As the sun sets on the night of the longest day, her cries pierce the dark skies reminding us of the inappropriate use of magic and the lack of forethought prior to its use. So many are too quick to revert to magic without first considering all possibilities and outcomes, or meditating and descending into vision to investigate all avenues before taking out the wand. The art of spell casting and conjuration are not frivolous opportunities to manipulate natural forces, we first need the ability to see the matter for what it truly is, to examine it and find balance. Is it the right thing to do? What are the consequences and are we prepared for the repercussions? Magic has its place, but its effective practise comes with experience and of learning the nature of transformation. Here at this time of battle between the waxing and waning year we learn to identify the need for magic and of its appropriate usage and integrate that knowledge into the framework of our spirituality.

CHAPTER 6
GWYL AWST/LUGHNASSADH

"There were three men come out of the west,
Their fortunes for to try,
And these three men made a solemn vow,
John Barleycorn must die.
They ploughed, they sowed, and they harrowed him in,
Throwing clods all on his head,
And these three men made a solemn vow,
John Barleycorn was dead.

They left him in the ground for a very long time,
Till the rains from heaven did fall,
Then little Sir John sprung up his head and so amazed them all.
They left him in the ground till the midsummer,
Till he grew both pale and wan,
Then little Sir John grew a long, long beard,
And so became a man.

They hired men with their scythes so sharp,
To cut him off at the knee.
They bound him and tied him around the waist,
Serving him most barb'rously.
They hired men with their sharp pitchforks,
To prick him to the heart,
But the drover he served him worse than that,
For he bound him to the cart.

They rolled him around and around the field,
Till they came unto a barn,
And there they made a solemn vow,

Of little Sir John Barleycorn.
They hired men with their crab tree sticks,
To strip him skin from bone,
But the miller served him worse than that,
For he ground him between two stones.

Here's little Sir John in the nut brown bowl,
And brandy in the glass.
But little Sir John in the nut brown bowls
Proved the stronger man at last,
For the hunt's man he can't hunt the fox,
Nor so loudly blow his horn.
And the tinker, he can't mend kettles or pots,
Without a little of Sir John Barleycorn.

(The Ballad of John Barleycorn, adapted from the traditional)

The earth lies golden and baked as the crops ripen under the waning sun, the aroma of breads and cakes adorn the countryside as the bounty of nature's larder is harvested. Gwyl Awst, the feast of August, is perhaps the prettiest of seasons, dappled with the first coming of the autumn colours and the dark green of leaves, matured by the summer sun. A sigh descends upon the land as it and we prepare for the end of summer and the culmination of our life's work since the winter solstice. We still have ample opportunity to bask in the warm days and cooling evenings, absorbing the last rays of the sun's warmth that tickles our skin. Many however, myself included are growing weary of the heat, humidity and brightness of the British summer and long for the days to cool as we near autumn. I am a child of winter, a child of the shadows and the unseen places, yet I appreciate the beauty and necessity of each season and connect to each one individually, allowing their influence to penetrate my body and mind. But at Gwyl Awst the tangibility of the coming decline becomes more apparent; we sense the waning of the year even though we are in the midst of life and fruition.

The opening ballad of this chapter tells the tale of the mythical John Barleycorn, a figure that represents the spirit of the harvest and of the season of Gwyl Awst. His legend is relatively modern, being only about four hundred years old, and does not have any Druidical significance as such. However the legend is probably inspired by the ancient harvest traditions of Britain and encapsulates within it the essence of sacrifice and of the harvest. Its appearance in this book is simply by personal choice and the fact that I find much mystery and truth of the season hidden within the lines of the ballad of John Barleycorn. The legend offers us a visual and easily identifiable method of acknowledging the vitality and necessity of the gifts of harvest, a mindset that is quite alien to the supermarket dependent society we live in. The ballad provides us with an opportunity to explore the dark and misunderstood nature of sacrifice, and also of our dependency upon the land. We live in a world where that dependency has been artificially removed, and in a manner of speaking we live because we are supported by an artificial life support system. Our utter dependency on the bounty of the harvest no longer has power over us, we no longer have to interact with the land and connect with its tide to sustain the quality of our lives. How sad and tragic that our society has de-programmed us from associating with the very entity that provides us with life. It is surprising how many people in Britain today would not be able to differentiate between a field of barley and a field of wheat, and have no concept of the sacrifice required for the success of our crops. We have become distanced from the land and no longer feel an aspect of it. It is only when we realign ourselves with the flow of nature and the wheel of the year that we relearn our dependency and interrelation with nature. By understanding the metaphors, such as those contained within the legend of John Barleycorn and connecting to the underlying energies of the season we fall back into sync with the planet's natural cycles and begin to live reciprocally.

The consequences of this realignment however is not so easy to swallow, it brings about a consciousness of positive morality and ethical living. When we understand the significance of the harvest and of sacrifice, and experience its effect deep within our spirit how can we continue to pursue the abusive relationship we all have with this plane? We begin to heal, the wound that was inflicted upon us with the dawning of the industrial revolution begins to scab over, and we awaken to consequence, responsibility and commitment. Are we indeed ready to commit to the path of the inspired and will our lives transform positively as a result of our commitment? With the baking of the earth and the sacrifice of the harvest we learn acceptance of cause and effect, it is too late now to change what we have seeded, they have blossomed and borne the fruits of our labours. We must accept the harvest as it manifests itself. We are then faced with two choices: total acceptance of the harvest of our spirituality and lives, or strive to change them during the next cycle. For the time being it is too late, the year is rolling down into the abyss and we are carried with it, the only option we have is to accept our crop whether it was successful of not. We accept responsibility for our actions during the year, there is no element of blame available to us. We have created a reality based on our experience of the world and must deal with the consequences. By committing to the life of a Druid we commit to a lifetime of transformation and change as our spirits and bodies work together to achieve balance, yet for this to effectively occur we must offer sacrifice.

The sacrifice of commitment is that we must not simply adhere to a part time spirituality; our chosen path becomes an integral aspect of our lives as we dedicate more and more time and effort to the exploration of our spirit and connection. It is no easy task, fraught with difficulties, contradictions and times of loneliness and despair. Committing to the Druid way forces us to look hard and deep at our own lives and initiate the process of transformation that will reflect the nature of our spirituality. We live busy lives where time is a precious commodity; therefore the sacrifice of time is perhaps the most difficult of our tasks that requires forethought and commitment. We no longer spend countless hours sacrificing time and effort ploughing the fields to ensure nourishment for the tribe, our sacrifice must be applicable to our lives in the twenty first century and requires imagination and selflessness. John Barleycorn speaks to us on a deep spiritual level, as the voice of the land that selflessly gives of itself in order to provide. Yet this process is reciprocal, it is not a one way thing, it requires the interaction of humanity in order to succeed.

Within the legend of John Barleycorn we can see similarities associated with the ancient practise of Regicide, the ritual slaughter of the King and the spilling of his blood upon the land in order for life to continue. In many cultures including our own Celtic ancestry the King was sometimes seen as a representation of a God and was required to die if the crops failed, his blood would be poured upon the earth in the belief that this would appease the Gods and safeguard future crops. John Barleycorn represents the God of the earth, who is transformed throughout the year through the process of birth and death, finally destroyed completely at the harvest to be reborn once again at the winter solstice. He is the spirit of the land, the lover and child of the great Mother Goddess upon whose flesh he is born and eventually sacrificed. Without him and his selfless sacrifice life would wither and die; he represents the essential aspect of sacrifice, giving of himself for the greater good, for the benefit of life here on earth.

The ballad describes how John is initially cast into the earth and condemned to death; the earth representing the body of the Goddess is first ploughed in preparation for his execution. He is then harrowed into the soft brown soil and pronounced dead, silently he lies there, lifeless and still. Eventually the rains come and life stirs within the body of the God and suddenly he appears as the first shoots that reach from the soil towards the warming sun of late spring. Eventually he is murdered, seemingly with cruelty and barbarism as he is reaped and cut, thrashed and dragged, and ultimately crushed between the two stones of the miller. But the nature of birth and death is not quite as simple as we imagine, for John Barleycorn continues to survive through the burning fire of fermentation transforming into wines and beers and through the proving of bread. Humanity then consumes the body of John Barleycorn in his many guises, and through his nourishment we grow strong, as the energy he provides courses through our bodies enabling us to carry on his tale of sacrifice and selflessness to the willing ears of the community. This process describes the nature of sacrifice but how and what do we sacrifice for the greater good today?

Is it enough to offer a libation to the spirits of the land as a sacrifice, even if that entails pouring an entire bottle of mead upon the earth? I believe not. Sacrifice requires effort, thought and premeditation; it is the wilful giving of an aspect of ourselves that causes inconvenience, pain, torment, time or great effort. John Barleycorn gave all he had, his birth, life and death, yet when we look closely at the ballad he is not the only individual mentioned. Three men came from the west who ploughed and harrowed him in; a miller, a hunter, a tinker, all these men sacrificed time and effort to provide the ground for Barleycorn's sacrifice. They sacrificed an aspect of their lives for the greater good of the community. Sacrifice is still an essential aspect of our modern community, I am sure you will be no stranger to the mundane comment from the general populace on discovery of your pagan beliefs: "Do you sacrifice people then?" It is a sad fact that through ignorance it is the only comment they believe has any validity with paganism, yet fail to see the sacrifice of our of the people who governments dispatch to be sacrificially killed on the battlefields of war. We as pagans may no longer practise the art of human sacrifice as our forefathers probably did, yet human sacrifice remains an aspect of our society in general. We may disagree with war and strive for a peaceful world, yet everyday our own people die on foreign land, sacrificed for some political 'greater good'. Our own sacrifice may manifest as the giving of ourselves in protest of the atrocities we perceive against humanity and the natural world, lobbying for a change in regulations, law or protocol. We may sacrifice ourselves to protect the natural world, by working for voluntary bodies that care for our forests, nature reserves and coastline. We may give of ourselves to teach the tradition of Druidry, plant trees to offset our carbon footprint, spend more money in order to buy only local produce from local producers for the table. Provide a home for chickens and geese that will require our care and management to sustain us with eggs and meat. However we choose to sacrifice ourselves, to give something back into the continuum we live within, we should feel it, whether it be through time and effort or through pain or joy. Sacrifice is essential for the continuation of life and a fundamental part of Druidry.

Acknowledging sacrifice is also an important and valid point, which can be as simple as honouring the food which nourishes us each day. Do we know where our food came from, can we even identify its origins? Whatever our kitchen cupboards and refrigerators hold, and what will eventually appear on the table are worthy of honour and gratitude for the sacrifice they offered, for the life that it has given, be it carrot or calf, lettuce or lamb, it has died so that you may live. By consciously honouring the food we consume and the sacrifice associated with it, we steadily develop an awareness of the ethical decisions that we can make to validate its honouring. I am not one to advocate any one lifestyle over another, it is a personal choice if one decides upon an omnivorous or vegetarian diet but hopefully we do so from thought, consideration and careful examination of the food products that we choose to eat. A few years ago I looked at my Gwyl Awst festival table in horror and embarrassment, the products were supermarket labelled and contained, well Gods know what they contained! How could we honour the land and its bounty from the forced products that appeared on the altar? How could we adequately acknowledge sacrifice when we had given nothing of ourselves to the harvest table, except for getting in the car and driving 15 miles to the supermarket, thus contributing to even more carbon emissions! I vowed that this would never happen again. Since that time, many moons ago, the festival table reflects the sacrifice of the land and also personal sacrifice; people take unpaid leave to gather foodstuffs from the wild, or from gardens and allotments. Folk pay for babysitters and spend hours in the kitchen, baking goods from the land, using local produce and organic materials. This entire process of honouring and preparing the foodstuff that we consume takes time and commitment, thought and consideration, but honours the fundamental sacrifice of all those organisms, be they animal or plant that die in order for us to live. Many cannot see beyond the aspect of death that sacrifice inevitably holds, yet death is merely a form of transport from one experience to another. It is not that bad! Life and death have a symbiotic relationship tied up to the enclosed nature of our planet, for all life to live death must occur, life needs death and death needs life, neither have severe or detrimental consequences for the spirit, they simply enrich the experience.

Sacrifice surrounds us each and every day, within the lives of our fellow human beings, within the land and the animal and plant kingdoms. Understanding the true nature of sacrifice cannot realistically be gained by reading a book it must be observed and allowed to filter through into the spirit. We need only stop, look and listen to the world around us, to the life and death that occurs in our own gardens to sense the importance and validity of sacrifice. As the earth bakes, wander into the fields that surround you and meet old John Barleycorn for yourself, watch him as his head sways and dances in the breeze of late summer, hear his voice in the rustling of wheat. Call to him, to the spirit of the harvest and listen to his story of birth and life and death.

As the breath of the second harvest speaks to us of decline and death, as we move towards the night of balance that manifests during the next season, we begin to learn the nature of the dark self. Having been immersed in the light since the winter solstice and transformed under the rays of the sun and the fertility of spring and summer, we are now challenged with the reality of our dark half. The year is waning down to darkness, and our dark half begins to manifest as it feels the steady decline, forcing us to deal with it and come to terms with that integral aspect of our spirits. To deny the existence of our dark half is to succumb to anxiety and worry, allowing it to torment us during the coming months. It is during this time that we first taste the darkness that lies within us and realise that it will seek manifestation whether we like it or not. When we experience the darkness and understand its mystery we achieve balance, yet the majority of us would rather ignore our dark half and deny its existence. But to do so is to deny the inspiration of the cauldron whose fires are just being lit. It will be Calan Gaeaf before the cauldron boils and its temptation calls us into its depths to be transformed within the great womb, but we feel it now under the waning strength of the harvest sun. As the earth burns in the oven of the Goddess, as the fire of fermentation takes hold, the dark half of our spirit leaps into action, as it feels the drawing of days and the coming of night.

And so the wheel continues its perpetual turning, teaching us the fundamental truths of life and connection. The rays of inspiration glow golden in the daggers of sunlight that ripen the first harvest, and corn dollies sway in the fields whispering secrets of sacrifice to the spirit of the land. We move upon the land like streams flowing down hill, occasionally we meet with other streams and for a while exchange and share the fruits of our productivity and expression. Rivers are formed from those slow, lazy streams, and that integration of spirit brings about an abundance of inspiration through the art of learning and listening, listening to the truths of others and within them hearing echoes of our own truth and the lyrics of Awen. Rivers eventually form lakes, dark, deep bodies of spirits joined for a while in unison, in singularity, learning the mystery of soul and connection. Those lakes separate after a while, becoming rivers once more and moving alone, the waters of our experience stem from us and nourish the fields of our spirituality and bring about the bounty of our harvest in its golden glory. Ultimately we meet as the sea and become lost in the blissfulness and rapture of oneness, of true singularity, each facet of spirit bringing to it the experience and individuality of life. We become the universe learning about itself through countless experiences that harmoniously sing the song of the universe.

Observing and interacting with the wheel of the year teaches us much of mystery, magic and transformation, we fall back in sync with her flow, learn the moods of our localities and the passage of sun and moon. However, it is all very well knowing and sensing the pull of the moon and sun on our planet and attributing them with spiritual qualities, we also need a physical understanding of their function. In the same manner that we need to learn the physical qualities of the trees and plants that bring us closer to their spirits, we need an understanding of the properties of our own planetary system, the fine balance of worlds that perpetually orbit our sun, the science of astronomy. Much magic lies in the science of our solar system, a science that even the ancient Druids were familiar with. Knowing on a deep spiritual level when each season manifests and when it declines enable us to synchronise with the energies of our planet, but to balance it we should also be aware of what happens on a physical level. How much do we know personally about the power of the sun and the gravitational pull of the moon? In which direction does our earth spin, and why does its axial tilting dictate our seasons? Many Pagans do not know the answers, yet I believe we should be aware of the science of our planetary system, the balance of which provides us with life.

The funeral pyres of summer have been burning since Alban Hefin, and this night they continue, the hilltops glow with the flicker of flames, the heads of corn, maize and barley dance in the valleys to the song of old John Barleycorn. High upon the hill a cartwheel is raised from the ground and set alight, it begins its sudden and fatal descent from the hilltop its flames leaping out behind it like the tail of a comet, it represents the decline of the sun, its flames diminishing as it nears the valley floor, its spin slowing. Its motion falters and it collapses to its side, its flames licking at the moist grass it lies upon. The tribe, breathless from running down the hill stand around it cheering, honouring the gifts of the harvest with offerings that are cast into the flames. The dawn arrives and with it the sound of machinery.

The tribe watch as the reapers and their machines descend upon the field of wheat that stretches out before them. They have arrived to kill the harvest God. One member of the tribe goes forth; a female Druid, and greets the tall man who stands by his mechanised harvester, they greet each other briefly, and the machines fall silent. Into the field the lone Druid walks, she casts aside her robe as the remaining tribe begin their steady chanting and drumming, naked and cold she walks amongst the tall wheat, a glowing scythe at her side. With a flash, the blade slashes at the wheat, in an instant she holds them high above her head, the tribe and men with machines cheer and whoop, John Barleycorn is dead. His executioner's scythe flashes once more and this time the Druid screams as she runs the blade across her thigh, the blood runs free from her soft white flesh, and drips to the ground beside the stumps of wheat. She dances wildly amongst the harvest and screams into the dawn "He is Dead, He is Dead, He is Dead, the great God is Dead, His blood runs free, his sacrifice has begun, blessed be the Golden God!"

Behind her the machines burst into life and move towards her, the field becomes a place of death, a war zone as the spirit of the land gives up its life. The Druid watches the machines speed past her tearing and slashing at the wheat, her leg stained with her own blood she falls to her knees and embraces the soft soil, tears of gratitude fall from her eyes. It is done, it is over. John Barleycorn is dead.

Chapter 7
Alban Elfed/Autumn Equinox

he life force catches within us, we begin to feel its fragility and incapacity to hold on, *"Just a little longer, don't give up!"* Yet within us, we begin to accept the impending and inevitable descent into the realm and kingdom of death, as we feel the dying process infect the land around us. Like the leaves that fall gently from tired branches we find ourselves falling into a different world, a different part of our psyche. As if with no direction we fall, not knowing where we will land or what to expect, not quite ready after the energy of summer to fall into the coming darkness and accept the devouring nature of the tomb and womb. We watch as nature responds; its breathing laboured and shallow it begins to shed the colours of summer, our land bursts into the glorious expressive colours of autumn, reds, golds, yellows and pinks. Yet we know that it is dying, infected with winter, darkness has penetrated the very heart of nature. Many, even Pagans, fight the coming tiredness and descent, antagonistically forcing them away from the mentality of accepting the dying process. Clinging on to the illusion of life and fertility that plagues our society, we struggle; we have been programmed to ignore the call of death. Yet we are infected by the darkness also, we find ourselves standing at the gates of balance, in opposition to Alban Eilir, we feel the tugging of the darkness pulling at our spirits, singing the land into a deep and blissful sleep. Many revel in the promise of winter and that slowing down to the grave.

This infection by darkness is not to suggest a process of disease; it is simply the method of taking us through the dying process and into the great womb of the mother, to be re-birthed at the Winter Solstice. It teaches us the treasures of truth and maturity, wisdom and understanding. The autumn equinox finds us at the gates of death, waiting for those formidable doors to open onto the darkness beyond. Around us the earth sighs as the golden, second harvest blesses the landscape, preparing us for the journey deep into the grave as the sun's rays weaken with the approaching descent into darkness. The light looses its long battle for supremacy; the smug nature of the approaching darkness taunts the glowing orb, knowing it has won the long battle.

As we enter the maturity of nature and the impending decline into reflection and contemplation, the earth continues to bless us with the fruits of the summer, her last bounty before the coming of death. There is no more to gather except for the few berries and fruits that our mother provides for the coming winter. Here at this season we learn the lessons of learning and with deep vision and intentional journeying we travel into our wisdom, discovering the teacher within that will reach out and inspire. At Alban Elfed we learn the sacred and silent art of observation, the still and quiet observer who moves amongst the realm of nature, learning from her cries as she accepts the coming doom of winter. As Druids we walk silently through the coloured landscape watching the changes that slowly penetrate the heart of our land, seeing the last bounty of the second harvest reaped for the long winter ahead. Through the continuous observation and interaction with the cycles of life, as expressed through the wheel of the year we develop a unique understanding of our growth, and we initiate the power of inspiration. We learn how to inspire effectively and honourably, displaying our connection to the three rays of Awen and singing the song of the universe in harmony with the voices of other Druids.

We have spent the year lost in the drama of the wheel, dancing with the sun and moon as they parade before us changing our season, cooling and warming our planet, we have been remarkably busy. Suddenly the wheel begins its steady decline and we are aware of its slow and steady fall into the dying time, do we fight or do we take stock of our year and of our development through our Druidry? Many may choose to utilise the dying time of Calan Gaeaf to take stock, but during that time we are too busy dying, too busy asleep in our graves of darkness to take heed, rather we simply reflect and digest, waiting for the coming inspiration of the new born sun at Midwinter. Alban Elfed allows us to be quiet and observe, be at one with nature once more and feel the pulse and drawing in of the earth within ourselves, and the abundance of nature that surrounds us. The threat of Alban Elfed is that we fall into senility and confusion, unready and unwilling to descend into winter, into the embrace of death. The danger of any form of spiritual exploration and development is that of insanity, the inability to control and allow positive transformation to sing to the heart. Druidry is no different; it is here at this time, on the verge of dying, hearing the death rattle within the throat of the earth, that we can lose our ability to be honourable. We must discover ways of becoming enraptured in the blissful loss of one's mind, rather than declining into blind insanity. Throughout the year we have learnt the lesson of paradox and of its applicability to life and spirit, the paradox of connection and loneliness, faced as we are with this paradigm of being at one through connection, but understanding the illusion of separation through density of matter that our society clings to.

When we look around us during this season, we see the beauty of declination and maturity, its wisdom and tranquillity and its sheer acceptance of the natural order of things as the earth, sun and moon dictates to it. During this season we ourselves accept the path we have taken during the previous

year and utilise the gifts we have harvested during the first
harvest at Calan Awst, implementing them into our lives and
enriching our tribes. By taking stock of our development and
what we have learnt through our connection we learn how
to adequately apply our spirituality into everyday life and the
life of our tribe. Here at the gates to the underworld we learn
what it truly means to inspire others and how that inspiration
becomes a reciprocal practise, enriching ourselves and the
world around us. Slowly we develop into the wisdom and realm
of the Druid, having experienced the essence of spirit and
connection, and observed the passing cycles of life throughout
the great wheel of the year; it is now time to evaluate how the
gifts of the Druid enrich the experience of life.

Personally I see the gifts of the Druid as one who inspires,
the Awenydd who walks through the world gently, inspiring
through words, acts and expression. The ancient Druids
worked within the frame of an oral tradition, the written word
was forbidden, but today we live in a very different world
where the written word holds precedence and the attitude of
many is *"If it's written down it must be true!"* Obviously words are
important to us in the twenty first century, they record myth
and histories and can inspire the people to imagine and seek
out their own truth through connection. However we are in
grave danger, especially in the Druid tradition of placing too
much emphasis on the written word, I can foresee that some
of our ancient works may well become gospels in the future if
we are not careful. Words have power, they have fluidity and a
magical quality when uttered from the human lips, they relay
emotion and feeling, they are the force that the bard utilises to
inspire and teach. However when words are written, myths and
allegories become static and unchanging, they lose their magic
and their ability to connect to the human mind and spirit. The
true magic of the oral tradition is the retelling of allegories
and truths, each applicable to any given tribe, space and time.
The stories of our lives and the lives of the other Druids in

our communities become new myths, the history of the heart and the people.

How can we hope to inspire our communities when the only contact we have with the majority of them is through mechanical and electronic methods? Are we succumbing to simple literalism and forgetting to use the power of the spoken word to inspire the tribe and each other? In recent times the World Wide Web has done a great deal in creating a vast interest in Paganism, with thousands of websites devoted to all matters mystical and magical, yet I cannot help but feel that they sidetrack us from true contact with each other. There is much that we can learn from the vast archives of information held on the internet, but many become trapped in the illusion that they represent infallible truths, preventing us from seeking out others on the same path and sharing sacred and inspired relationships with them. Here at his feast of the second harvest it is important that we reach out to our tribe and encourage the coming together of other tribes to share inspiration, wisdom and knowledge. We live in a material society obsessed with the written word, as priests of the natural world and of inspiration surely we should be encouraging the return of the oral aspect of our tradition, balancing it with words that appear in books and on computer screens. The Druid's role is to bring the people together in a celebration of spirit and connection, to teach and to learn, to inspire and to cry, to laugh and feel pain at the tales and trials of the tribe, to walk in honour, with the inherent ability to perceive the spirit of the person standing across the circle from you, as an aspect of the great soul that we all share.

This is the season of the Mabon's maturity and release from confinement, whereupon the earth ripens and the final harvest blesses the land. In the mythological hero tale of *Culwch ac Olwen* we first encounter the archetypal figure of Mabon, son of Modron, the great Mother. He is imprisoned when only three days old in a mysterious location. Mabon translates roughly as 'The son' and has become synonymous with the season of Alban Elfed. It is said that upon his release the earth bloomed into the fruits of the harvest and nature's bounty was endless that year, as it celebrated the release of the Goddesses son. What intrigues me about the tale of Culhwch ac Olwen is the fact that the relevant information needed to discover and subsequently release Mabon from his imprisonment was the wisdom of the natural world. Mabon's liberators sought the advice of five sacred creatures from the realm of nature, creatures that epitomised the spirit of the animal kingdom and the wisdom of nature. These creatures were the Blackbird of Cilgwri, the Stag of Rhedynfre, the Owl of Cwm Cawlwyd, the Eagle of Gwernabwy and finally the Salmon of Llyn Llyw, their knowledge combined led them to the prisoner.

The blackbird, a creature of the undergrowth, flitting through bush and shrub, she is both tame and harsh, and sings clearly of the wonder and beauty of the world she inhabits. She is a creature of the hidden places but is not shy to show her face, she is placid and fierce. The Stag, a creature that changes through the seasons by casting off its antlers, and in this tale a creature that had outlived even the life of an Oak, he is knowledgeable and strong, and represents man's affinity with the natural world. Our old gods are still depicted wearing antlers. He is a creature of transformation and of power and the ability to roam free, inspired by the world around him. The Owl a creature of the night time, she understands the true nature of the powers of darkness and of its potential, she is cunning and wise, and displays intelligence and intimidation, she is powerful and mighty, a merciless killer, she is the ghost that takes to the night sky, she is illusion and reality, and a symbol of magic. The Eagle roams the high places in search of his prey, his eyes see all things that grace the earth below, he has a different perspective than those forced to live upon the ground. The Eagle has the ability to see beyond the obvious and into the heart of a matter; he is majestic and noble with a hint of vanity. And finally we come to the Salmon, the wise and ancient creature of water that plays a significant role in ancient Celtic tales and folklore. He is the spirit of the water, wisdom and above all inspiration. He is the embodiment of the primary ability of the Druid, that ability not only to receive inspiration but to give it.

During this time of stillness as we wait before the gates of death we are able to digest the skills and qualities of the Druid and evaluate which ones we hold, and how those skills are to be implemented. We are nearing the completion of the cycle, we have awoken from the sleep-like state of the mundane world, and now see a world filled with enchantment and magic, mystery and wonder, we are imbued with the Awen filled wisdom of the salmon. Whichever path of inspiration we choose to take is irrelevant, what is relevant is that we inspire! Some of us may express our connection through paint on canvas, through selfless acts of sacrifice or through poetry and writing. How we utilise our expression of connective inspiration is not the issue. What is important is that we never forget to inspire, each and every day of our human lives, until the call of the cauldron summons us from this world and into the next.

No one experience of Druidry is better than another, no one Druid is better than the next, we are here walking the dappled woods alone, yet in unison, aware of each other through the whispering leaves. All our paths and expressions of Druidry are valid; there is no grand old ancient text, no dogma to adhere to, except for the call of the wild and the song that our Gods sing to us. After nearly two thousand years Druids once more grace the green and fertile lands of Britain, and we are those people. We may not resemble the Druids of old, may not know of their practises, yet we strive to invoke the magic of their inspiration, however romantic that may seem it is still valid. What makes one a Druid, does reading this book or any other book make one a Druid? No. Druidry cannot be found within the pages of books, cannot be found in the libraries of our nation or upon the screens of our computers. Those words can and do inspire us to go out amongst the wilderness and feel the essence and language of this land, and hear the voices of the ancient past that continue to speak to us through the mountains and fields. That is where we find the true teachings of Druidry, in the landscape, in the song of earth.

The magic that is Druidry is beautiful because of its uniqueness and sense of anarchy; it is the people who practise it that bring wonder to the very name. We may be judged for associating ourselves with a spirituality deemed dead by academia and historians. We may be labelled as cranks by the general, torpid public. We may also be judged by our own kind, by those who do not see beyond the cerebral aspect of spirituality. But we are here, and no-one can strip us of the wonder we feel and the heart breaking bliss that knowing the rays of Awen brings to the spirit. No one can invalidate the experiences of connection that we encounter during vision and ritual. We are here and intend to stay, listen to the song that ripples through your being, do not be intimidated by others and do not succumb to judgement, lift your head up high and take to the woods, for that is your home. We are the Druids, the Awenyddion, the Gwyddon, those who belong to the trees and harbour the wisdom of the wild.

We are all the Mabon, the child who reaches out from imprisonment to bestow inspiration upon the land, to make music and dance to the rhythms of the earth. Even here at the near closing of the year, lost in the confusion of maturity, strive to keep the child alive. The Mabon that burns the very fabric of your spirit, allow it to shoot the darts of wisdom from the trunk of the old yew to impale the world with wonder and awe. He is the wren, the smallest, most inconspicuous creature yet he is the king of birds, he is the wisest of creatures and can see beyond the afflictions of mankind and the illusions the modern world presents as reality. The Mabon within us is the Bard, the teller of lies and of truth, the expert of satire and comedy and drama, keeping alive the history of our culture's heart and soul. The Mabon within you is the song of the universe that sings so loudly that planets burn and implode before the shining rays of Awen, and that song burns within your heart. You are the stars that twinkle in the most distant galaxy, their light taking a million years to reach us; you are a light that will never die, and yet a light that understands the essential aspect of darkness. You are a child of this universe and your eyes shine like a million stars for you know the secret, the truth that hides within all things, and nothing can prevent you from singing that truth from the tallest building. Those who see or hear you, may stop for a moment and wonder why you seem so content, so in awe of the world, and that is perhaps all it takes. You may never encounter the people you inspire, your meeting may last only seconds, or maybe hours only to part for ever. But the Mabon within you, that child of Awen, might have plucked their heart strings and caused them to enter the woods and listen to the wonder that lies there, leading them straight to those glorious rays and into the arms of connection.

As you become that which you strive to be, remember this, enjoy every, single bloody minute of it, loose yourself in the rapture of Awen, and sing until your heart will burst! So before we enter the wonder of the next season, whilst we are here at the point of balance once more, allow yourself the opportunity to stop and reflect and smile a little. Look back upon the year, or upon the years that the Druid path has called you, and see it for what it truly is, not an opportunity to be fundamental or anally retentive, to criticise that *"that Druid isn't doing it right!"* But look into your heart and spirit and see how it has changed you, what transformations you have been through since you first started out. Read your journals or diaries to discover how you have progressed, and be inspired by your own inspiration. I have met such wonderful people on this path, and to be honest quite a few arseholes as well, but they are happy with themselves, why should I worry about them! Druidry is a magnificent community to be a part of, an ever growing community of wonderful people, whose eyes sparkle with the joy of connection.

At Alban Elfed, the high point of autumn; I remember those who I have met across the years, and honour them in my own peculiar way for inspiring me. And to you all here in the words of this chapter, I thank you. We are all pure potential locked within the confines of a temporary body, do not abstain from the pleasures of the world, it maybe your only visit, enjoy it while it lasts.

Find the Druid within your heart, that part of you that cannot resist bathing in the light of Awen, and adores the descent into the darkness before their initiation each Calan Gaeaf. Find the voice of the Bard, the magic of the Ovate and express them however you can. And above all enjoy it! We are aware of the end now, as the balance tips and the land falls under the spell of the coming winter, and we ourselves take to our deathbeds. Will you regret anything, lying there, waiting for the darkness to encroach upon you, the darkness that your dark half will be unable to resist? Or will you think quietly to yourself, *"That was bloody marvellous, I can't wait to do it all again!"*

CHAPTER 8
CALAN GAEAF/SAMHAIN

"I am the crone,
I am death and destruction,
I am pestilence and plague,
War and terror,
I am the dark face of the mother,
I am corruption and decay,
But from decay comes regeneration.
I am the crone,
You may fear me, but also love me"

(The Call of the Crone, Betty Powell, 2003)

e have almost come full circle, the harvest is in, what we have sowed we have now reaped, the leaves fall gently from tired limbs that sigh in anticipation of the long sleep and the silence of the earth tomb, as the life force withdraws from its colourful expression and the theatre of summer. As if in one final dramatic dance nature displays perhaps its most glorious of faces, the preparation for winter. As leaves parade from deep brown and reds to the gold of late autumn, squirrels and hedgehogs busy themselves for their long awaited sleep. The tender fingertips of winter's approach reach out, gently at first, subtle, caressing the land with the first frosts and encouraging the trees to shed their attire and display their skeletal nakedness. Calan Gaeaf lures us into a false sense of security, it is the last hooray before the day of dying, days may still be warm, but suddenly, snap!

In an instant winter is upon us, and death comes careering through the door, surprising those who have not prepared for its coming.

Calan Gaeaf, Welsh for "The Calends of Winter", is ancestor night, the end of the previous year and heralds the long darkness before the new light. Traditionally the 1st of November was the day of Calan Gaeaf heralded by the sunset of the previous evening known commonly as *Noson Calan Gaeaf* and *Ysbrydnos* (spirit night). This is the night which preludes the coming of the Gods as they draw nearer to our physical reality, allowing us to perceive them through the shadowy darkness of the coming winter, where we forge new relationships within the primordial nothingness of the day that does not exist. Here we find ourselves truly within the mists, trapped between nothing and everything in a time and a place that has no firm cohesion, no fixed boundaries or perimeters. Night has truly conquered day and the earth succumbs to the powers of darkness as they enthrone themselves upon our landscape and touch the very fabric of our spirits. At this time we fall into the womb of the dark Goddess, the crone, the lady of Death and destruction, contemplation and inspiration. Here we remain, listening to the snapping reins of the horned hunter as he travels the skies in his dreaded chariot collecting the spirits of the dead. Although we find ourselves at the end of the year, the beginning of the next is not yet tangible, unlike the sudden transition we find on the 31st of December when the new numerical year begins. *Our* year begins on the Winter Solstice, a long and tired six weeks away. Until then we find ourselves at the borders of the gates to the west, standing just outside the great hall of the dead, listening to their whispers permeating to us from beyond the veil, a veil which grows thinner with each passing hour. Calan Gaeaf or as it is commonly referred to, Samhain pronounced 'Sow-een' allows us the unique opportunity to reflect on the previous year, its gifts and tribulations and to honour our dead. It is also an opportunity for celebration and mischievousness, our rituals should ideally reflect both traits during this time, the spirit of gratitude and reflection combined with the chaotic nature of the approaching winter.

We find ourselves entering the most feared aspect of human life and existence, the uncertainty of death and darkness. But through our Druidry we have prepared the spirit for the nature of sleep and of death, of that slow descent into nothingness and potentiality, into slumber and sighing. Having worked with the energies of the year, and progressed through the facets of life, and the ever flowing rays of Awen, we have arrived prepared and willing, arms outstretched to embrace the cold darkness of death. In many ways Calan Gaeaf represent the shamanic descent into the otherworld where our bodies are consumed by the cauldron of the Goddess, and we return transformed having experienced the process of death and the rejuvenation of the spirit. Calan Gaeaf teaches us to listen with deep intent to the hushed whispers of the dark mother as her reign approaches. Who is this dark mother and what does she represent?

The Black Sow

In Wales during the feast of Calan Gaeaf there is an ancient tradition known as the *"Hwch ddu gwta"*, (The tailless black sow). It is believed the black sow pursues those who dare be outdoors during her reign. Children would run screaming through the villages to their homes, followed by their parents, in the hope that they would not be the last one in line and fall victim to the deadly jaws of the black sow. A chant would echo through the streets as folk ran in fear of their lives from the sow *"Adref, adref, am y cyntaf, Hwch ddu gwta a gipia'r olaf."* (Home! Home, be the first! The tailless black sow will snatch the last.) In some districts an individual would dress in black cloth and give chase, forcing the children into their homes and to bed, the tradition eventually becomes one of joviality but beneath it there possibly lies a deeper message, one of transformation and death, rebirth and rejuvenation. The origin of this tradition has puzzled historians for generations, and no amount of research have resulted in conclusive evidence of its origination, or in fact its antiquity, yet I believe that within this curiosity lies a mystery that links us to the ancient past.

In recent years the sow has become synonymous with the Goddess Cerridwen, yet very little evidence suggests that this should be so. However she can be seen as a representation of the dark mother, the vessel which initiates the shamanic death and descent into the underworld. The sow is connected with stiles and other structures which define a boundary or a crossing, on the eve of Calan Gaeaf she would be seen atop stiles waiting for passers by to fall into her grasp, like a spider in a web, waiting patiently, biding her time. Another mysterious figure would be seen with her, the ghostly apparition of a headless woman, clothed in white called *"Ladi Wen"* (The White Lady), nothing much is known of the lady in white, one can only assume that she also represents the goddess in her guise as the bringer of death. For one night only the sow would run amok, seeking out those whose feet could not outrun her, catching them in her teeth, tearing flesh from bone, destroying the body as she drags her victims to the underworld. Victim, a word popularly associated with anyone unfortunate enough to be caught by the *Hwch ddu gwta,* but its usage is through misunderstanding, and the declining nature of our own indigenous shamanic traditions. Those who are caught by the sow are not victims, but willing participants who understand the transformative qualities of what the sow represents, as an embodiment of the great, dark Goddess. Death and rebirth is the message of the sow, she is the initiator of the shamanic death, the being who tears apart the physical body and completely destroys the initiates' perception of reality and ordinary experience. Immersed in the cauldron of life, death and inspiration, the body is reconstructed and the adept emerges from the cauldron inspired, his experiences of all things physical and spiritual having integrated and fused together to form a cohesive new body, an Awenydd is born. The three rays of Awen shine from the brow of he who succumbed to the power of the dark Goddess, and allowed his flesh to be torn apart, his spirit cast to the four winds in pursuit of the truth that lies beneath the mystery of death.

Noson Calan Gaeaf can be perceived as a night between nights, a perilous border between realities, and the sow occupies a similar state, never actually seen, only in shadows, guarding stiles, bridges and stepping stones, those places of magic and enchantment neither on the ground, in water nor in air. She is the guardian of the great cauldron that lies within the halls of the Goddess and the vehicle that provides the only means of getting there, death. By approaching her we volunteer to feel the merciless sharpness of her teeth, and succumb to the tearing of our flesh, ridding ourselves of the obstruction of human form, as she eats our bodies and casts our spirits into the vast cauldron, to be churned and dissolved in that wondrous nothingness of the womb. From her excrement our bodies are reconstructed, our spirit realigned with the physical, refreshed and replenished, inspired and transformed. The sow can be seen in our native tales, for instance in the fourth branch of the Mabinogi in the tale of Math fab Mathonwy we meet Lleu Llaw Gyffes (Light and skilful hand). His death can only occur when in a state of flux, neither on water or on land, indoors nor outdoors, yet when he suffers a fatal wound dealt by the hands of an enemy, he does not die. Lleu transforms into an eagle and ascends into the branches of a mighty oak that lies between two lakes. A magician named Gwydion is alerted to Lleu's predicament by following the trail of a large black sow (a recurring theme in Welsh mythology of humans being led by otherworldly animals) as she trundles towards the tree eating the remnants of Lleu's flesh that have fallen to the ground. The destruction of the profane body is apparent in this tale as Lleu undergoes his transformation and is eventually returned into human form, more powerful and more skilled than previously.

Sadly the message of the sow dissipated through the mists of time, and her allegorical significance paled into joviality and frivolity, yet her power remains. Locked within our cultural consciousness she speaks to us through the shadows of Calan Gaeaf, on that night between nights, in a time that does not exist, inviting us to test the waters of the cauldron and awaken inspired, with the dawning light of Alban Arthan. I believe we have a duty as modern Druids and seekers of Awen to awaken these ancient traditions and utilise their power to transform the spirit and heighten the experience of this life. Modern Pagan practice is in danger of succumbing to the fluffy nature of many new age movements where the rapture of the spirit through intense experience is replaced with the insipid nature of commercial spiritual tourism, which lacks integrity and depth of spirit. I ask you to join me in reawakening the sow, approaching her each Calan Gaeaf eve and journeying with her to inspiration.

The night is dark and moonless, deep and silent; your feet slither in wet mud as you approach a dense forest that lies before you, the skeletal arms of the mighty trees reach up a silent gesture towards the stormy skies. Something calls to you from the hidden depths of the vast forest, your heart quickens and your breathing becomes erratic as primal fear sets into your bones. There is a familiarity to the voiceless whisper that calls to you from the deathlike trees, something within you remembers, remembers something, but you cannot be sure what it is and why it feels familiar.

Slowly you approach the perimeter of trees and with a heavy exhalation you step into their midst, the air changes instantly, there is magic in this place. Oh but you fear it! A thousand images float into your minds eye, an echo of long ago, an echo of yesterday. Voices reach out to you, broken and distorted by the ripples of

time and space, calling to you, preparing you for what lies waiting
in the heart of the forest. Your feet can barely keep you upright
as you slip and slide over dead and dying leaves, picking your way
towards the centre. As you walk a clearer sound reaches your ears,
and you realise that it is the same sound you heard calling you
from the forest's edge and you remember!

It is the snorting of a Sow that you hear; the rustle of leaves
as her snout stirs the ground in search of food. On Noson Calan
Gaeaf deep in the woods it can only be one Sow that you hear,
only one Sow that waits for you. As you enter the clearing in the
centre of the forest, your memory awakens and clarity fills your
being. There stands a large dead oak, its torn branches scattered
about the damp and muddy grove. It is pale in the darkness
almost bone-like and it seems to whisper to you, secrets of long
ago. There beneath its decaying trunk stands the Sow herself
the "Hwch Ddu Gwta"! You watch the trail of her breath that
leaves the warmth of her body to join the cold of night. You glare
into the black emptiness of her eyes, she has no pupils, and no
sclera, nothing, her eye sockets open onto an emptiness of swirling
blackness. Your heart pounds even harder threatening to leap from
your chest, but you advance, one step after another towards her,
your head held high.

She knows you, and you know her, you have seen her in vision
and dreams. A panic rises to your throat as the realisation of
what is to be, dawns upon you. Before your mind has time to think
she leaps! A blur of black crashes into your body, and suddenly
you feel the sharpness of teeth sinking into your right leg. She has
you in her grasp and begins to drag your screaming body towards
a shadow beneath the old dead oak. The pain is unbearable as
her teeth crunch through bone and muscle tearing at tendons that
snap like elastic, warm blood floods to the ground leaving a trail
of carnage as you are pulled into the shadow beneath the tree. In
the darkness the Sow releases you, and for a moment you feel relief,
but in an instant she is upon you again, tearing at the flesh of your
abdomen, clawing at your belly, her grunts and squeals piercing the

shadows that surround you. You feel a deep tug as you intestines are torn from your body, you beg for unconsciousness to release you from the terror of pain and torment. But oblivion does not come; neither does the punching or thrashing help in any manner, the Sow eats regardless. You feel your own blood spatter your face as flesh and sinew and gut are strewn into the darkness. Your arms and legs lie in tatters, a slimy, bloody mess as her legs thrash wildly. You hear the crack of your ribs as she bites into your sternum, you can scream no more. Air and damp rush into the space your lungs should occupy, you try to cry, scream, anything, but no sound comes, all you hear is the munching of the Sow as she devours your flesh.

As her mouth clamps around your heart, you pray the end will come, with a pop your life muscle bursts free of its sack and into the merciless mouth of the Sow. Death, however does not come. At last the great black sow chews at your neck and somehow you sense your heads detachment from its body, blood fountains from your severed arteries, spraying the sows face. Then suddenly a light shines beneath you, your head turns in the mouth of the Sow and you realise that you are falling, your head and your torn body, flesh and bone fall down towards the glowing contents of a large cauldron deep beneath you. The Sow cracks open your skull with one bite and the darkness comes just as you sense the warm liquid of the cauldron, as your head and your flesh and the Sow crash into it.

You have arrived at the gates of death, into the embrace of the primordial Goddess, your body destroyed. Only your spirit remains in the warm amniotic fluid of the mother. Listen to her mysteries.

It is the God of the land that summons you back with a tap of his wand upon the cauldron's rim, and your new body lifts gracefully from the depths, with eyes of wisdom you smile at him. Naked and inspired you climb into his chariot, with a crack of his whip, the nine white hounds with their blood red ears take to the air. Through the darkness you travel, back to the empty field

near the forest, the moon is shining, bathing the land in silver.
You leave the hunter's chariot; with a bow he resumes his course,
his arms gathering the spirits of the dead as he rushes through the
moonlit sky. You remember the pain inflicted upon you by the Sow,
and silently you reach out to her, spirit to spirit with a voiceless
thank you.

The Cauldron

In the twenty first century we have been programmed to ignore
the hidden message of winter, and the inspiration that the
cauldron of transformation offers to those who are capable
of reaching into the murky depths of its body. Through our
Druidry we learn to disable the antagonistic nature of modern
society and use the powers of the approaching darkness as
nature herself does, with reverence and clear intent. Within
the cauldron of the Goddess, free from our bodies, we learn
truth and mystery; the previous path-working may effectively
take you there, otherwise devise your own method of reaching
the cauldron. At the gateway to winter we find ourselves
standing beside the tree of life, her branches barren and bare
reaching towards the stormy skies. There at its base we find
the doorway that will lead us to the realm of the dark mother,
she who is clothed in darkness and shadows, waiting for us
to approach her cauldron. We have been lead to believe that
life carries on as normal during the dying time, but does it?
Our bodies respond to the darkness and stillness of winter
as cold and shadows seep into our bones, calling us to listen
to the voice of death and the secrets of life that lie concealed
beneath its cloak of mystery. As we enter the doorway of the
tree of life and descend the spiral staircase we enter the dark
world of the mother's womb, our footsteps echoing through
her vast halls. Here we see the spirits of the other creatures
that inhabit our world, from the hibernating mammals to the
deathlike appearance of roots that reach down from trees and
plants that stand silently absorbing the essence of winter.

It is here that we meet the dark Goddess herself, the mother of all life, travelling to her realms through songspell and meditation we see her. Her cloak of shadows reaches out like tendrils as she approaches, her face filled with beauty and terror, darkness and the spark of new life. The Goddess gestures for us to approach the great cauldron of inspiration, standing upon its eternal fire, its rim decorated with glimmering pearls as nine maidens dance gracefully around it, warming the bubbling surface of the cauldrons contents with their breath. No coward may approach and take from this cauldron, the Goddess of winter and darkness challenges the spirit, tests our stamina and integrity, daring us to peer into the depths of her womb. When we do, free from the bondage of flesh, swimming with her, spirit to spirit, aware of the connection of soul, we learn the secrets of winter and of the dying time, and the gift of death is presented to us, clear and vivid.

Working with the ever present energies of the cycle of life, and the perpetually spinning wheel of the year, and accepting our part within the shining rays, we learn to take from the cauldron that which is conducive to our transformation and development, that will gradually awaken during the coming year. No fool may enter the realm of the Goddess and sip from the cauldron of inspiration, only those who have integrated the experience of the divine and the mystery of Awen into their lives may partake, to others the image is simply imagination. The importance of working with the subtle energies of the year and allowing them to infiltrate our lives provides us with the ability and integrity to drink long, dark draughts from the magical cauldron, here in this place and time of non-doing and nothingness. Journeying within and down into the deepest recesses of life, the maidens part briefly and allow us to approach the mysterious vessel of the Goddess. Her face transforms, becoming skeletal and deathlike, offering us a glimpse into the world of the dead and the true mystery of death and rebirth. We reach into the blackness of the cauldron, feeling the cool liquid within, that primordial soup of the universe seeping into our flesh, inspiring each molecule that inhabits our being, and relaying mystery and understanding to the spirit. Calan Gaeaf provides the unique experience of being and non-being all at once. As we enter this cycle of the year, mimicking the natural energies of nature, we slow down, reflect and travel to that divine cauldron, taking from it the inspiration we require to transform with the coming light as the inertia of the ever spinning wheel quickens.

Within our rites the cauldron becomes an instrument of deep mediation and vision, as individuals or groups we journey into the stillness and potentiality of the mother's womb. Having experienced the maturity and the inevitability of death during the previous season we sink slowly into the security and transformative quality of the womb, where we bask in the blissful nothingness of pre-conception and birth. Within the amniotic fluid of the universe we rest, our daily tasks reduced only to those actions deemed exceptionally necessary for our human survival. This void before the springing forth of the rays of Awen allows us the luxury of basking in the very essence of our spiritual tradition, reflecting on the previous year and the new life that lies ahead.

Seeing, The Gift Of Divination

The setting of the Calan Gaeaf sun offers a time highly advantageous for successful prophesy and divinatory practises, whether to benefit the individual or to offer advice and counselling to the tribe. With the veil at its thinnest it is traditionally believed that psychic abilities are heightened on this night alone, offering us a brief window to easily communicate with the otherworldly inhabitants and perhaps be guided regarding future events. Obviously those of the Druid tradition are no strangers to the otherworld or those who reside there, but this night does provide a fast track method, if you'll forgive the term, to reach through the veil easily and without distraction. The Ovatic skills of the Druid tradition come to the fore during this season.

There are countless techniques for divining the future and offering the gift of prophesy, each one suited to a different individual, each method will speak to the spirit in a very personal manner. Those who use the tarot may have no attraction for scrying, whilst a rune reader may have no interest in the tarot. Methods of divination are highly personal and develop with time, as mentioned in a previous chapter we must develop a relationship with something for it to be successful. You may know everything there is to know about the tarot and memorised the meaning of each card to perfection, does that make you a good soothsayer, no! We require a sacred relationship with our chosen tool to ensure accuracy and success. During this night use the ambient energies of the season to deepen your relationship and skills at prophesy and divination.

It is important during any method of divination that the mind is set free from the confines of the body to readily and freely explore the realms of spirit. A key may be used as a signal to the subconscious mind that something extraordinary is about to take place. This key is a symbol with which you have developed a relationship to focus the mind on the exercise at hand. We use the key to open the gates to the gift of sight and then to firmly close them at the conclusion of the session. I personally use the image of an Oak leaf. Upon my altar I have a single oak leaf that has remained with me for many years, now old and rather fragile; we share a history that reaches back to my early years on the path through the forest. The oak leaf has been imbued with an energy specifically created and directed for the gift of sight. Before any divinatory session, I allow my eyes to gently close and within my mind I recall the image of the oak leaf, allowing it to filter through until its form becomes clear. After many years of working with the oak leaf I am aware of every single pattern and shape upon its body, allowing me to recall the image easily. When the image is clear in my mind, I state a simple affirmation, something on the lines of *"From this moment forth I am perceptive and able to see beyond the mists of life into the realm of spirit."* My subconscious is instantly open to the subtle energies that vibrate just below the density of matter. The oak leaf is my key, opening my mind to the wellspring of knowledge that allows us to perceive and see beyond the borders of normality. I am now ready for the act of divination. To reverse the effect, I simply close my eyes and watch as the key fades into the darkness, taking with it my openness to perceive the world of spirit. You may use any key that resonates with you, any object that may epitomise your abilities or represent them in some manner or form. Allow the key to become your personal friend and guide that encourages your link to your own Ovatic skills, the guiding hand that opens the doorway between the seen and unseen worlds.

For effective divination we need only instruct the mind to switch off from the static of normal life, allowing the non-conceptual mind to reach into the darkness beyond normality. From this point onwards without the restrictions of the logical, rational mind we find ourselves open to advice, suggestions and information that will not be questioned or rationalised by the restrictive finite mind. Do not be misled that divination and other Ovatic skills are beyond your reach, listen to the shadows that speak to you during the dying time, trust that what you sense and hear are real, tune your ears and mind to the wonder of divination and the sight.

Death And Dying

"The Druids hold that the soul of a dead man does not descend into the silent, sunless world of Hades, but becomes reincarnate elsewhere; if they are right, death is merely a point of change in perpetual existence."

Lucan.

Many ethical questions arise during this time of year, mostly those concerning the process of dying and the mortal remains that we leave behind. To what degree have you thought or pondered over your own death and of the death of those who surround you, family, friends and loved ones, what consequences will their deaths have on your own and what negative effects will the disposal of their bodies have on the planet herself? The process of dying is perhaps the most feared aspect of death itself; the mode of death, the manner in which we leave this world, but of death, our spiritual experiences teaches us not to fear it. Death is simply a mode of transport from one reality to another, a journey beyond the gates of life into the blissfulness of the universe and the brilliance of Awen.

The modern death industry persuades us to partake in damaging procedures that contribute towards the destruction of our planet's ecology. Cremation pollutes and consumes untold amounts of natural gas, embalming poisons the land, and pollutes the air. There are other options available to us in the twenty first century, woodland burials are increasing in popularity and provide a natural alternative to conventional disposal. A woodland burial ensures the protection of the land, having trees planted in memory rather than gravestones, which are formed from precious minerals and stones that our earth needs! General conversations regarding death and dying, especially amongst family groups are normally avoided or discouraged, death has become a taboo subject, yet ironically it remains the primary life event that we cannot hope to control. As a society we have grown to fear it, with the decline of religious and spiritual thinking in the last hundred years or so, and the emphasis on modern society's importance of the physical, we fear death even more. Society no longer emphasises the importance of the human spirit and its survival after death, instead we have in place an irrational obsession with the preservation of the human body, especially within the multi million pound funeral industries.

The reality of death and the subsequent decomposition process has become abhorrent to the modern human mind and we find ourselves in a society compelled to protect the density of matter and reject the impeding fact that we will ultimately rot! The resurgence of personal spirituality and concern for the environment at large has prompted the movement commonly referred to as "alternative or green funerals", a movement that is positively impacting the funeral and death industries. Rather than attempting to preserve the human body and inadvertently polluting the environment we can and are able to die and be dead in an ethical and bio-diversified manner. In a manner that positively reduces the impact and ecological footprint of man upon the earth. Actively arranging and involving oneself in the funeral and disposal of dead human remains is not only psychologically comforting and healing, but offers opportunities to safeguard a part of this world, a part that will stay forever green because of our legacy. As individuals within the neo-pagan culture we must be aware of the ecological damage the death industry not only contributes towards but actively encourages as an illusion of immortality and comfort. At no other time of year are these thoughts more apparent to the pagan than during Calan Gaeaf, when we stand before the gates of death and discover our place within its sacred process.

As an exercise during this time of year consider your own death and the consequences on the environment that your death may have. What methods do you have in place to safeguard the security of the land with your impending demise? Talk to your relatives and loved ones, ensure that those that care for you are aware of your wishes and will honour your decisions when your time comes to sail to the western shores, beyond the veil of this life. Death is a personal journey, one which we must embark upon alone, it has no preference for age or creed, sex or wellbeing, and it may well visit tomorrow. Think of your own death as the portals of Calan Gaeaf lie open before you, what ethical decisions can you make to ensure your death reflects your life in Druidry?

Many find the challenges of Calan Gaeaf perhaps a little too challenging, or maybe a little too close to the bone, with its message of death and darkness, the grave, stillness and memories of ancestors who have long since passed into the halls of the dead. In fact the modern commercialisation of the feast we have come to know as Halloween seems to trivialise the sacred attributions of the season, yet within them are the hidden truths and allegorical attributions of Calan Gaeaf. Made ever more popular by our American cousins, Halloween has become mischief night, the night of trick or treating, of glamorous parties and social activities, and the opportunity of inducing hyperactivity in our children! Yet within the seemingly innocent and childlike symbols of the modern Halloween we can find ancient traditions that have metamorphosed over the centuries. Calan Gaeaf is the blending of both Pagan and Christian traditions that have fused together to become the feast that we are familiar with today. The tradition of fancy dress and the mimicking of ghosts and ghouls, mirror the tradition that upon this night the veil between our world and the next is at its thinnest, allowing the spirits of the dead to move amongst us with greater ease. In Wales men would cross dress as female spirits called *"Gwrachod"* (Hags) and parade the streets, representing the spirits from beyond the veil. They would knock on doors and demand appeasement; if none was given they would wreak havoc and trickery upon the unfortunate victim. Their song was sung as follows; note within it a reference to the strange lady in white and the *"Hwch ddu gwta"* mentioned previously.

"Nos G'langaea, twco 'fala',
Pwy sy'n dod mas I chwara?
Ladi wen ar ben y pren,
Yn naddu croes ymbrelo,

Mae'n un or gloch, mae'n ddau or gloch,
Mae'n bryd I'r moch gael cinio!"

"Its Hallow's eve, falling apples,
Who is coming out to play?
The white lady upon the stile,
Hacking at an umbrella stick,
It's one o clock, its two o clock,
Its time for the pigs to have dinner."

The celebratory aspect of the season is as important as the acknowledgement of its attributions; we have much to be grateful for, the previous year having been filled with experiences that enrich the spirit, however positive or negative. Calan Gaeaf allows us the unique opportunity to honour those experiences and integrate them into our development. The harvest is in, in the olden days the weakest animals would have been slaughtered for the winter larder, what do we harvest in the twenty first century? How fruitful was your harvest this year or did your crops fail, what did you find in the cauldron?

Having traversed the mighty wheel of the year, embracing the human experience in conjunction with the commands of nature, we have encountered birthing, development and maturity and the beauty that these transitional periods relay to us. Finding the hidden beauty within death is perhaps a little less easy, we spend the majority of our lives avoiding anything related to death, but this path of avoidance and denial is not an option for those on the Druid path. Death is a vital aspect of life and the catalyst for regeneration and rebirth, her whispers and secrets hum from tree to tree, shrub to shrub, animal to animal and we are not excluded. Death teaches us the mystery of listening deeper with finely tuned senses and the intentional streaming of consciousness, we stop and prick up our ears, listening through spirit to the voice of the underworld and the connection we have to it. To listen to the message of death we need only look to nature for direct evidence of her interaction with it. Nature responds to this vital calling by shrugging its shoulders and assuming the form of death and of stillness, moving deep within itself to discover the secrets of death and its applicability to the living. Without death there can be no life, without contemplation and reflection there can be no positive expression and inspiration, death is as vital to our life force as the air we breathe.

The stage of death presents two differing acts, the physical experience including the effect of death, and the allegorical message within it. On the surface we see its physical attributions, decay, decomposition, silence and stillness. However abhorrent some of these may appear they contain within them a hidden beauty and the seeds of new life. As the mortal forms of all life on earth die they leave behind a mass of rotten matter, unpleasant and extremely smelly. Yet without this decomposition nothing would ever live, this is the beauty of physical death, whether it be the old oak blown down by the winter gales or a death of a human being, each provide stable ground for the development of new life from trees and plants to simple bacteria. Life emerges from the rot of death. Allegorically we see the truth of death through our experience of it and our passage through the realms of life, and as we become accustomed to the mystery of death a burden lifts from our shoulders. We all carry this burden, this attitude of abhorrence towards death, impregnated within us since infancy; our Druidry shatters this illusion and teaches us the truth behind the grave.

Together we can counter-attack the commercial face of Calan Gaeaf and working within our communities attempt to undo the damage of "Mischief Night". As those who understand the relevance of the season we have a duty to inform and educate others, to bring back the sanctity of Calan Gaeaf and the truth that lies within its public face. As night gains supremacy over day and the shadows deepen, our roles within our communities become ever more apparent, as healers and comfort givers, soothsayers and inspirers. Calan Gaeaf offers us an opportunity to move amongst the people as our ancestors did before us, reclaiming the role of those who move from one world to another serving those whose eyes have not yet opened to the mysteries of life and death.

During the sacred weeks of Calan Gaeaf we retreat inwards, experiencing the wonders of the 'little death', embracing the mystery of winter and the dying time. We journey through myth and tradition to the very border of the underworld and encounter our own shamanic death and the rejuvenation of spirit. Our bodies and minds slow in response to the weakening sun, like the flowers and trees we retreat into the womb of the earth, falling gently into a state of contemplation. What achievements and developments occurred during the growing time, how have we enriched our development and to what extent do we actually live? The mystery of death is the secret of life, and the embracing of life and living, knowing that the experience with all its torments, sadness and happiness is the miracle and wonder of a living universe exploring and expressing itself through our lives. Calan Gaeaf offers us the opportunity to travel beyond the three illuminations of Awen and into that darkness and truth that lies beyond them. Taking time out from the conflicting nature of human life in the twenty first century, we allow ourselves the privilege of moving into the darkness, to learn the near impossible task of stillness, and the art of undoing, of unmaking and the pure blissfulness of nothing as we swim, wrapped in the rapture of our song, as it sings the song of the universe, in unity and singularity. Within this unity and the pure indulgence of nothingness, we do nothing, become nothing and like the sleeping earth beneath our feet, and the skeletal trees that dot our landscape we learn to simply 'be'. Without decision, without major plans or events, absconding the antagonistic approach that has become normal for man, we allow ourselves to become the sacred brew of Awen deep in the mother's womb. And we wait, patiently lost in the nothingness, sipping the darkness of Awen as we await the coming of the light and the reconstruction of our bodies that will stir us from this place of non-doing.

Through the experience of our Druidry there is no confusion or apprehension regarding this season and the metaphoric attributions it presents. Instead we approach with reverence and understanding, allowing the secrets of sleep and the silent places to be gradually revealed to us as we prepare for the journey inward, deep into the recesses of our spirit. Having sung the song of life we now learn the lyrics to the tune of death and travel deep beneath the gates of life and into the transition and wonder of the cauldron of transformation and the inspiration that lies hid within it.

And so the journey ends, the wheel of the year slows only enough for us to transform, we await the coming of a new dawn, a new day that will see a new us. The journey of this book is over, yours hopefully is just beginning. Thank you for sharing my journey through the year and my ramblings! And remember *"Druids do it with trees!"*

Brightest of blessings to you all.

Other titles from Thoth Publications

THE DRUIDIC ORDER OF THE PENDRAGON
By Colin Robertson

The Druidic Order of the Pendragon reveals the rituals and secrets of a Druid order active in Derbyshire from the mid-nineteenth century until the 1940s.

The author was sworn to secrecy during his lifetime but wrote down all his knowledge of the Order's ceremonials and symbolism for posthumous publication. He describes this, that and a whole lot of other things. There are surprisingly few parallels to other Druidical, magical or pagan groups. The initiation rituals are not for the faint-hearted and, to initiates, eggs will never seem the same again.

The Druidic Order of the Pendragon is a delightful insight into an all-but lost world of powerful magic and profound self development. At a time when paganism is increasingly diluted by teen witches, this is a reminder that ritual magic can be an effective tool for personal change.

ISBN 978-1-870450-55-3

THE WESTERN MYSTERY TRADITION
By Christine Hartley

A reissue of a classic work, by a pupil of Dion Fortune, on the mythical and historical roots of Western occultism.

Christine Hartley's aim was to demonstrate that we in the West, far from being dependent upon Eastern esoteric teachings, possess a rich and potent mystery tradition of our own, evoked and defined in myth, legend, folklore and song, and embodied in the legacy of Druidic culture.

More importantly, she provides practical guidelines for modern students of the ancient mysteries, 'The Western Mystery Tradition,' in Christine Hartley's view, 'is the basis of the Western religious feeling, the foundation of our spiritual life, the matrix of our religious formulae, whither we are aware of it or not. To it we owe the life and force of our spiritual life.'

ISBN 978-1-870450-24-9

*   *   *   *   *

A MODERN MAGICIAN'S HANDBOOK
By Marian Green

This book presents the ancient arts of magic, ritual and practical occult arts as used by modern ceremonial magicians and witches in a way that everyone can master, bringing them into the Age of Aquarius. Drawing on over three decades of practical experience, Marian Green offers a simple approach to the various skills and techniques that are needed to turn an interest into a working knowledge of magic.

Each section offers explanations, guidance and practical exercises in meditation, inner journeying, preparation for ritual, the arts of divination and many more of today's esoteric practices. No student is too young or too old to benefit from the material set out for them in this book, and its simple language may help even experienced magicians and witches understand their arts in greater depth.

ISBN 978-1-870450-43-0

THE GRAIL SEEKER'S COMPANION
By John Matthews & Marian Green

There have been many books about the Grail, written from many differing standpoints. Some have been practical, some purely historical, others literary, but this is the first Grail book which sets out to help the esoterically inclined seeker through the maze of symbolism, character and myth which surrounds the central point of the Grail.

In today's frantic world when many people have their material needs met some still seek spiritual fulfilment. They are drawn to explore the old philosophies and traditions, particularly that of our Western Celtic Heritage. It is here they encounter the quest for the Holy Grail, that mysterious object which will bring hope and healing to all. Some have come to recognise that they dwell in a spiritual wasteland and now search that symbol of the grail which may be the only remedy. Here is the guide book for the modern seeker, explaining the history and pointing clearly towards the Aquarian grail of the future.

John Matthews and Marian Green have each been involved in the study of the mysteries of Britain and the Grail myth for over thirty-five years. In THE GRAIL SEEKER'S COMPANION they have provided a guidebook not just to places, but to people, stories and theories surrounding the Grail. A reference book of Grail-ology, including history, ritual, meditation, advice and instruction. In short, everything you are likely to need before you set out on the most important adventure of your life.

This is the only book that points the way to the Holy Grail Quest in the 21st. century.

ISBN 978-1-870450-49-2

THE FORGOTTEN MAGE
The Magical Lectures of Colonel C.R.F. Seymour.
Edited by Dolores Ashcroft-Nowicki

Charles Seymour was a man of many talents and considerable occult skills. The friend and confidant of Dion Fortune, he worked with her and his magical partner, Christine Hartley, for many productive years.

As one of the Inner Circle of Dion Fortune's Society of the Inner Light, Seymour was a High Priest in every sense of the word, but he was also one of the finest teachers of the occult art to emerge this century.

In the past, little of Seymour's work has been widely available, but in this volume Dolores Ashcroft-Nowicki, Director of Studies of the Servants of the Light School of Occult Science, has gathered together a selection of the best of Seymour's work. His complex scholarship and broad background knowledge of the Pagan traditions shine through in articles which include: The Meaning of Initiation; Magic in the Ancient Mystery Religions; The Esoteric Aspect of Religion; Meditations for Temple Novices; The Old Gods; The Ancient Nature Worship and The Children of the Great Mother.

ISBN 978-1-870450-39-3

LIVING MAGICAL ARTS
By R.J. Stewart

Living Magical Arts is founded upon the author's practical experience of the Western Magical Traditions, and contains specific teachings from within a living and long established initiatory line of British, French, and Russian esoteric tradition.

Living Magical Arts offers a new and clear approach to the philosophy and practice of magic for the 21st century, stripping away the accumulated nonsense found in many repetitive publications, and re-stating the art for contemporary use. This book offers a coherent illustrated set of magical techniques for individual or group use, leading to profound changes of consciousness and subtle energy. Magical arts are revealed as an enduring system of insight into human and universal consciousness, combining a practical spiritual psychology (long predating materialist psychology) with an effective method of relating to the physical world. Many of the obscure aspects of magical work are clarified, with insights into themes such as the origins of magical arts, working with subtle forces, partaking of esoteric traditions, liberating sexual energies, magical effects upon the world of nature, and the future potential and development of creative magic.

ISBN 978-1-870450-61-4

THE DRUID WAY
By Philip Carr-Gomm

In The Druid Way, Philip Carr-Gomm takes us on a journey through the sacred landscape of Southern Britain, and as he does so, we learn about Druidry as a living tradition of the land and its people, a tradition that is as relevant today as it was for our ancestors.

As we walk the ancient tracks across the South Downs we encounter dragons and giants, ancestral voices and ancient places that speak to us of the beauty of a spiritual way that still exists and can still be followed. We learn how Druidry can help us to sense again our kinship with Nature, and how following the Druid Way can lead us towards a profound sense of oneness with all life.

This new edition has been extensively revised and includes the complete ceremonies of three Rites of Passage, a guide to the sacred sites of Sussex and a Foreword by Cairisthea Worthington.

This whole book is a delight. It is the diary of a sacred journey, through sacred space, and through the heart and mind - a book to use, to keep and to remember.

Wood & Water

This book provides inspiration, soul-food and encouragement to those who long to be part of the richer life of this beautiful planet.

Caitlin Matthews

ISBN 978-1-870450-62-1

THE ARTHURIAN FORMULA

By Dion Fortune, Margaret Lumley Brown & Gareth Knight

The Arthurian Formula, was the last major work of Dion Fortune, and formed the corner stone of the inner work of her Society of the Inner Light for the following twenty years, supplemented by the remarkably gifted psychic Margaret Lumley Brown. It later formed the basis for work by Gareth Knight with the Company of Hawkwood and allied groups in later years, inspiring his book The Secret Tradition in Arthurian Legend.

Dion Fortune`s contribution explores the remote sources of the Arthurian legends and the mission of Merlin, played out in the polar relationships between Arthur, Guenevere and Lancelot in both human and faery dynamics, and leading to aspects of the Grail. Margaret Lumley Brown develops the threads in the labyrinth formed by the archetypal patterns of the knights and ladies, including particular reference to Morgan le Fay. Gareth Knight`s commentary pulls together these strands with an overview of the various traditions back of the Arthurian Formula – of Glastonbury, Atlantis, the world of Faery, Merlin, the Troubadours, the cult of Queen Venus, and their application in the practical Mysteries of today.

An introductory commentary by Gareth Knight includes a guide to recent academic and esoteric scholarship and is supplemented by Appendices on the Glastonbury legends, clairvoyant impressions of Atlantis, (from which archetypal principles behind the Arthurian legends are held ultimately to spring) and a remarkable perspective on Queen Gwenevere and the Faery and Grail traditions, by Wendy Berg.

ISBN 978-1-870450-90-4

THE FOOL'S COAT
By Vi Marriott

The story of Father Bérenger Saunière, the poor parish priest of Rennes-le-Château, a remote village in Southern France, who at the turn of the 19th century spent mysterious millions on creating a fantastic estate and lavishly entertaining the rich and famous, is now as well known as "Cinderella" or "Eastenders". He would never divulge where the money came from, and popular belief is that in 1891 he discovered a priceless treasure; yet Saunière died penniless, and his legacy is a secret that has continued to puzzle and intrigue succeeding generations.

Since *The Holy Blood and the Holy Grail* hit literary headlines in the nineteen eighties, hundreds of solutions have been suggested. Did he find documents that proved Jesus married Mary Magdalene? Was he a member of The Priory of Sion, a sinister secret society that knew the Da Vinci Code? Did he own the equivalent of Harry Potter's Philosopher's Stone?

A ragbag of history, mystery, gossip and myth, THE FOOL'S COAT investigates Father Saunière's extraordinary life against the background of his times, and suggests that the simplest solution of his rise from penury to riches is probably the correct one.

Vi Marriott is a theatre administrator, writer and researcher. Her play *Ten Days A-Maze,* based on Count Jan Pococki's *Tales of the Saragossa Manuscript,* had seasons in London and Edinburgh; and she contributes regularly to three "house" magazines concerned with the mystery of Rennes-le-Château and other esoteric matters.

ISBN 978-1-870450-99-7